SAYLES TALK

CONTEMPORARY APPROACHES TO FILM AND TELEVISION SERIES

A complete listing of the books in this series can be found online at http://wsupress.wayne.edu

General Editor

BARRY KEITH GRANT
Brock University

Advisory Editors

PATRICIA B. ERENS
School of the Art Institute of Chicago

LUCY FISCHER
University of Pittsburgh

PETER LEHMAN
Arizona State University

CAREN J. DEMING
University of Arizona

ROBERT J. BURGOYNE
Wayne State University

TOM GUNNING
University of Chicago

ANNA MCCARTHY
New York University

PETER X. FENG
University of Delaware

New Perspectives on Independent Filmmaker John Sayles

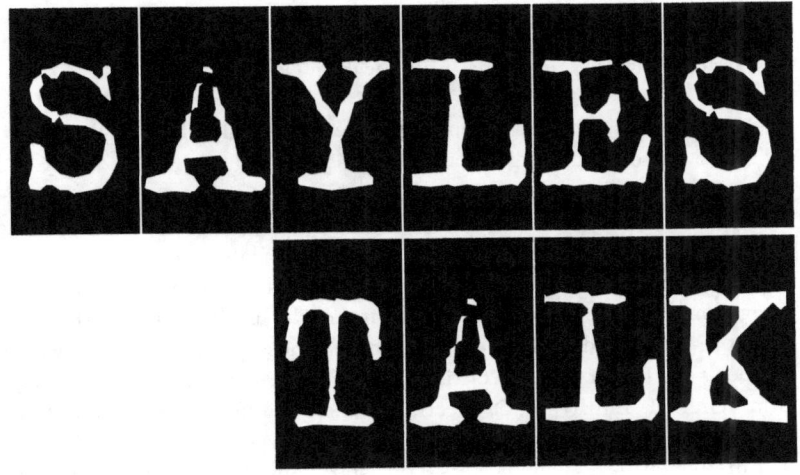

SAYLES TALK

EDITED BY
DIANE CARSON
AND
HEIDI KENAGA

WAYNE STATE UNIVERSITY PRESS   DETROIT

© 2006 by Wayne State University Press, Detroit, Michigan 48201.
All rights reserved.
No part of this book may be reproduced without formal permission.

10 09 08 07 06   5 4 3 2 1

Library of Congress Cataloging-in-Publication Data

Sayles talk : new perspectives on independent filmmaker John Sayles / edited by Diane Carson and Heidi Kenaga.
p. cm.
1. Sayles between the systems : bucking "industry policy" and indie apolitical chic / Cynthia Baron — 2. Breakups and reunions : late realism in early Sayles / Alex Woloch — 3. The false salvation of the here and now : aliens, images, and the commodification of desire in The brother from another planet / Mark Bould — 4. The theo-political landscape of Matewan / Martin F. Norden — 5. Passersby and Politics : City of Hope and the Multiple protagonist film / Greg M. Smith — 6. Of spectral mothers and lost children : war, folklore, and psychoanalysis in The secret of Roan Inish / Maureen Turim and Mika Turim-Nygren — 7. Oedipus edits (Lone star) / Susan Felleman — 8. Men in context : gender in Matewan and Men with guns / Klaus Rieser — 9. Tourism and territory : constructing the nation in Men with guns (Hombres armados) / Hamilton Carroll — 10. Psychic borders and legacies left hanging in Lone star and Men with guns / Rebecca M. Gordon — 11. The space of ambiguity : representations of nature in Limbo / Laura Barrett.
Includes bibliographical references and index.
ISBN 0-8143-3155-6 (pbk. : alk. paper)
1. Sayles, John, 1950—-Criticism and interpretation.
I. Carson, Diane.
II. Kenaga, Heidi, 1960–
PN1998.3.S3S28 2006
791.4302′33′092—dc22
2005014983

   The paper used in this publication meets the minimum requirements of the American National Standard for Information Sciences—
Permanence of Paper for Printed Library Materials, ANSI Z39.48-1984.

CONTENTS

Acknowledgments vii

Introduction 1
    Heidi Kenaga

1

Sayles between the Systems: Bucking "Industry Policy" and Indie Apolitical Chic 16
    Cynthia Baron

2

Breakups and Reunions: Late Realism in Early Sayles 51
    Alex Woloch

3

The False Salvation of the Here and Now: Aliens, Images, and the Commodification of Desire in *The Brother from Another Planet* 79
    Mark Bould

4

The Theo-Political Landscape of *Matewan* 103
    Martin F. Norden

5

Passersby and Politics: *City of Hope* and the Multiple Protagonist Film 117
    Greg M. Smith

6

Of Spectral Mothers and Lost Children: War, Folklore, and Psychoanalysis in *The Secret of Roan Inish* 134
> Maureen Turim and Mika Turim-Nygren

7

Oedipus Edits (*Lone Star*) 158
> Susan Felleman

8

Men in Context: Gender in *Matewan* and *Men With Guns* 174
> Klaus Rieser

9

Tourism and Territory: Constructing the Nation in *Men With Guns* (*Hombres Armados*) 194
> Hamilton Carroll

10

Psychic Borders and Legacies Left Hanging in *Lone Star* and *Men With Guns* 215
> Rebecca M. Gordon

11

The Space of Ambiguity: Representations of Nature in *Limbo* 238
> Laura Barrett

Annotated Resources   261
List of Contributors   271
Index   275

ACKNOWLEDGMENTS

We would like to thank our contributors for bringing this project to life and helping us to see John Sayles's work in new ways. We appreciate and applaud their perseverance, diligence, and timeliness through the successive phases of the production process. For perceptive commentary and suggestions on various stages of the project, we thank the participants and attendees of the 2001 Society for Cinema Studies panel on Sayles that we cochaired and the students in Dr. Kenaga's spring 2002 Contemporary Cinema class on Martin Scorsese and John Sayles at the University of Memphis. The two anonymous reviewers of the manuscript provided very thoughtful and incisive critiques of the first draft of the collection.

Several individuals merit special recognition: University of Memphis graduate student Joseph Watson, who provided Heidi with research assistance in the preparation of the bibliography; and Jane Hoehner, our initial acquisitions editor and director of Wayne State University Press, who encouraged and supported us with enthusiasm through every step of the process. We would also like to extend heartfelt thanks to Annie Martin, acquisitions editor, who guided us through the publication process with clear and quick answers to our numerous questions; to Carrie Downes, our production editor, who explained succinctly and tracked perfectly the many details of production; and Dawn Hall, freelance editor, who has an admirable talent for fashioning a consistent and lucid style. Our anthology has benefited enormously from our production team; moreover, we have learned from and enjoyed the entire experience.

Heidi adds thanks to her spouse, Pradeep Sopory, who cannot quite agree with her on *Limbo* but will watch *Men With Guns* anytime, and to coeditor Diane Carson, whose insight, guidance, and good humor never flagged.

Diane adds thanks to her best friend and husband, Willis Loy, for his wholehearted involvement in numerous conversations about Sayles's films as we talked through the complexities and the ideas of these provocative works that reveal added facets the more they are examined. With such engagement, intellectual endeavors are thrilling as well as rewarding personally and politically. And deep thanks go to coeditor Heidi Kenaga, without whom *Sayles Talk: New Perspectives on Independent Filmmaker John Sayles* would never have been produced. It always benefited from her passion for excellence in scholarship and her commitment to meaningful education. We hope this volume contributes to many more discussions that bring Sayles's films to the forefront of conscientious study and constructive debate.

Introduction

Heidi Kenaga

> I want people to like the stuff I do, but not enough to lie to them. . . . I can take a lot of risks that the studios won't talk about. I can talk about things in depth. I can make the audience uneasy.
> John Sayles, 1987

For twenty-five years, first as a screenwriter and then as a writer-director, John Sayles has created films that are consistently distinguished in their treatment of character, place, and perspective. He has received both critical acclaim and institutional approbation: his movies often secure places on yearly "Ten Best" lists; his scripts (such as for *Lone Star* and *Passion Fish*) are nominated for Oscars and given screenwriting awards; his first film, *Return of the Secaucus Seven*, was named to the National Film Preservation Board's Film Registry in 1997; and he is the recipient of the John D. and Catherine T. MacArthur, John Cassavetes, and John Steinbeck awards, among others. Still, within modern visual culture Sayles remains relatively unrecognized as an "innovator" in comparison with other filmmakers such as Martin Scorsese or Stanley Kubrick. In *Mike, Spike, Slackers, & Dykes*, for example, John Pierson notes that while young filmmakers recognize Sayles as one of the earliest articulators of the kind of counter-Hollywood ethos they support, few cite him as either a "catalyst" or source of "creative sparks" (18–19).

In part, this neglect reflects the extent to which auteurs have become an extension of celebrity culture. Too often, the students we teach become most familiar with directors via sound bites on *Entertainment Tonight* or video clips on the Internet. To varying degrees, figures like Steven Spielberg, Francis Ford Coppola, Oliver Stone, Spike Lee, and Quentin Tarantino enacted in the 1980s and 1990s (and perhaps still do) what Tim Corrigan has called "the commercial performance of being an auteur." Corrigan argues that contemporary American filmmakers are "defined by their commercial status and their ability to promote a film, sometimes regardless of its distinction" (42). In contrast, it is Sayles's resistance to the marketing of directors like brand names within industry and public discourse that marks him as an outsider. And it is his work, rather than that of commercial auteurs, that exhibits greater affinities with those postwar European art cinemas they claim as their influences. Such thematically complex and stylistically individualized films sought to challenge the dominance of Hollywood representation by offering spectators "counterhegemonic alternatives" (Lears 574) mobilizing a variety of narrative structures, aesthetic possibilities, and character realizations, often in service of a progressive politics. Correspondingly, this anthology offers a detailed examination of a director whose work consistently explores such alterity rather than merely serving to promote the auteur as star and reduce his or her films to a set of iconic moments, spiced with self-referentiality. In addition, this collection may well constitute for readers a key supplement to Sayles's films akin to that critical apparatus (for example, interviews, academic journals, film festival program notes, other materials of cinephilia) that arose as a means to understand the art cinema and art cinema directors as committed to an expressive praxis.

While film scholars have long acknowledged Sayles's significant role in the history of independent production in the United States, relatively few have devoted serious critical attention to his oeuvre. This anthology—which had its origin in a 2001 Society for Cinema Studies panel that I cochaired with Diane Carson—is a preliminary attempt to address this lack. Our presenters analyzed how across the 1990s Sayles increasingly explored aesthetic possibilities in *City of Hope, Lone Star, Men With Guns,* and *Limbo.* In the course of organizing and presenting this panel, we discovered an informal network of scholars who were, like us, eager to reconceptualize Sayles's work. This is not to say, of course, that his films have gone unexamined in film studies literature, especially *Lone Star* and *Men With Guns* (see the annotated resources found at the end of this collection). But our goal was to collect a set of essays that would help establish the range of Sayles's innovation and singularity. Here, nationally and internationally known film and media scholars working in the United States and Europe interrogate a remarkable group of films, using a variety of conceptual approaches: industrial and historical study (Cynthia Baron and Martin F. Norden); formal, narratological, and generic analysis (Greg M. Smith and Alex Woloch); psychoanalytic and critical theory (Maureen Turim and Susan Felleman); and poststructuralist and postmodern frameworks (Klaus Rieser, Mark Bould, Hamilton Carroll, Rebecca M. Gordon, and Laura Barrett). We hope this range suggests to other scholars the venues by which the director's oeuvre might be examined, specifically those films our collection does not directly address (*Lianna* [1983], *Eight Men Out* [1988], and *Passion Fish* [1992]), those released while this book was in preparation (*Sunshine State* [2002], *Casa de los Babys* [2003]), and *Silver City* [2004]), as well as those yet to come.

The anthology opens with Cynthia Baron's comprehensive essay "Sayles between the Systems: Bucking 'Industry Policy' and Indie Apolitical Chic," which situates Sayles's narratological and aesthetic choices (detailed in individual films in subsequent essays in the book) in relation to Hollywood's long history of circumventing if not censoring material about political issues. For Baron, the director's films "seem to be the isolated work of an auteur rather than part of a larger social or aesthetic movement in large measure because American cinema has been created according to the blueprint of political censorship." Thus, an extended examination of Sayles's work may tell us as much about the ideological operations of Hollywood practice as it does about Sayles's worldview. Baron provides crucial context for another supposition implicit across the entire collection, that the director's work as a whole occupies a liminal position in relation to *both* popular commercial filmmaking, which functions hegemonically to denaturalize any critique of capitalism and class relations, and the contemporary independent movement, which commonly relies on "art-house designer violence" (Pribram 176) and hyperbolic stylization. Accordingly, Baron supports E. Deidre Pribram's proposition of a new descriptor for Sayles's films—the "narrative avant-garde"—as a way to locate within the realm of independent cinema a space for his singular vision.

Baron's concluding suggestion leads us into the balance of essays, many of which contest the critical commonplace that Sayles has little interest in the possibilities of form. Focusing on individual films, these contributors would agree that despite his status as the "father" of contemporary independent cinema, Sayles's work is generally incompatible with the nonclassical aesthetic trends (for example, *Reservoir Dogs* [1992], *π* [1998], *Memento* [2000]) of this film movement. This is a frequent observation made by indie chroniclers. For example, in *Cinema of Outsiders*, Emanuel Levy refers to the director's declaration that "my main interest is making films about people . . . I'm not interested in cinematic art" (82). The fact that Sayles came to the cinema as an acclaimed writer of fiction,[1] and that he only makes films based on his own screenplays, perhaps supports this view. Yet a key feature of this collection is the extent to which the essays undermine the judgment that, as Levy puts it, his films are "basically photographed scripts" (85). Clearly the aesthetic that emerges across Sayles's work is more realist than expressionist in orientation, indicating a greater concern with "content" than "style." Yet his films reveal an artist with a sophisticated grasp of realism as a practice, involving the selection and arrangement of formal elements in order to construct verisimilitude, in tandem with a complex understanding of the ideological implications of the "seamless" classical Hollywood style.

As Alex Woloch discusses in the second essay, "Breakups and Reunions: Late Realism in Early Sayles," a close analysis of *Return of the Secaucus Seven* (1980) and *Baby It's You* (1983) demonstrates Sayles's sustained commitment to "representing social reality [as] always informed by, or intertwined with, a sense that lived reality exceeds whatever aesthetic representation has been constructed." Drawing upon the work of the principal theorists of literary and cinematic realism, Georg Lukács and André Bazin, Woloch analyzes how Sayles's films consciously engage realist representation as both derived from a referential ground and always partial, always incomplete. The notorious ending of *Limbo* is one of the most literal demonstrations of how a "formal principle of withholding seems built into the very conception of Sayles's realism," but this was evident in early Sayles as well. *Secaucus* is both about political activism in the 1960s and how such action is (mis)represented, via the film's depiction of a weekend reunion of former "radicals," which trades in nostalgia (the lost, the irretrievable) both in terms of narrative and at the level of form. Woloch argues that a similar kind of reflexivity is evident in *Baby It's You*—a film that would seem to have little similarity with Sayles's first—which scrutinizes the staging of "breakups and reunions" in the teenpic and thus Hollywood's investment in the illusion of plenitude and completeness in this and other genres.

Challenging the comfortable alliance between the popular cinematic text and its consumers, Sayles's complex characters, unpredictable story trajectories, narrative disjunctures, and unresolved endings reveal the calculated packaging of the commercial product. Yet his approach seldom undermines the accessibility of the stories he wants to tell; he deliberately draws upon such familiar genres as the sports film (*Eight Men Out*) or the melodrama/woman's film (*Passion Fish*, and to some extent *Lianna* and *Casa de los Babys*), among others, even as he works to undermine their assumptions. Sayles's revision of the teenpic in *Baby It's You* was in fact a little too subversive for Paramount executives. Extensive postproduction struggles between director and studio over creative control resulted in lackluster distribution and marketing, while it only reinforced Sayles's commitment to producing outside the studio system.[2] His strategy unmasks the putatively "safe" status of the genre film in ways that go beyond the revisionism of the 1970s and 1980s (for example, *Chinatown*, *The Long Goodbye*, *Body Heat*) through more recent examples of formula reworkings (such as the sly interrogation of film noir in the Coen brothers' *The Man Who Wasn't There* [2001]). This tactic is perhaps clearest in *The Brother from Another Planet*, Sayles's contribution to the science-fiction genre. While media corporations have long mined the science-fiction product for financial gain, its most skilled practitioners have approached the form allegorically, creating futurist narratives that critique contemporary political, cultural, or environmental issues. In his essay "The False Salvation of the Here and Now: Aliens, Images, and the Commodification of Desire in *The Brother from Another Planet*," Mark Bould counterposes the "alien arrival" opening of Sayles's 1985 film to the highly ironic beginning of Barry Sonnenfeld's first *Men in Black* (1997). Trying to evade detection, an extraterrestrial masquerades as an "illegal" Mexican attempting to cross the U.S. border but is caught by the Men in Black—a scene designed to prompt a humorous response and establish the movie's slick comedic tone early on. As Bould comments, "imagining [alien] Otherness in terms of racialized difference has long been a major strategy of both literary and cinematic science fiction," but in *Brother* Sayles eschews such easy mapping by alluding to the more complex and interrelated origins of individuals' oppression within capitalist social relations. Sayles's irony in the final scene of the film is powerful: although the original "Men in Black" are vanquished, the Brother is still not free, enslaved by an economic system that reduces human beings (especially people of color) to the status of commodities.

Like nearly all of the director's work, *The Brother from Another Planet* articulates a leftist political sensibility, although the extent of Sayles's progressivism, particularly in terms of his representation of historical events, has been the subject of some controversy. *Matewan*, based on the "Matewan Massacre" of 1920, sympathetically documents the struggles of West Virginia coal miners to unionize against ferocious company opposition. While the movie was critically hailed for its narrative power and technical achievements, its historical veracity was much debated among labor historians. Left unaddressed, however, was the film's powerful use of Christian religious imagery to articulate a vision of social justice achieved through nonviolent means. As Martin F. Norden notes in his essay on "The Theo-Political Landscape of *Matewan*," the union organizer, Joe Kenehan, is both "Christ-like" and a proselytizer, although not in the service of a reactionary ideology; rather, his death compels Danny's pursuit of a "new gospel of unionization." In this way, Norden suggests, the film critiques Reagan-era religious fundamentalism as much as it targets the administration's infamous antagonism to union organizing. Here Sayles seeks to pry apart the imbrication between Christian moral philosophy and a conservative politics, representing this uneasy alliance in the figure of the Hardshell Preacher (played, ironically, by the director himself) who is a de facto company shill.[3]

The complexities of contemporary urban life and political culture depicted in *The Brother from Another Planet* are center stage again in *City of Hope* (1991). Like several other contributors to this collection, Greg M. Smith focuses on how Sayles develops and sustains a structured dependence between topic and method. In his essay "Passersby and Politics: *City of Hope* and the Multiple Protagonist Film," Smith analyzes the use of long Steadicam shots (which Sayles called "trades") to follow a set of characters, eventually switching emphasis in midshot to trail another set. For Smith, *City of Hope* is a "veritable catalog of inventive ways to move our attention from one character to another," yet they are never arbitrary nor the result of a reluctance to cut. Rather, "his stylistic choices serve narrative, political, and moral goals": to convey how otherwise disparate city dwellers are connected to one another, their environment, and their personal and public history. While many of Sayles's films feature ensemble casts, the fact that *City of Hope* is set in an urban environment mandated an innovative technique such as the "trades" in order to reveal this web of political and social interrelatedness. Further, Smith convincingly illustrates the iconoclasm of Sayles's method, his "leveling of the traditional character hierarchy of mainstream cinema" in ways that go beyond even art-cinema precursors such as Ophuls's *La Ronde* (1950) and Buñuel's *The Phantom of Liberty* (1974).

The Secret of Roan Inish (1994) would seem to be a departure for Sayles. Primarily a movie for children, it lacks the political orientation of his previous work. Still, like *Matewan, Eight Men Out, City of Hope,* and *Passion Fish, Roan Inish* explores a regional community (or "tribe," as Sayles calls them), their spaces and cadences, particularly the stories they tell about life and legacies in that terrain. Myth increasingly comes to the fore in Sayles's work in the 1990s, and it is his specific use of folktale that is of interest to Maureen Turim and Mika Turim-Nygren in their essay "Of Spectral Mothers and Lost Children: War, Folklore, and Psychoanalysis in *The Secret of Roan Inish.*" Using her young daughter's intense first response to the movie as a starting point, Turim analyzes this complex narrative of loss, memory, and nostalgia, which embeds tale within tale as a means to comment upon the therapeutic function of storytelling. She draws upon psychoanalytic theory as well as comparative sources such as Greek myth and Japanese folktales as a means of interpreting the universality of Sayles's story. Turim concludes with a discussion of how *Roan Inish* treats the village milieu and its folklore fantasy tradition as a lost heritage that young war orphan Fiona seeks to recover as she constructs the fable of her *own* identity as a survivor.

The intricacy of those stories we tell each other and ourselves about our own "myths of origin" and the ways they are intertwined with those of the nation are central to Sayles's most critically hailed as well as financially successful film to date, *Lone Star* (1996). After garnering a place on many national "Ten Best" lists and a very influential rave from Roger Ebert, the film eventually grossed $13 million. Sayles also earned Golden Globe, Writer's Guild, Independent Spirit, and Oscar nominations for his screenplay (losing the latter to the Coen brothers for *Fargo*), which has appeared in print several times.[4] Its complex temporal structure and use of long tracking shots to seamlessly interweave the past and present in the course of a murder-mystery in a Texas border town exhibited Sayles's mature grasp of technique. Again, the director develops his approach in tandem with topic: *Lone Star* depicts the contiguity of events long past with those in the present in order to convey the dense topography of racial, ethnic, and class relationships that characterize individual and national identity in the United States. As a result, the film's sophisticated address of the problematics of "borders" along a number of parameters has received much attention from cinema and media scholars; the last five years has witnessed a veritable subindustry of analyses and commentary, in conference and published formats, devoted to *Lone Star*. Americanists in particular have shown considerable interest in the film. In two successive yearly addresses (1997–98), presidents of the American Studies Association referred to *Lone Star* as a document of American multiculturalism par excellence, a "prophetic allegory" for the century to come as historians continue to examine the very meaning of "American" in their scholarship (Washington 16; Radway 6).[5]

It was, therefore, a bit of a challenge to find an original essay on the film for our collection, but we have. While a number of scholars have taken a psychoanalytic approach to the story—a Texas lawman seeks to solve the forty-year-old murder of one of his predecessors, a notoriously corrupt sheriff, all the while suspecting his own father is responsible—in her essay "Oedipus Edits (*Lone Star*)" Susan Felleman innovatively combines explication with an analysis of intertextual, "generational" relationships across films. Drawing upon Sayles's praise of Freud as a master metaphoricist who nonetheless has had little influence on his work, Felleman points out that the movie's most striking formal feature, languorous takes with mobile framings that fluidly move from action in the past to the present, effectively collapse historical time and geographic space in a precise cinematic rendering of the Freudian unconscious's ineffable and omnipresent qualities. Further, she argues that in *Lone Star* Sayles enacts what Harold Bloom might call *Tessera*, "antithetically completing his [stylistic and generic] precursors" such as *Grand Illusion, Touch of Evil, Chinatown,* and *The Man Who Shot Liberty Valance,* in order to express what Felleman describes as "demystification with an oedipal attitude."

Assessing Sayles's depiction of "fathers and sons" in slightly different terms, Klaus Rieser examines the paradoxical ways in which the director has constructed masculinity across time, selecting two films made roughly ten years apart. In his article "Men in Context: Gender in *Matewan* and *Men With Guns,*" Rieser argues that Sayles clearly recapitulates hegemonic elements here, featuring oedipal narratives and "lone heroes" (Joe Kenehan and Dr. Fuentes) who exemplify male narcissism via their exclusion from women and culture that grants them a naturalized authority and legitimacy. Yet the director concurrently undermines such depictions, emphasizing the influence of context and region, the complexity of social relations, and ersatz communities built from diverse character ensembles. Thus, for Rieser, Sayles's films "implicitly present a codependent concept of masculinity that is at one remove from a conventional patriarchal heroic individualism." This refigurement suggests an alternative to the glamorized mise-en-scène of violent retribution (for example, as enacted by the action hero as "patriot"), articulating a pacificist agenda ultimately more resistant to oppression. Most importantly, that these films end in the deaths of Kenehan and Fuentes does not signify they have failed; rather, it endows their "sons," Danny and the young soldier, with a legacy of social justice and altruism, not exclusive gender or racial privilege.

Like Rieser, Rebecca M. Gordon addresses the construction of patriarchy in Sayles's work in her essay "Psychic Borders and Legacies Left Hanging in *Lone Star* and *Men With Guns.*" Gordon focuses on how these films problematize links between manhood and nation in ways that unmask their mutual ideological investment in a coherent, uncontested myth of origin. She argues that the "masculinized" nature of historical metanarratives cannot exist for long in a hybrid society, for once a culture recognizes itself as comprising many stories, the psychic identifications that subtend a singular view may fail. Sayles's work interrogates the paternal legacy not only to comment on the exhaustion of the motif but also to suggest it is bankrupt as a source of cultural formation. Given *Lone Star*'s engaging qualities, we might find its expression of contemporary American cultural hybridity particularly useful in the classroom, as it suggests to students the insufficiency of one national story, one "paternal legacy."

Sayles followed his most accessible film with what is probably his least, *Men With Guns* (*Hombres Armados*), although it is less temporally complex and densely plotted than *Lone Star*. An aging physician from the city (Dr. Fuentes, played by Federico Luppi) returns to the countryside to reunite with the young doctors he trained for work in the Alliance for Progress program, only to find they have disappeared or been killed. Several aspects of this occasionally perplexing film render it a challenge to those not acquainted with the traditional norms of art cinema: a slower, measured pace, with an aleatoric narrative and reflexive narratological mode; an allegorical presentation of an unspecified "Central American" conflict between state government and rural insurgents; use of English subtitles for Spanish and indigenous dialects; and deemphasis on stars. In his essay "Tourism and Territory: Constructing the Nation in *Men With Guns* (*Hombres Armados*)," Hamilton Carroll argues that the film's very refusal of categorization—its lack of specificity, cultural markers, stylistic familiars, or identifiable performers—make it an exemplar of what he calls "postnational cinema," a product of ambiguous domestic origin that critiques the hegemony of the United States' national imaginary and the practice of cultural imperialism. He focuses on the role of tourism in these processes, embodied by Andrew and Harriet, two American travelers who while quite aware of the country's mythic precolonial history are completely blind to its contemporary sociopolitical realities, refusing to see the parallels or their own complicity as privileged national subjects. At the same time, Dr. Fuentes is also a tourist, traveling to rural areas as if a visitor from another country, so foreign to him are these regions, its cultures, languages, and struggles. Whereas the Americans can leave, Fuentes cannot. His journey culminates in an epiphanic, indeed fatal moment as he understands the culpability of the Alliance for Progress program for the ravaged conditions he has seen.

Yet as Carroll points out, viewers are never as it were "let off the hook," able to comfortably disengage their identification with the unpleasant realities the film unmasks. He argues that in *Men With Guns*, Sayles employs various distanciating tactics—for example, lack of a linear narrative trajectory, clear-cut character motivation and psychology, resolution of all enigmas—to suggest links between the exploitative gaze of the tourist imagination and viewers' parallel desire for "illusion" in the cinema, in all senses.[6] In this way, Carroll comes to the same conclusions drawn by other contributors in the course of discussing otherwise dissimilar movies: in terms of *both* form and content, Sayles's work continually critiques Hollywood's optimal investment in producing an "all-consuming" spectatorial experience focused on plenitude and pleasure. At the same time, he avoids reducing the story to the twin tropes common in contemporary independent cinema—aestheticized violence and nihilist sensibility—never failing to situate his characters and their actions in context, in community, and in history.

The question of spectatorial gratification as well as the political and cultural economy of tourism returns in *Limbo* (1999). The "missing" ending of this romance/survivalist tale about individuals from disparate "tribes" who inhabit the Alaskan wilderness caused some viewers distress. Yet as Laura Barrett notes in her contribution "The Space of Ambiguity: Representations of Nature in *Limbo*," many other Sayles films end without definitive closure—or offer closing moments that precisely contradict what has gone before, as in *Lone Star*'s "Forget the Alamo" line. Barrett notes that *Limbo*'s infamous nonending accords with the general features of postmodern narrative, which reflexively comments upon the illusory representations of a diegetic world while at the same moment constructing a world and characters about whom we are asked to suspend disbelief. Drawing upon a wide array of theorists who have written about the social and cultural processes by which we assign (often contradictory) meanings to "nature," Barrett demonstrates how throughout this film Sayles is centrally concerned with the process of representing nature, how images and stories "help to constitute nature itself," in this case the putative "last wilderness" in America. Although several characters are enthralled by a modernist attachment to experiencing "the thing itself"—the best example perhaps being Joe Gastineau's (David Strathairn) quasi-religious engagement with the act of fishing—Sayles investigates nature as, in Peter Goin's phrase, more a "cultural idea than physical reality," and particularly as expressed in language. Thus, Barrett argues that although *Limbo* would seem to reify the traditional modernism/postmodernism binary, in which postmodernism is affiliated with the replacement of nature and reality by simulation, and modernism evokes the truth and authenticity that evolves through a relationship with the natural world, ultimately this schism is problematized. She specifically points to the last third of *Limbo*, when three protagonists, suddenly stranded on a remote island and unsure of their survival, are transformed not through an encounter with savage nature but with language, the pained and cruel diary entries Noelle invents to communicate with her mother. For Barrett, ultimately the title of the movie refers not just to his characters' uncertain status at the close of the narrative but also to Sayles's aesthetic aspiration: to make us uncomfortable, "uneasy" (as in the quote that opened this introduction) with media representations that too often and too easily structure political, historical, and social realities in terms of simplistic binaries.

If the essays in this collection represent something like a "first word" on Sayles's body of work to date, they certainly should not be the last. He continues to make films: *Sunshine State* was released in June 2002, *Casa de los Babys* in June 2003, *Silver City* (a political satire and murder mystery set in the "New West") debuted in theaters less than two months before the 2004 U.S. presidential election, in a bid to impact its outcome.[7] The movie targets the inegalitarian character of American political life and civic culture and especially the fourth estate's culpability in perpetuating rather than interrogating this state of affairs. *Silver City* elicited perhaps most attention for its employment of an allegorical mode: Bush *père* and *fils* appear in the guise of conservative ideologue Colorado senator Jud Pilager (played by Michael Murphy) and his hapless son Dickie (played by Chris Cooper), a born-again, linguistically challenged gubernatorial candidate who is the jovial puppet of corporate interests.

In addition, developments in the last three years may encourage renewed attention to Sayles's earlier movies. In March 2002, IFC Films sponsored a Sayles retrospective at the South by Southwest Film Festival and helped launch a tour of *Secaucus Seven*, *Lianna*, and *The Brother from Another Planet* during the spring and summer of that year. IFC also subsidized the reissue of these films (and *Men With Guns*) in both video and DVD format with director's audio commentary (see the annotated resources for a complete listing of those Sayles films now available with commentary). Scholars should also find helpful the recent archiving of Sayles's papers in Williams College's Chapin Library (see the annotated resources for the archive URL).

Further, Da Capo Press has published a new edition of Sayles's 1987 book on the making of *Matewan*, *Thinking in Pictures* (now subtitled "How Movies Really Get Made"), with a new introduction by the director. Purchasers of the new Da Capo edition might find this anthology a most insightful and encouraging companion piece—especially our students, who often express an interest in both the art and craft of alternative filmmaking. Sayles's praxis provides us with one workable model for such activity in the United States today. Like many independent and art-cinema directors, he has established a "creative family" of talent and production personnel with whom he repeatedly works. However, Sayles takes it a step further, adhering to a nonhierarchical model that privileges collaboration and exchange. His team also exhibits respect for the communities within which they work, hiring local personnel and avoiding injuries to structures and environments (too often the norm in location shooting) as much as possible.

At the same time, Sayles has a pragmatic understanding of the economic codependence of independent and mainstream cinema. Using the substantial fees he earns as a script doctor for studio productions (including *Apollo 13*, *The Quick and the Dead*, *Mimic*, and *Jurassic Park IV*) to help support his own projects, he has found a way to inventively exploit the synergetic relationship between artisanal forms of film practice and the commercial industry. Overall, Sayles's work suggests how a creative individual can make a significant contribution to film art within a commercial context that carefully markets "innovation" according to the dictates of a celebrity culture or in service of a technologically driven, spectacular aesthetic. We hope that this collection, perhaps as part of students' introduction to Sayles's work in a film or media course, may spark similar ambitions in future filmmakers.

NOTES

The epigraph to this chapter is cited in Carson 95–98.

1. Sayles's stories "I-80 Nebraska, M.490–M.205" and "Golden State," published in the *Atlantic Monthly* during the mid-1970s, both won O. Henry Awards, and his second novel, *Union Dues* (Little, Brown, 1977), was nominated for both the National Book Award and the National Book Critics

Circle Award. He continues to publish fiction and short-story collections, including *Los Gusanos* (Penguin, 1991) and *Dillinger in Hollywood: New and Selected Short Stories* (Thunder's Mouth/Nation Books, 2004).

2. For more detailed discussions of Sayles's problems with Paramount over *Baby It's You*, see Ryan, chapter 6, and Molyneaux, chapter 11.

3. The relevance of such a critique when I write this—the fall of 2004, as the Iraqi war occupation under the auspices of George W. Bush's administration continues—renders Sayles's work prescient. Perhaps we might see Danny Radnor as the spiritual, if fictional, progenitor of some Christians who, at this moment, have expressed dissent over the course of current events. In the April 2003 issue of *The Progressive*, journalist Colman McCarthy offered an engaging profile of one of Danny's "grandchildren," theological ethicist Stanley Hauerwas, for whom part of "nonviolence is . . . the attempt to make our lives vulnerable in a way that we need one another. To be against war . . . is a good place to start. But you never know where the violence is in your own life. To say you're nonviolent is not some position of self-righteousness—you kill and I don't. It's rather a way to make your life available to others in a way that they can help you discover ways you're implicated in violence that you hadn't even noticed" (24). In many ways, it is this ethical stance that Sayles specifically explores in *Matewan*, and indirectly in many of his other films.

4. The scripts for *Men With Guns* and *Lone Star* were published in a set from Faber and Faber (1998), and those for *Return of the Secaucus Seven*, *Matewan*, *Lone Star*, *Passion Fish*, and the recent feature set in Colorado appear in *Silver City and Other Screenplays* (Thunder's Mouth/Nation Books, 2004).

5. However, in an essay on the popularity of *Lone Star* as a model of historical counternarrative, Handley (2004) suggests that "the relevance of [*Lone Star*] to American studies has been misread" by scholars' privileging of the border-crossing trope. He argues persuasively that "[a]s much as the intended aim is to move away from American exceptionalism, if we categorically shun any examination of the unique particulars of U.S. history, any celebrations of discovered kinship across borders will only reflect a renewed narcissism" (161).

6. The prospect and implications of Sayles's own complicity in the creation and circulation of *Men With Guns* as postcolonial narrative is productively explored in Embry and Rodriguez (see the annotated resources).

7. *Silver City* was nominated as best film of 2004 by the Political Film Society; in previous years, Sayles's films *Matewan*, *City of Hope*, and *Men With Guns* were nominated or won awards in various categories from this organization.

WORKS CITED

Carson, Diane, ed. *John Sayles: Interviews*. Conversations with Filmmakers Series. Jackson: UP of Mississippi, 1999.

Corrigan, Timothy. "Auteurs and the New Hollywood." *The New American Cinema*. Ed. Jon Lewis. Durham: Duke UP, 1998. 38–63.

Embry, Marcus. "A Postcolonial Tale of Complicity: The 'Angel of History' and *Men With Guns*." *Discourse* 21.2 (1999): 163–80.

Handley, George B. "Oedipus in the Americas: *Lone Star* and the Reinvention of American Studies." *Forum for Modern Language Studies* 40.2 (2004): 160–81.

Lears, T. J. Jackson. "The Concept of Cultural Hegemony: Problems and Possibilities." *American Historical Review* 90.3 (1985): 567–93.

Levy, Emanuel. *Cinema of Outsiders: The Rise of American Independent Film*. New York: New York UP, 1999.

McCarthy, Colman. "'I'm a Pacifist Because I'm a Violent Son of a Bitch': A Profile of Stanley Hauerwas." *The Progressive* 67.4 (2003): 23–25.

Molyneaux, Gerard. *John Sayles: An Unauthorized Biography of the Pioneering Indie Filmmaker*. Los Angeles: Renaissance Books, 2000.

Pierson, John. *Spike, Mike, Slackers, & Dykes: A Guided Tour across a Decade of American Independent Cinema*. New York: Hyperion, 1995.

Pribram, E. Deidre. *Cinema and Culture: Independent Film in the United States, 1980–2001*. New York: Peter Lang, 2002.

Radway, Janice. "'What's in a Name?' Presidential Address to the American Studies Association, 20 November 1998." *American Quarterly* 51.1 (1999): 6.

Rodriguez, Ralph. "*Men With Guns*: The Story John Sayles Can't Tell." *The End of Cinema as We Know It: American Film in the Nineties*. Ed. Jon Lewis. New York: New York UP, 2001. 168–74.

Ryan, Jack. *John Sayles, Filmmaker: A Critical Study of the Independent Writer-Director*. Jefferson, NC: McFarland, 1998.

Washington, Mary Helen. "'Disturbing the Peace: What Happens to American Studies If You Put African-American Studies at the Center?' Presidential Address to the American Studies Association, 29 October 1997." *American Quarterly* 50.1 (1998): 16.

1

Sayles between the Systems:
Bucking "Industry Policy" and Indie Apolitical Chic

Cynthia Baron

The salient features of the films and televisions programs directed by John Sayles come into view when one compares Sayles's body of work with films produced by both Hollywood and American independent cinema during the last twenty-five years.[1] To assess the significance of the thematic and aesthetic qualities that distinguish Sayles's work, it is useful to consider the context in which Sayles's films have been produced and distributed, viewed and analyzed. In part, that context has been shaped by the economics and stylistic conventions of American cinema's two industrial systems, Hollywood and American independent cinema. That context has also been influenced by social and political developments in the United States during the last twenty-five years, in particular, the rise of neoconservatism.

When one compares Sayles's films to ostensibly apolitical films produced by Hollywood, it is impossible not to notice the progressive political perspective of Sayles's work. One should remember, however, that the political stance in Sayles's films is a distinguishing trait largely or perhaps only because contemporary mainstream American films rarely express a progressive perspective. As we will see, the unusual political dimension of Sayles's films serves to illuminate an important aspect of the mainstream system, namely, that Hollywood's long-standing policy of censoring screenplays and films critical of unbridled capitalism and governmental corruption has had a profound impact on the films that Hollywood produces and the expectations that American audiences bring with them when they watch movies.

At the same time, when compared with ostensibly political films produced by American independent cinema, Sayles's work does not have an obvious connection to the modernist film traditions that are often associated with left-leaning politics. Sayles's films are not marked by self-reflexivity, direct address, sound-image disjunctions, and incoherent or disrupted narrative patterns. They do not depend on shock, spectacle, or violence. Instead, in contrast to dominant trends in American independent cinema, Sayles's films draw on modernist and realist traditions. They employ long-take aesthetics and nonlinear, layered narrative designs that create multiple, shifting perspectives of characters and their social environments. Here again, the distinguishing features of Sayles's films indirectly illuminate the conventions of a system in American cinema, this time the system of American independent cinema.

Looking at America's independent film system from the vantage point of Sayles's body of work, one can see that in terms of economics and aesthetics, the Hollywood and independent film systems are not separate but instead entirely intertwined. The routine process of political censorship in Hollywood has increasingly shaped the economics and aesthetics of American independent cinema. Moreover, independent cinema's promise of unrestricted authorial freedom seems to have become publicity double-talk to cover up the fact that independent films help to sustain mainstream industry policies. Rather than producing scores of films from a progressive political perspective, today American independent cinema often generates products that display "a marginal difference in styling" without challenging the conservative political orientation of Hollywood entertainment products (Rosenbaum, *Movies as Politics* 1).

Along with the context defined by American cinema's two industrial systems, the social and political realignment that has taken place in the last twenty-five years is arguably one of the most salient features of the production and reception context for Sayles's films from *Return of the Secaucus Seven* (1980) to *Silver City* (2004). Ronald Reagan's election in 1980 signaled neoconservatives' success in transforming civil-rights demands—for individuals' equal protection under the law—into property owners' right to private, unfettered economic enterprise.

With the fragile union between liberalism and democracy broken, with demands for individual rights decoupled from communal obligations, for the last twenty-five years neoconservatives have won support for their policies from even working-class people by promoting a philosophy that eschews "New Deal visions of government assistance or working-class democracy" (Bodnar 213). Keeping this social and political realignment in mind, one can see how Sayles's focus on communities of college friends, union members, baseball players, and disenfranchised reporters, and on fragile coalitions in neighborhoods, border towns, and isolated outposts seems anachronistic to some, a welcome relief to others (see Zieger and Zieger 67–68).

Sayles's films are out of step with right-leaning American culture, but that is not to say that they are entirely unique. Films such as *Blue Collar* (1978), *F.I.S.T.* (1978), and *Norma Rae* (1979), which provide disparate views of working-class characters, were produced in the years leading up to Sayles's *Return of the Secaucus Seven*. Films such as *Wag the Dog* (1997), *Primary Colors* (1998), and *Bulworth* (1998), which explore various connections between corruption and political power, were released at about the same time as Sayles's *Men With Guns* (1998). Still, in spite of the many contemporary films "inspired by Nixon-inspired distrust" of politics and politicians (Bruzzi 19), Sayles's body of work is in fact distinct from mainstream and independent American cinema because throughout his films, one finds "inherently political recurrent themes: sympathy with working-class and poor people, cynicism about authority, and a view of wealth as being corrupting" (Meyer and Hoynes 33).

The progressive political focus in Sayles's films prompts David Meyer and William Hoynes to compare them to "populist films" such as *It Happened One Night* (1934), *Mr. Deeds Goes to Town* (1936), and *You Can't Take It With You* (1938) directed by Frank Capra (33). Sayles's sustained interest in working-class people also invites comparison between his films and the diverse collection of working-class films produced in the Progressive Era—before the construction of movie palaces, the influx of middle-class audiences, and the "shift from highly polemical films that explored conflict between the classes to far more conservative films that emphasized fantasies of love and harmony among the classes" (Ross xiii).[2] Comprehensive studies by Steven J. Ross and Michael Slade Shull of silent-era working-class films allow one to see important connections between Sayles's work and the collection of films produced in the early years of

American cinema by "workers, radicals, and labor organizations . . . that challenged the dominant ideology of individualism and portrayed collective action . . . as the most effective way to improve the lives of citizens" (Ross 7; see Foner 103–11).

Ross's account of films such as *A Martyr to His Cause* (1911), *From Dawn to Dusk* (1913), and *What Is to Be Done?* (1914) actually reveals a tangible connection between Sayles's films and Progressive Era working-class films. In 1923, following the 1921 murder of Matewan sheriff Sid Hatfield, the subsequent acquittal of his murderers, and the theft of the mine workers' only copy of *Smiling Sam* (a one reel reenactment of Sid Hatfield's legendary gun battle with the Baldwin-Felts agents who had been hired to crush miners' attempt to unionize), Sid's brother, C. Willis Hatfield, and members of United Mine Workers Local 323 attempted, unsuccessfully, to secure funding for a feature film that would depict the events leading up to the shootout between Hatfield and the Baldwin-Felts agents (see Ross 226–27, 253–54, 343–44; see also DeKoven 143). Ross points out that the release of *Matewan* in 1987 represented the completion of that project first conceived in 1923.

The salient connections between Sayles's films and working-class films produced in the Progressive Era (1909–17) point to important distinctions between Sayles's work and Hollywood films produced according to industry censorship policies publicly in place since 1924. The link between Sayles's work and silent-era working-class films that "promoted the ethos of mutualism" also suggests differences between Sayles's films and dominant trends in American independent cinema, for as Ross explains, "social realism and political commentary are not the hallmarks of the modern movie industry," mainstream or independent (93, 5). Marianne DeKoven confirms that point in her discussion of Sayles's concern with characters in given social circumstances. She explains that postmodern visions of "temporality, reality, consciousness and the subject" make Sayles's serious realist fiction seem anachronistic (129). While Sayles's work might be out of step with certain prevailing trends, the political perspective in Sayles's work invites examination, if only because it indirectly tells us a great deal about developments in the Hollywood film industry, American independent cinema, and the country's political realities.

Political Cinema

In some sense all films are political, even and perhaps especially if they are marketed as entertainment (see Combs and Combs 7; Christensen 2). At the same time, one can identify films that belong to a loosely defined genre of political films, which includes thrillers and social-problem films that focus on politicians and government scandals (see Christensen 3–11). A film like *Force of Evil* (1948), which draws "an explicit parallel between corruption and racketeering, and the 'normal' operation of American business" (Neve 133), exemplifies the political cinema of its era because it underscores class conflicts and the effects of materialism in American society. Today, vestiges of the left-leaning political thriller genre can be seen in studio pictures like *JFK* (1991), *A Civil Action* (1998), *Erin Brockovich* (2000), and *Paycheck* (2003), which use bowdlerized accounts of government scandals to generate entertaining narratives.[3]

Steven Ross argues that "a film is 'political' if it depicts the uses and abuses of power by one individual, group, or class against another" (41). Echoing that point, M. Keith Booker proposes that political cinema is best understood as film practice that dramatizes the belief that there should be "economic, social, and political justice for all people, regardless of their class, ethnicity, or gender" and shows that "capitalism is fundamentally incompatible with this" objective (ix). Ross notes that "films do not have to offer solutions to be political, nor do they have to devote their entire story to exploring political issues" (41). He explains that "some of the most political films of the [Progressive] era never referred to political movements. They simply showed ordinary men and women standing up for themselves" (41).

Ross's observation that films become political simply by showing ordinary people standing up for themselves is crucial to understanding the political nature of Sayles's films. In sharp contrast to the apolitical madmen and beautiful losers often found in contemporary mainstream and independent cinema, the underdogs in Sayles's films demonstrate not only the willingness to work for change. They also possess the intelligence and personal dignity to find solutions—even if, as it did for Shoeless Joe Jackson, it means joining a bush-league team.

Sayles's films often exemplify long-standing traditions in left-leaning political cinema. They consistently depict characters that are relational entities and a "responsible part of a collective" (Ryan and Kellner 274). As such, Sayles's films are entirely distinct from right-leaning films that present the individual hero as an "isolated unit [and] lone survivalist warrior battling others" (Ryan and Kellner 274). Sayles's films also often show official history to be a lie or a myth. While that objective is demonstrated perhaps most clearly in a film such as *Eight Men Out* (1988), Sayles's interest in exposing the falsity of official stories forms the spine of *City of Hope* (1991) and *Lone Star* (1996), and it can be found in all of his films—beginning with the group of characters being detained on suspicion of "bambicide" in *Return of the Secaucus Seven*.

Following traditions in left-leaning political cinema, Sayles's films repeatedly present history as "a domain of struggle . . . in which the outcome is undecided" (Ryan and Kellner 275). That perspective, found throughout Sayles's work, is eloquently expressed in the closing scenes of *Sunshine State* (2002). Beginning with a glimpse of the townspeople's collective success, the sequence starts at the almost-bulldozed Native American burial ground that has stopped the developers' plans to transform the area. Then, by showing us the developers leaving town for another destination, Sayles emphasizes that the corporation already has its envoys right back at work to take control of another tract of land. Intertwining connotations in the two scenes, Sayles concludes the sequence with a long take. The shot, which begins as a tight, low-angle shot of the wealthy golfers casually teeing off, pulls back to become a wide shot of the men standing on a sliver of boulevard median. The congested street illustrates the human cost of the real estate developers' financial profit. Still, seeing the golfer-developers squeezed in by the congestion reminds one that even they will not escape the consequences of their actions. Moreover, the fact that the men pulling the strings are boxed into a small plot of their own turf even seems to suggest that the future holds promise for disenfranchised people if they work together to create equitable environments.

While right-leaning films tacitly share the progressive view that the future depends on the actions of concerned people, they invariably express an entirely different vision from Sayles's films. Often appealing to notions of tradition, conservative films suggest that the best future for everyone depends on the powerful remaining in power. They propose that safety depends on everyone staying in their proper place. Right-leaning films intimate that history and power relations of the past are a legitimate basis for existing relations of power. Valorizing the wisdom, courage, and strength of those in power, right-leaning films repeatedly warn of the dangers inherent in departures from existing relations of power. The present represents a time of danger precisely because power held in the past can be lost. Given that perspective, right-leaning films frequently feature fantastic heroes whose battles against external forces are legitimized by the heroes' own power and by the threat external forces pose to the heroes' property, identity, and power (see Ryan and Kellner 275).

Sayles's films present an entirely different picture of the present's significance. Echoing progressive visions of the individual and history, Sayles's films seem to suggest that the best of all possible worlds is one in which society is "a source of cooperation and mutual help . . . a network of multiple, interconnected, expanding relations" (Ryan and Kellner 275). And in films like *Return of the Secaucus Seven*, *Matewan*, and *Sunshine State*, Sayles presents audiences with clear instances of self-defined communities serving as a "source of cooperation and mutual help." In other films, Sayles makes the point that human society must be a network of cooperation by showing us nightmarish environments that lack cooperation and mutual help.

As if responding to the initial ascendancy of neoconservatism, Sayles created striking visions of dystopian societies in a series of films from the early 1980s, *Lianna* (1983), *Baby It's You* (1983), and *Brother from Another Planet* (1984). Then, turning to a more utopian vision in films from *Matewan* forward, Sayles has produced thoughtful studies of characters who work together to further the good of all. Yet along with the films that have provided glimpses of a progressive future, Sayles has also continued to create work that reflects a keen awareness of political realities. Exposing the consequences of weapons proliferation, in *Men With Guns* Sayles vividly captures the horrors of a world in which cooperation and mutual help are almost entirely absent. In *Silver City*, Sayles returns to his focus on dystopic American society, this time looking at a world in which corporate moguls control the government and the press. Released two months before the 2004 presidential election, *Silver City* affirms the value of underground, investigative reporting. It also damns the monstrousness of corporate America. Its closing image, one that reminds

Elma (Mary McDonnell) and Joe (Chris Cooper) in *Matewan* (1987), a film indicative of the connection between Sayles's films and working-class films of the Progressive Era.

me of Sayles's piranha and alligator exploitation film allegories, reveals thousands of dead fish floating in the lake that had, moments before, provided the scenic backdrop for the cynical and bombastic campaign ad produced by the self-appointed handlers of corporate stooge and dim-witted political heir Dickie Pilager (Chris Cooper).

There are, as M. Keith Booker points out, "a number of ironies and difficulties inherent in" the project of identifying any film as politically progressive (ix). He explains that the "attempt to tease out the presence of leftist ideas in films that are in general not overtly leftist places the investigator in a position weirdly reminiscent of that of the House Un-American Activities Committee (HUAC) of the late 1940s and 1950s" (ix). When considering the work of John Sayles, it is probably useful to note that Sayles sees his films not so much as political films but as films that are "politically conscious" (Phipps 4).[4] He also points out that his films are at odds with mainstream representations largely because of the conception of character and character relations underlying his work.

Whereas Hollywood high-concept films' simplified character types ensure instant audience recognition (see Wyatt 53–60), Sayles's films challenge conservative visions of society in part by establishing connections between sympathetic and unsympathetic characters. They also challenge right-leaning positions by being structured in ways that create dramatic space for characters' dissonant perspectives. In contrast to high-concept films like *American Gigolo* (1980) that valorize "the mindless obsession with self in contemporary America" (Lipsitz, *American* 85), Sayles's films present audiences with a progressive view of the individual as a relational entity, a progressive view of history as a domain of struggle, and a progressive view of society as a network of interconnected relations that requires individuals to be concerned with the common good.[5]

Industry Policy as Political Censorship

In discussions about censorship in American cinema, censorship is consistently equated with legal censorship of violent or pornographic texts. Questions about political censorship in the film industry are rarely raised, and if they are, the focus is often on state censorship in countries other than the United States. Yet, as Jonathan Rosenbaum points out, one form of political censorship, namely the "refusal to discuss capitalism itself," is "more prevalent in the United States than in Europe" (*Movie Wars* 159).[6] Echoing and expanding on that point, Sue Curry Jansen argues that throughout its history, censorship in the United States has been primarily state and corporate political censorship. In her study of American censorial practices that rarely make headlines in U.S. news coverage, Jansen links developments in American commercial practice with identifiable governmental actions that are seldom seen as censorial in a democratic, free-market society. Her study reveals that Americans need to recognize forms of censorship that are "routinely undertaken by state bureaucracies in the name of 'national security' [as well as] censorships routinely sanctioned by the 'profit principle'" (15).[7]

In the United States, the government has not needed to engage in political censorship of Hollywood films because the industry's corporate associations have been so efficient in their policing of film content (see Lewis, *Hollywood* 180–81).[8] With institutions and individuals working at various levels, the industry has effectively censored cinematic representations of legitimate labor concerns, the effects of unbridled capitalism, and the potential power of organized laborers. Steven Ross points out that political censorship in the American film industry developed in the early years of the twentieth century because powerful constituencies across the country considered films dealing with class struggle "more threatening than cinematic displays of sex and violence" (87–88). Employers and government officials feared the influence that films like *By Man's Law* (1913), *The Jungle* (1914), *The Strike at Coaldale* (1914), and *The Blacklist* (1916) could have on working and poor people (see Shull for photos and plot summaries of representative films from the period).[9]

Political censorship in the American film industry was quickly effective. By the mid-1920s, filmmakers "hesitated to make labor-capital films because censors threatened to ban them" (Ross 196; see Gianos 2). Film censorship boards in one hundred cities had shown that they would act "against any producer—labor film company or Hollywood studio—who made features or newsreels that criticized capitalists or offered sympathetic depictions of working-class life and struggles" (Ross 196). Francis Walsh explains that in subsequent years, any films "involving organized labor acted as a lighting rod, attracting criticism from any number of sources" (570). Walsh notes that "local boards of censors throughout the country were particularly sensitive to scenes showing labor violence" (567).

To circumvent disruption by local censors, industry executives in the studio era made political censorship an integral part of Hollywood cinema. Ruth Vasey explains that censorship in this period did not exclusively or primarily concern filmic representations of sex and crime. Instead, it concerned representations that did not conform to "industry policy." Gregory Black notes that Production Code Administration head Joseph Breen "coined the term 'industry policy' for dealing with those films that, while technically within the moral confines of the code . . . were adjudged 'dangerous' to the well-being of the industry . . . because they dealt with politically sensitive topics" (245). Breen labeled "anything that might be construed as overt criticism of the government, the free-enterprise system, or the police and courts [as] Communistic propaganda" and required that it be "banned from the screen" (Black 246). Screenplays about racism, poverty, unemployment, or labor-management conflicts in America were altered to meet industry policy guidelines because candid treatment of such subjects was thought to involve "communistic" criticism of existing structures of power (see Black 246).[10]

Public pronouncements by the evolving industry association that established the Production Code Administration and later the Code and Rating Administration (known as the Classification and Rating Administration after 1977) have led many observers to believe that the film industry's censorship institutions are morally conservative and that they have only been concerned with protecting film audiences from offensive or ethically harmful representation of sex and violence. Yet since 1916 politically sensitive topics have been consistently eliminated from screenplays before they can be moved into production and Hollywood has continued to make fewer and fewer films about class issues or social problems. Those facts suggest that the industry's corporate associations are politically conservative and that they have been primarily concerned with protecting the increasing profits industry leaders make in an environment shielded from realistic representations of labor-management conflicts and depictions of the positive capabilities of working people.[11]

Interestingly, just as the Motion Picture Producers and Distributors of America (MPPDA) covered up its connections to the labor battles of the 1910s and 1920s, the Motion Picture Association of America (MPAA) created in 1945 has downplayed its roots in the labor battles of the 1940s (see also Lewis, *Hollywood* 13, 182). In more recent stages of the association's evolution, that public relations strategy has been executed with remarkable finesse. For example, the emphasis on representations of sex and violence built into the Code and Rating System developed in 1968 perhaps ensured that filmmakers seeking to challenge the defined status quo would not even think about unemployment or union organizing as radical subjects.

Moreover, while the arrival of the rating scheme seemed to suggest that American films were freer than ever before, since that time appeals to marketplace forces have made political censorship a central feature of contemporary film practice. Litigation or protest initiated by local politicians, civic leaders, or special interest groups such as the American Legion present themselves as forces to contend with (see Lyons, Chapters 2–5; Miller 125, 160–61). The consolidation of power that has taken place in the entertainment industry during the last twenty-five years also serves to delimit the range of expression in contemporary American cinema (see Lewis, *New American* 87–120). In the current environment, political censorship is simply an effective negotiation of the marketplace. As Jon Lewis notes, "in Hollywood content regulation does have its political dimension. But the political is subsumed by or conflated with the economic" (*Hollywood* 7).

It may be possible to compare Sayles's work to films by directors such as Douglas Sirk, Nicholas Ray, and Abraham Polonsky (see Andrew 74, 94, 109). There is, however, a profound difference between the political climate for American filmmakers in the 1940s and 1950s, and the economic and cultural milieu for filmmakers today. For the earlier generation, "even in the darkest days of McCarthyism, social movements, cultural practitioners, [filmmakers,] and traditional intellectuals continued to draw on the legacy of the past to preserve oppositional thought" (Lipsitz, *American* 22). Now, progressive filmmakers like Sayles must contend with the routinized political censorship that is the consequence of the industry's long-standing, highly effective opposition to any person or any representation that challenges existing relations of power. Today's left-leaning filmmakers must also reckon with the fact that for the last thirty years "the most important mass mobilizations" have come from the right (Lipsitz, *American* xv). By the time Sayles's first film was released in 1980, the conservative coalition had already discredited the social movements of the Progressive, New Deal, and Civil Rights eras by pitting people who had once been beneficiaries of union organization (usually white male laborers, now unemployed or economically insecure) against people identified with the civil rights movement (also unemployed or economically insecure).

Sayles's Films and Censorship in the Corporate Era

Sayles's studies of characters in social environments do not conform to industry policy because they deal candidly with government corruption, labor-management conflicts, class difference, racism, and the limitations of people's social understanding. Corporate Hollywood's enforcement of industry policy makes it difficult to distribute and exhibit even independently produced films that might be dangerous to the well-being of the film industry, which profits from media-related products that equate freedom and happiness with wealth and prosperity (see Horne 6). A small sampling of film reviews of *Baby It's You*, the only Sayles film distributed by a major studio (Paramount), illustrates the dynamics of the market-driven censorship process.

When the film was released, several reviewers called attention to Sayles's concern with "the politics of class" (Bonavoglia 38). Ronald Simon discussed the way Sayles subverted the teen romance genre by including the lovers' "painful separation caused by class differences" (302). Sheila Benson told readers that the film explored "the question of class and unequal opportunity with humor and tender insight" (1). David Denby proposed that the film had been "nurtured by tough, anti-romantic notions of how class and money work in America" (72). David Ansen discussed the film's "trenchant social details" and explained that Sayles was "attuned to every nuance of class" (78).

Equally important, reviewers also often noted that the studio seemed intent on keeping the film out of circulation. Sheila Benson argued that the performances of Rosanna Arquette and Vincent Spano made the film "well worth searching out, even in the no-fanfare release to which Paramount [had] consigned it" (1). Chris Auty wrote, "kept on the shelf for two years by UIP, *Baby It's You* joins *Over the Edge* as one of those films whose distribution history seems genuinely inexplicable on commercial grounds" (330). Denby told readers, "it's a minor, badly flawed movie, but it's also charming, tender, and funny, and it deserves better treatment than the quick dump Paramount is giving it" (72).

While these passing observations do not demonstrate a connection between the film's tacit critique of the free-enterprise system and Paramount's disinterest in promoting the film, they do point to the routine character of Hollywood's political censorship. The critics' comments about the film's limited distribution also show how even reviewers, who are employees of newspapers and magazines that stand to gain economically from the continued well-being of the film industry, are sometimes prompted to intimate that a film's distribution history has been shaped by political rather than commercial forces. The reviewers' passing observations on the studio's distribution methods reveal how effective censorship is when it depends on the simple process of minimizing consumers' exposure to politically sensitive material.[12]

In her study of contemporary American independent cinema, E. Deidre Pribram observes that routine political censorship may be one of the most significant effects of studios' ownership of independent distribution companies (39). Considering that question, *Variety* reporter Dan Cox explained in a 1998 article that "in the last year, lone wolf production companies like Arnon Milchan's New Regency, Peter Guber's Mandalay Entertainment, Armyan Bernstein's Beacon Communications and Mike Medavoy's Phoenix Pictures [had] become integral to the corporate studio filmmaking process" (1). That business configuration leaves MPAA members as the final arbiters of film content (see Cox 102).[13]

The corporatization of mainstream and independent American film is intertwined with national social-economic developments that crystallized in the 1980s. Michael Rogin points out that Reagan's "landslide election to a second term . . . consummated the first lasting electoral realignment since FDR's second term" (33–34). Rogin contrasts the ideological perspective that became dominant in the 1980s with "interest group liberalism—the labor, business, ethnic, and public interest coalition centered in the Democratic Party—[which had been] the governing American political system from Roosevelt's New Deal to the election of Ronald Reagan" (xvii–xviii). This realignment has played a crucial role in shaping the cultural and industrial context of John Sayles's films.

Outlining points made by Sidney Plotkin and William E. Scheuerman, George Lipsitz explains that "a key goal of conservative political work over the past three decades has been to . . . encourage people to think of themselves as taxpayers and homeowners rather than citizens and workers" ("Academic Politics" 84). Summarizing developments that have effectively discredited interest-group liberalism, Lipsitz explains that conservatives have been able to label the "demands for redistributive justice by women, racial and sexual minorities, and by other aggrieved social groups as the 'whining of special interests'" (84). In contrast to the period of interest-group liberalism that fostered the unprecedented rise of union representation, the neoconservative movement has ensured that the United States has the lowest percentage of workers represented by labor unions in the world (see Puette 159).[14]

The effects of the current conservative political environment are far reaching. In part it means that the perspective of ostensibly left-leaning Hollywood films needs to be examined carefully. As Lynn Garafola points out, since the commercial success of *The Godfather* (1972), Hollywood films have framed narratives about working-class characters, not as studies of class conflict, but instead as conventional portrayals of ethnic identity. Garafola sees films like *Mean Streets* (1973), *Taxi Driver* (1976), *Saturday Night Fever* (1977), and *The Deer Hunter* (1978) as exemplifying this conservative strategy. Locating the conservative ideology at the foundation of seemingly political films, she points out that in films like *Rocky* (1976), *Blue Collar* (1978), and *F.I.S.T.* (1978), "under a mask of critical liberalism, Hollywood projects onto the union and its membership the moral paralysis and cynicism associated with the government" after Vietnam and Watergate (543). Succinctly describing dominant trends in contemporary film practice, Garafola explains that "for Hollywood's new breed of filmmakers, the working class is ultimately a pretext in whose name corporate media voices the vague discontents of the [neoconservative era while at the same time] discrediting the politics of change" (544).

Sayles's narratives do not conflate economic class with ethnic identity but instead examine the two factors as they overlap in the experiences of individual characters. Even in an early film like *Baby It's You*, Sayles does not reduce the complications between Sheik (Vincent Spano) and Jill (Rosanna Arquette) to ethnic differences between Italians and Jews or the very different opportunities available to working- and middle-class teenagers growing up in Trenton, New Jersey, in the 1960s. Similarly, Sayles's films do not let the U.S. government off the hook by presenting unions as the locus of institutional misconduct. In *Matewan*, union organizer Joe Kenehan (Chris Cooper) is the ethical and spiritual guide for the sometimes quick-to-judge mine workers. Moreover, Sayles's films do not present audiences with characters whose vague discontent has no connection to pragmatic politics of change. In *City of Hope*, council member Wynn (Joe Morton) is a salient counterexample to the many discontented, apolitical characters in contemporary mainstream and independent cinema because he is prepared to work on behalf of his neighborhood, knowing full well that his fractious community is invariably outvoted and outmaneuvered by more established bases of power in the city.

Like many American films in the post-Watergate era, Sayles's films buck the system defined by Hollywood's industry policy by violating the stricture against "depicting public officials as criminals" (Lyons 13). Yet unlike other contemporary American filmmakers, Sayles's focus is on public officials who belong to systemically unjust institutions. Sayles's films explore links between politicians and organized crime, between police officers and criminals, between city officials and powerful private interests in ways that leave two lasting impressions. First, in contrast to mainstream political thrillers, Sayles's films do not prompt audiences to identify with vigilante lawmen who reestablish order by eliminating some isolated transgressor. Instead, exemplifying a thread that runs through all of Sayles's work, in films like *City of Hope* and *Lone Star*, the search for truth leads the councilman and the sheriff back to themselves as the solution to the problems they have uncovered.

Second, in contrast to mainstream political thrillers that vacillate between the vision of the lone hero saving the day for all the lesser humans and the vision that social ills are caused by forces so evil, so pervasive, and so mysterious that society cannot be changed for the better, Sayles's films serve as a series of picaresque vignettes of groups comprised sometimes of only a couple of people whose cooperation makes a small, sometimes inadvertent, but still potentially positive impact on their environment. Sayles's depiction of the mutual assistance that emerges out of conflicts between characters in films like *Matewan* and *Sunshine State* gives expression to the effect ostensibly private interactions can have on larger social-political circumstances.

Sayles's films violate the policy that films must confirm that bankers, lawyers, and businessmen are "the very backbone of our country" (Vasey, "Beyond" 107) in part because any and all of the characters in his stories have the potential to be the backbone of the country and in part because Sayles's bankers, lawyers, and businessmen are often no more or less well intended, no more or less fallible, no more or less accountable, no more or less deserving of circumspect compassion than other characters in the stories. The consequent moral ambiguity of films like *Eight Men Out, City of Hope,* and *Lone Star* makes them very different from films that "publicists feel equipped to hype" (Rosenbaum, *Movies as Politics* 184).

Sayles's work presents audiences with more than "a marginal difference in styling" (Rosenbaum, *Movies as Politics* 1). Discussing *Shannon's Deal,* the NBC television series that Sayles wrote and directed in the 1990/1991 season, David Meyer and William Hoynes explain that the series presented a "radically unconventional picture of the legal system and the role of the lawyer" (40). They contrast Sayles's television series with *LA Law.* While *Shannon's Deal* "suggests that idealistic visions of the American legal system as a site for dispensing justice [are misplaced, on *LA Law*] rarely is there any recognition of the larger political and economic forces which [public interest attorney Jack] Shannon confronts" (Meyer and Hoynes 40). Meyer and Hoynes point out that *LA Law* attorneys "do not acknowledge the structural inequalities built into the criminal justice system" (40). By comparison, Shannon recognizes that "the legal system is stacked against his clients" but works to get them the best deal possible (38).

Like all of Sayles's work, the television series presents audiences with a vision of social reality that is more critical of bankers, lawyers, businessmen, and politicians than industry policy would allow precisely because Sayles examines systemic and institutional problems rather than isolated, individual problems that can be solved by punishing the particular individual. Equally problematic from a corporate perspective, the series also offers an empowering vision of ordinary people who form egalitarian relationships to help each other and the people around them. Exemplifying the progressive political perspective that distinguishes Sayles's body of films, *Shannon's Deal* violates industry policy on two counts, for the series presents the life-sustaining effects of rational, social cooperation in the interest of the common good as a viable counterweight to the stultifying consequences of individual and institutional self-interest.

Outside the Fashionable Trends in Independent Cinema

The factors that have shaped mainstream American cinema have also had an effect on contemporary American independent cinema. As a consequence, while Sayles's films are not suitable as mainstream fare, his films also fall outside dominant trends in independent cinema. Pribram notes that in contemporary American independent film, concerns about marketability have had three related consequences: limited aesthetic experimentation, limited expression of political perspectives, and a focus on formal elements that ostensibly distinguish an independent film from mainstream fare (see 52). The lucid, often leisurely visual style of Sayles's films stands in sharp contrast to the flamboyant visuals of films that define "edge" in independent film (see Merritt 398–403). Even setting aside other considerations, Sayles's signature shot—"a long unbroken take meandering from group to group, picking up phrases and showing how all these people connect up" (Kemp 223)—distinguishes his work from the "jagged, rock-scored, in-your-face, wildly gestural mode" that has become a key feature of indie film aesthetics (Hoberman 31).[15]

Sayles's films also exist at a distance from central trends in independent film because they feature naturalistic narrative design. Observers have seen connections between Sayles's work and the social analysis found in films directed by Wayne Wang, Spike Lee, and Todd Haynes (see Andrew 362). Yet, as Emanuel Levy points out, "Sayles is one of the few filmmakers, inde and Hollywood, who is concerned with the diverse and complex structure of American society" (101). In Sayles's work, that concern is expressed largely by Sayles's naturalistic conception of "character as a product of accumulated social and cultural influences" (Kemp 221; see Carson "Plain and Simple"). That view of the individual as a relational entity violates the narrative norms of American independent cinema, which for the last two decades have followed mainstream conventions by presenting audiences with characters that are defined by formulaic psychological quandaries that emerge during conflicts with threatening outsiders.

The marked difference between Sayles's films and independent cinema's prevailing stylistic trends makes some observers question Sayles's place in the indie field. Pribram explains that "if a film is aesthetically experimental it is likely to be considered independent even if it is not in any way alternative in content or social agenda" (71). By comparison, "if a film is alternative in social agenda but formally conventional, it is the least likely to find acceptance within the boundaries of independent film" (71). That conceptual scheme causes labor history films such as *Union Maids* (1976), *Harlan County* (1977), *Babies and Banners* (1978), *Northern Lights* (1978), and *The Wobblies* (1979) to exist at the margins of independent film practice, even though *Harlan County* received an Academy Award for Best Documentary in 1978 and *Northern Lights* was named the Best First Feature at the 1979 Cannes Film Festival (see Demeter 545–57). It also means that films directed by John Sayles are difficult to classify as independent "because his work is not formally experimental" in a way that is widely recognized (Pribram 51).

The fact that Sayles's films do not represent central trends in American independent cinema is curious. *Return of the Secaucus Seven* is often described as a seminal film in the independent movement (see Pribram 15; Ferncase 15–28) cited after, for example, *A Woman Under the Influence* (1974) and *Stranger Than Paradise* (1985) (see Pribram 19). John Pierson proposes that Sayles's *Brother from Another Planet* belongs (together with *Stranger Than Paradise, Stop Making Sense, Choose Me, Blood Simple, Streetwise,* and *Paris, Texas*) to the group of films released in the fall/winter of 1984/85 that constituted a "veritable golden age for independent films" (28).

The marginal status of Sayles's films might have something to do with box-office figures. In the early to mid-1980s, the grosses for Sayles's films did not match those for foreign art films like *Fanny and Alexander* (1984) or *My Life as a Dog* (1987), which both grossed over $4 million. In the late 1980s and beyond, the grosses for Sayles's films do not begin to compare to independently funded entertainment films like *Dirty Dancing* (1987) or *Teenage Mutant Ninja Turtles* (1990), which grossed $25 million and $62 million, respectively. The box office for Sayles's films also does not compare to the remarkable success of Michael Moore's work from *Roger & Me* (1989) to *Fahrenheit 9/11* (2004). Only one Sayles film, *Lone Star* (1996), has had a better box office than indie favorite *sex, lies, and videotape* (1989) by grossing almost $13 million.

Sayles's films belong to trends in independent cinema if one considers their low budgets, nonstudio funding and distribution, limited release pattern, nonstar casting, specialized audience, socially conscious subject matter, complex mode of storytelling, and director who has made a commitment to working independently (see Pribram 5–9). Yet Sayles's films do not embody trends in independent cinema if one equates independent cinema with filmmaking that is clearly marked by modernist, avant-garde aesthetic experimentation (see Pribram 9, 58–76). Modernism's significant influence on contemporary American independent cinema is disclosed by the premium its practitioners and critics place on explicit authorial signatures and on films that can be readily identified as original, shocking, and strange (Pribram 76). Pribram points to the very narrow conception of modernism and postmodernism that informs the majority of independent films. Noting the "dominance of gangster and crime genres" in Hollywood and independent film, Pribram explains: "what has variously been called art shock, violent chic, and art house designer violence is the single most prevalent, one could well say overrepresented, genre in independent film" (176). Of course, not one of Sayles's films falls in the art-shock genre.

To understand how avant-garde aesthetic experimentation in independent cinema could have become identified with the designer violence of films like *Bad Lieutenant* (1992), one needs only to remember that "the movies that people hear about are precisely those that publicists feel equipped to hype" (Rosenbaum, *Movies as Politics* 184). Commenting on the marketing campaigns of the "major independent" distributors now linked to the conglomerates of mainstream cinema, Rosenbaum notes that a few independent film titles are "smeared across public consciousness like lowfat margarine" while other independent films "never get mentioned in the infotainment universe" (184). He reminds readers that commercial success and critical influence do not "operate independently of advertising" and that box-office figures do not reflect "some sifting through of popular consensus" (184).

Rosenbaum's points are especially pertinent to discussions about the place of Sayles's work in American cinema because the contemporary political climate makes it very difficult to sell Sayles's work. Sayles recognizes that the politically conscious subject matter he and his collaborators want to explore does not suit the Hollywood system. It fails to provide mainstream "vehicles for trendy young stars who are being rushed into yet more movies about trendy young subjects for trendy young audiences" (Carson, *John Sayles* 96). The films' progressive political perspectives also fail to provide vehicles for actors in independent films about trendy subjects.

While films like *Matewan* and *Eight Men Out* might be "spurned by studios for their political content" (Carson, *John Sayles* xiv), the subject matter of Sayles's films also presents difficulties for independent distributors who have found ways to sell films "associated with identity politics: gay and lesbian cinema, African American cinema, Asian and Asian American cinema, Latino/Latina cinema, women's cinema and so on" (Pribram 9; see xiv, 52). With *Brother from Another Planet* being the most obvious example, Sayles's films integrate the perspectives and concerns of different underrepresented social constituencies into their narratives. Yet Sayles himself does not belong to one of the identity groups and his narrative focus changes with each film. These factors have stymied small distributors' efforts to market the films effectively to any one of independent cinema's various target audiences.

Writing about the unfashionable aspect of Sayles's films, Gavin Smith explains that they are "unified chiefly by a realistic, unsentimental sympathy; a rational, almost-journalistic sensibility; an animating spirit of inquiry; and by a shrewd underlying awareness of the political implications of his material" (xiv). He argues that "if Sayles has an overarching impulse, it is to investigate the complex, shifting relationship between individuals and their communities and social orders, or put another way, the dynamic between the personal and the political in ordinary life" (xiv). Pribram echoes that perception, arguing that Sayles has made "a career-long commitment to exploring narratives of multiple, and shifting, perspectives" (51).

Critics have called attention to this aspect of Sayles's work from the beginning of his career. Writing about the design of *Return of the Secaucus Seven*, Naomi Glauberman and Claudia Fonda-Bonardi notes, "there isn't a linear narrative line; there is a layering effect" (32). Edwin Kephart characterizes the multiple perspectives that emerged in the film by pointing out that "as the characters reappear in scene after scene, their collective quirkiness develops into recognizable patterns of behavior that become identifiably and indelibly real" (566). Richard Corliss discusses the film's "discursive, episodic format" and, comparing Sayles's methods of scene construction with those used by Billy Wilder, explains that Sayles had created "more than a dozen complex, contradictory characters [simply] through their speech rhythms, the way they walk and sit and prepare food" (101). Andrew Sarris is impressed by "the ultimate intricacy of the various personality patterns and life styles expressed through the elaboration of once-or-twice-in-a-lifetime ensemble acting" (41). Comparing *Return of the Secaucus Seven* to Jean Renoir's *Rules of the Game* (1939), Orson Welles's *The Magnificent Ambersons* (1942), and Jacques Prevert's *Children of Paradise* (1945), Sarris argues that Sayles's film was "one of the few American films in recent years with a multiplicity of perspectives" (41).

Echoing those sentiments, Pribram explains that one could locate Sayles's films at the vanguard rather than margins of American independent cinema. She notes that "alternative film is defined, and continually redefined, in contradistinction to changing forms of normative cinematic practices and changing conceptions of the hegemonic" (50). Pribram's point here is key to ascertaining the significance of Sayles's work. Their alternative formal design comes into view when they are compared to Hollywood high-concept films and to indie films that feature art-house designer violence. Their alternative political perspective becomes apparent in relation to the politically conservative orientation of mainstream and even independent American cinema.

Pribram debunks the equation between alternative film and avant-garde formal strategies. She proposes that "a looser, more floating notion of alternative artistic activity would be better in keeping with the multiple, vast potential of the permutations that artifacts can and do take" (50). Citing Rainer Werner Fassbinder's films as examples of "narrative avant-garde" cinema, Pribram suggests that "the concept of alternative narrative practice might open up a space [in independent cinema] for a filmmaker like John Sayles" (50, 51). The term "narrative avant-garde" is a useful way to describe the design of Sayles's narratives that break with conventional views of the individual and society. The politically avant-garde conception of character in Sayles's films does not depend on a simple return to nineteenth- or mid-twentieth-century naturalistic conceptions of character. Instead, the conception of character in Sayles's films is colored by a contemporary vision of society that integrates progressive perspectives from across the twentieth century.

George Packer's analysis of Sayles's films helps to clarify the significance of their alternative narrative design. In a comparative study of John Sayles and Oliver Stone, Packer notes that both filmmakers have, since the 1980s, "been turning out movies that attempt to portray and interpret America with some consistent degree of sympathy for the downtrodden and suspicion of the powerful" (105). Packer proposes, however, that Stone's more successful career shows "the attraction of glamorous muck over common decency, and the difficulty of saying something serious about politics through the vehicle of mass culture" (109). More specifically, he argues that Stone's riveting narratives join "the shallowest instincts from the sixties—paranoia, grandiosity, romantic primitivism—to the skillful manipulation of images and celebrity of our own decade" (109). By comparison, even though Sayles is from the same generation as Stone, Packer finds that Sayles "belongs temperamentally to an earlier period of radicalism [because] his main characters aren't alienated rebels, but working people ensnared in mundane obligations to family, job, town" (106).

Packer explains that Sayles's films are "reminiscent of the Popular Front era, and of films by directors like Capra and Ford" because one finds "ordinary people in all-American settings struggling for courage, justice, tolerance" (106). While Packer's point is apt, Sayles's films are different from the work of Capra and Ford. They also differ from the postwar films directed by the generation of filmmakers that Brian Neve analyzes in his study of Elia Kazan, Joseph Losey, Abraham Polonsky, Nicholas Ray, Robert Rossen, Orson Welles, John Berry, Cy Endfield, Martin Ritt, Edward Dmytryk, John Huston, and Jules Dassin. The films directed by these sometimes-erstwhile leftist filmmakers were shaped by socialist or communist perspectives in the 1930s, but Sayles's politically conscious films reflect the caution of post-Stalin and post–civil rights progressives. Rather than seeing class as the sole cause of division within a community, Sayles's films explore ways in which a town, team, region, profession, or family can be divided by class, ethnicity, gender, sexuality, political views, or disparate share of power.

Conclusions

Sayles's alternative narrative style depends on and gives expression to a politically conscious perspective that directly challenges the divisive strategies the neoconservative movement has deployed so successfully for the last thirty years. Sayles's films draw on political perspectives from the Progressive Era, the New Deal, and the civil rights movement without equating or simplifying them. The films' intimate and unadorned study of what seem to be ordinary people invokes the "cult of the common person" found in the popular culture of the 1930s (see Lipsitz, *American Studies* 21). At the same time, their multiple and shifting perspectives provide a dramatic space in which the claims for social justice by women and nonwhite workers, who were consistently shut out of New Deal social welfare programs, are woven into a complex picture of American identity (see Lipsitz, *American Studies* 85). Packer suggests that because of their seriousness, cinematic plainness, sense of political responsibility, and moral decency, one would simply not expect Sayles's films to satisfy the tastes of today's consuming public whose expectations have been shaped by industry policy (106–7).

Sayles's films are out of place in the current marketplace because they do not suit the demands of the commercial entertainment industry, which has become increasingly geared to distributing media products that enhance corporate profits in what had been ancillary markets in the television, cable, video, music, toy, and publishing industries (see Lewis, *New American* 97). Sayles's films also become more difficult to promote in the independent market as evolving profit strategies in the mainstream sector become increasingly part of the indie system. Peter Biskind notes that Sayles has remarked, "It's getting harder to get our movies financed. . . . Anything over $1 million or $2 million sends distribution companies into their litany of the five or six hot actors who can allegedly 'open' a picture" (472–73). Outlining prevailing economic trends, independent screenwriter-producer James Schamus explains that "the companies that distribute and finance art house fare have had to remake themselves in the light of successes such as Miramax's *Pulp Fiction* (1994) and *Il Postino* (1994)" (104). Today, American independent cinema is a "victim of its own success, a success that has made the independent film game look more and more like a microcosm of the studio business" (Schamus 103).

That type of success is one reason Sayles's films exist outside dominant trends in the independent system. Another is that perceptions about Sayles's work seem to be influenced by modernist polemics that continue to shape ideas about progressive cinema and the political avant-garde. The modernist notion that left-leaning political positions can only be expressed through nonrealistic formal strategies has prompted some observers to see the naturalistic elements in Sayles's films as signs of their conservative political perspective. An ongoing reliance on modernist polemics has led some contemporary scholars to dismiss Sayles's work because they assume that "it is impossible to have a cinema of politics without an accompanying practice of nonconventional signifiers" (Pribram 54). While many filmmakers, scholars, and critics would agree that the "progressive character of a text" is best determined by ascertaining "how well it accomplishes its task in specific contexts of reception" (Ryan and Kellner 268), the absence of overt self-reflexivity and extreme narrative intransitivity in Sayles's films has been seen as evidence of their nonprogressive character.

It is interesting that Sayles's films occupy a position outside the terrain of the Hollywood industry and outside dominant trends in contemporary independent American cinema. The films' outsider status reflects the fact that political censorship has long shaped mainstream American cinema. That Sayles's films also exist outside the independent system suggests that the industry's political censorship has been so effective that it now influences audience expectations for mainstream and independent film. Sayles's films seem to be the isolated work of an auteur rather than part of a larger social or aesthetic movement in large measure because American cinema has been created according to the blueprint of political censorship.

Still, Sayles's body of work has secured an audience that responds to the films' political acuity, narrative depth, and integrated visual style. Audiences looking for films that go beyond the familiar formulas of Hollywood's high-concept films find an alternative aesthetic experience and political perspective in the multilayered narratives of Sayles's films. Audiences interested in filmmaking that goes beyond the droll allusions and designer violence of American independent cinema find an alternative aesthetic experience and political perspective in the long unbroken takes in Sayles's films. Writing about the films Jean Renoir directed in the 1930s—when poetic realism reflected the "optimism created by the Popular Front Movement of 1935–1936 [and] the despair created by the movement's failure and the realization that Fascism in some form was at hand" (Cook 316)—André Bazin found that Renoir's deep focus aesthetic disclosed "the hidden meanings in people and things without disturbing the unity natural to them" (38). While it does not suggest a connection between aesthetic approach and philosophical perspective, Bazin's remark seems to reveal that a leisurely visual style has been known to express the salient social-political experiences of an audience interested in films that reflect on the tacit systems of power.

NOTES

1. There are two important caveats to note at the outset. First, while Sayles has written novels, short stories, screenplays, and teleplays, and has produced and acted in films and television programs, my analysis focuses on the films that Sayles has directed. Second, while Sayles has consistently worked in collaboration with other people, especially Maggie Renzi, my analysis will discuss the films under the rubric of "films directed by John Sayles."

Sayles was the creator, writer, and director of the NBC television series *Shannon's Deal*, which premiered in 1990 and was cancelled in 1991. To date, the fifteen films Sayles has directed include: *Return of the Secaucus Seven* (1980, distributed by Libra Films), *Baby It's You* (1983, distributed by Paramount), *Lianna* (1983, distributed by United Artists Classics), *Brother from Another Planet* (1984, distributed by Cinecom), *Matewan* (1987, distributed by Cinecom), *Eight Men Out* (1988, distributed by Orion), *City of Hope* (1991, distributed by Goldwyn), *Passion Fish* (1992, distributed by Miramax), *The Secret of Roan Inish* (1994, distributed by First Look), *Lone Star* (1996, distributed by Sony Classics), *Men With Guns* (1998, distributed by Sony Classics), *Limbo* (1999, distributed by Sony Pictures' Screen Gems), *Sunshine State* (2002, distributed by Sony Picture Classics), *Casa de los Babys* (2003, distributed by IFC Films), and *Silver City* (2004, distributed by Newmarket Films).

Lone Star is Sayles's most commercially successful film, with a North American domestic theatrical release record of $12,883,149. *Brother from Another Planet* is second with a box-office record of $3,700,000. *Sunshine State* is third with a domestic release record of $3,064,000. *Limbo* is fourth with a domestic theatrical release of $2,121,569. *Matewan* is fifth with a record of $1,000,000. After being in release for a month, *Silver City*'s box office gross was over $1,000,000. It appears that Sayles's other nine films made less than $1 million in their domestic theatrical releases, although *Return of the Secaucus Seven* is estimated to have grossed $2 million (see Rosen 181; Cohn 1990 and 1991, "Top Rental Films for 1992"; Klady 1994, 1995, 1996, 1997, 1998, 1999; D'Alessandro 2000 and 2001; *Sunshine State; Casa de los Babys; Silver City*). One reason these figures are far below the box office of studio films is that Sayles's films have had very limited releases and very limited print and advertising budgets. In contrast to the 2,000-plus screen releases of Hollywood blockbusters, during its two-and-a-half-month domestic theatrical release *Casa de los Babys* was in fewer than seventy-two theaters at any given time. During the first two weeks of its release, the film was shown in fewer than ten theaters each week.

2. Ross explains that working-class films in this period "generally fell into three categories" (45). One group included romances, comedies, and melodramas whose protagonists were workers and immigrants. Social-problem films depicting the hardships of working-class life were another. A third group included "highly politicized labor-capital films . . . that focused on the often violent confrontations between employers and employees" (45) and featured stories about "adult male workers who labored in the nation's most contentious and highly organized industries: miners, steel workers, railroad workers, and skilled industrial laborers" (57).

3. In the last twenty-five years, it appears that many if not most right-leaning and left-leaning Americans have lost faith in collective action and turned instead toward "the search for personal identity and change" (Neve 232). Increasingly, radio and television have provided venues for conservatives to evangelize and share their vision with like-minded audiences. The far more delimited realms of independently funded documentary and fiction filmmaking have been the venue for left-leaning political expression, which, until the 2004 presidential campaign, had shifted its focus to concentrate on the subjective experiences of previously underrepresented individuals. A film such as *Daughters of the Dust* (1992), which explores women's experiences, intergenerational relationships, the economic legacies of slavery, and the abiding influence of transnational culture, is emblematic of an important development in independent cinema. Linked to a film like *Force of Evil* by its candid recognition of class and caste in America, Julie Dash's film also gives expression to perspectives emerging from the women's movement and the rise of black consciousness sparked by the Los Angeles rebellion (see Bambara 118–44).

4. Sayles's list of important political films of the last twenty years appears in "The Big Picture: John Sayles." Studies of political films include different ranges of material. Steven J. Ross and Michael Slade Shull focus on films in the Progressive Era. John Bodnar and Phillip L. Gianos examine working-class and/or political films in the studio and corporate eras. M. Keith Booker and Tom Zaniello have prepared research guides for studying left-leaning and working-class films.

5. The films' meandering studies of everyday social circumstances present a sharp contrast to the "beautiful, mouth-watering surfaces" of Hollywood's high-concept films that sell high-tech style as "a utopian way of life" (Wyatt, *High Concept* 25). The ordinary characters in Sayles's films implicitly falsify the two-dimensional characters in high-concept films that are presented "as models, selling the film and, more significantly, the lifestyle to which the film offers entry" (Wyatt, *High Concept* 53). Rather than promoting the "upscale lifestyles promised in many ads" (Wyatt, *High Concept* 25), Sayles's films examine the consequences of that social agenda. The result is that Sayles's work is precisely the sort of cinema that has provoked political censorship in the film industry ever since 1907, "when a Cleveland union man shot and exhibited films of the strike-ravaged Cripple Creek (Colorado) area to enthusiastic audiences" (Ross 87).

6. Rosenbaum notes that while Neil Labute's *In the Company of Men* examines "the effects of aggressive competition via business on notions of masculinity and romance," it "is almost never described as a film about capitalism and its effects" (*Movie Wars* 160). Similarly, while Atom Egoyan's *The Sweet Hereafter* "evokes the effects of aggressive competition via litigation on the functioning of a community," the anticapitalist views are glossed over in reviews (160).

7. Charles Lyons outlines key pieces of political censorship that have been enacted in the name of U.S. national security in the last twenty-five years (see 47–48).

8. Lyons explains that government censorship of films under the Foreign Agents Registration Act of 1938 continues to occur (see 26–52). Discussing the film industry's self-censorship, producer Irwin Winkler notes, "films that have a safe political message have a much better chance" of being awarded the Oscar for Best Picture (Kipen 44).

9. These films and films like them were repeatedly "banned in their entirety . . . in cities like Chicago, Detroit, Boston, and Springfield, Massachusetts, where censorship was controlled by the police, or in Ohio, where it was controlled by the Industrial Commission" (Ross 109). Summarizing the period, Ross explains that the relatively few films "produced by individual workers, labor unions, worker-owned companies, or members of radical, worker-oriented organizations like the Socialist party . . . precipitated bitter struggles over the political content and direction of American cinema" (86–87).

10. To describe the function of the Production Code Administration (PCA) established by the Motion Picture Producers and Distributors of America in 1934, Vasey explains that the role of the PCA "in guiding the representational practices of the studios can be more fully understood within the wider context of 'industry policy'—a set of constraints that gradually took shape throughout the 1920s and 1930s in response to factors originating outside the industry itself" ("Beyond Sex and Violence" 102). Those outside forces included foreign governments, state and local censorship bodies, individuals or organizations with the power to generate negative publicity, and, most especially, "other institutions of corporate capitalism" (Vasey,

"Beyond" 103). Vasey explains that "industry policy not only covered the depiction of foreigners and foreign locales . . . it ensured the general probity of onscreen public officials, as well as the benevolence of cinematic bankers, lawyers, doctors, teachers, social workers, newspapermen, and police" (*World* 194). She notes that "political subjects, including any discussion of the relationship between capital and labor," were precluded by the conventions of industry policy (*World* 195). Also off limits were revolutionary themes and "explorations of social conflict" (Vasey, *World* 195). Vasey argues that "it was in these little-publicized areas of the MPPDA's activities that its effects were, in practice, most censorious" (*World* 195). For studies that examine bowdlerized narratives, the continual decline in the number of social problem films, and political censorship under CARA (Code and Rating Administration, or, after 1977, Classification and Rating Administration), see Maltby 471–90; Vasey, "Beyond" 105, 112; Black 247–87; Lipsitz, *Rainbow* 282; Jones 196–233; Roffman and Purdy 296; Miller 167; Behlmer 136–37; Lewis, *Hollywood* 165, 181–87, 289, 298; Leff and Simmons 276, 281; "Save Our Films from the MPAA" 1; Wyatt, "Formation" 80, 86; Lyons 30–31; Pribram 37–38.

11. The political basis of film censorship is suggested by the history of the association that enforces film censorship. The film industry's first trade association, established in 1916, was an open-shop (antiunion) organization. The MPPA (Motion Picture Producers' Association)—a precursor of the MPAA (Motion Picture Association of America) established in 1945—was formed by twenty-five of the largest film producing companies. It was a corporate response to "the creation of Actors' Equity and the more radical Photoplayers' Union in 1916" and to the American Federation of Labor's (AFL) efforts to organize "the studio crafts (stage hands, electricians, cameramen, and laboratory workers) into a single union" in 1916 (Ross 61). Following major strikes by the International Alliance of Theatrical Stage Employees (IA) in 1918 and 1919, a series of strikes against theater owners by "projectionists, musicians, and attendants," and the IA's control of "motion picture machine operators, stage hands, carpenters, plasterers, electricians, painters, grips, and other studio workers," in 1921 eleven studios retaliated by issuing "a drastic set of wage cuts" (Ross 132). The studios "locked out all disgruntled workers and refused to meet with federal mediators or negotiate with AFL national representatives" (Ross 132). While striking workers responded with a nationwide boycott of Hollywood films, by 1922 many IA workers had returned to work without winning concessions, and "by the end of 1922, the new era of labor militancy had come to an end" (Ross 133). With labor demands crushed, executives replaced the MPPA with the MPPDA (Motion Picture Producers and Distributors of America). At the time of its widely publicized creation in March of 1922, the MPPDA was presented as a direct response to scandals that involved sex and drugs (see Cook 185–86). In reality, it represented consolidation of corporate control and the fact that executives would delimit the bargaining power of workers—without government interference.

That same consolidation of antiunion power marks the transition from the MPPDA to the MPAA in 1945. In response to a series of strikes by the Conference of Studio Unions (CSU) in 1945, the studios locked out workers and refused to negotiate, claiming that the labor dispute had arisen from jurisdictional conflicts between rival unions. With members of the Screen Actors Guild opting to cross picket lines and IA members more than willing to take positions formerly held by CSU workers, the studios were not adversely affected by the strikes. Studio executives received assistance in their efforts to eliminate the power of organized labor. The *Hollywood Reporter* published articles that suggested the strikes were caused by communist agitators. In 1945, the head of the California Fact Finding Committee on Un-American Activities, California senator Jack B. Tenney, held hearings to air allegations that Herb Sorrell, head of the CSU, was a communist. In 1945, these efforts and those of the antiunion Motion Picture Alliance for the Preservation of American Ideals were rewarded when the HUAC opened its investigation of communist activity in Hollywood (see Baron 143–62).

Following the pattern established in the 1920s, executives crushed labor unrest by their coordinated efforts behind the scenes, but they portrayed their public actions as moral responses to ethical misconduct, in this case, membership in the Communist Party. They served as friendly witnesses at the HUAC hearings and produced the 1947 Waldorf Statement, which prohibited employment of known communists, to establish the identity of the new association. The MPAA gained power by blacklisting employees on the grounds of their communist affiliation. That power translated into the MPAA's new effectiveness in regulating film content. Backed by the threat of HUAC intervention, the MPAA could focus on "apolitical film entertainment" (Lewis, *Hollywood* 24; see 25, 38).

12. That method of political censorship is, of course, used by other corporate entities. As John Nichols notes, prior to the 2004 Super Bowl, "CBS refused to permit MoveOn.org to buy time during the game for a commercial criticizing the Bush deficit" because, in contrast to the ads for "beer, R-rated movies and Bob Dole's solution to erectile dysfunction," CBS executives found the MoveOn.org commercial "too controversial" (8).

13. More visibly, independent films are now consistently required to feature stars. For specific aspects of this development, see Roman 11, 22.

14. William J. Puette explains that in 1989 "only about 15 percent of the nation's work force [was] unionized, which means that organized labor is a remote experience to the vast majority of Americans" (4). In this environment, media representations of labor shape Americans' view of organized labor. The usual picture portrays labor conflicts as senseless contests caused by unions' unwillingness to negotiate in good faith. There is a focus on company offers rather than workers' grievances, and there is no coverage of management salaries, and such. Stories focus on the impact rather than cause of the strike and overlook the harm that will come to workers if they give up their strike. There is little coverage of union solidarity, and

the government is portrayed as a neutral arbiter even when it is protecting corporate interests (see Puette 10).

15. As one might expect, observers do not agree about Sayles's influence. Gerard Molyneaux believes that Sayles has been an inspiration for "film majors, graduate students, and novice directors" (11). Yet Greg Merritt and E. Deidre Pribram place Sayles's films outside central developments in independent cinema (398; 51). Michael Ryan and Douglas Kellner see connections between Sayles's work and films like *Norma Rae* (1979), *The China Syndrome* (1979), *Missing* (1982), *Silkwood* (1983), *Under Fire* (1983), and *Salvador* (1986); they see such films as examples of progressive political cinema in the conservative era (see 266–87).

WORKS CITED

Andrew, Geoff. *Stranger Than Paradise: Maverick Film-Makers in Recent American Cinema.* New York: Limelight, 1999.
Ansen, David. "Baby It's You." *Newsweek,* 11 April 1983: 78.
Auty, Chris. "Baby It's You." *Monthly Film Bulletin* (November 1984): 330.
Bambara, Toni Cade. "Reading the Signs, Empowering the Eye: *Daughters of the Dust* and the Black Independent Cinema Movement." *Black American Cinema.* Ed. Manthia Diawara. New York: Routledge, 1993. 118–44.
Baron, Cynthia. "'As Red as a Burlesque Queen's Garters': Cold War Politics and the Actors' Lab in Hollywood." *Headline Hollywood.* Ed. Adrienne L. McLean and David A. Cook. New Brunswick: Rutgers UP, 2001. 143–62.
Bazin, André. "The Evolution of the Language of Cinema." *What Is Cinema?* Berkeley: U of California P, 1967. 23–40.
Behlmer, Rudy. *Inside Warner Bros. (1935–1951).* New York: Viking Press, 1985.
Benson, Sheila. "Baby It's You." *Los Angeles Times,* 22 April 1983: Calendar 1.
"The Big Picture: John Sayles." http://www.motherjones.com/mother_jones/MJ96/sayles.html. 17 February 2005.
Biskind, Peter. *Down and Dirty Pictures: Miramax, Sundance, and the Rise of Independent Film.* New York: Simon and Schuster, 2004.
Black, Gregory. "Film Politics and Industry Policy." *Hollywood Censored: Morality Codes, Catholics, and the Movies.* New York: Cambridge UP, 1994. 244–91.
Bodnar, John. *Blue-Collar Hollywood: Liberalism, Democracy, and Working People in American Film.* Baltimore: Johns Hopkins UP, 2003.
Bonavoglia, Angela. "Baby It's You." *Cineaste* 13.1 (1983): 38.
Booker, M. Keith. *Film and the American Left: A Research Guide.* West-

port, CT: Greenwood, 1999.
Bruzzi, Stella. "The President and the Image." *Sight and Sound* (July 1998): 16–19.
Carson, Diane, ed. *John Sayles: Interviews*. Jackson: UP of Mississippi, 1999.
———. "Plain and Simple: Masculinity through John Sayles's Lens." *More Than a Method: Trends and Traditions in Contemporary Film Performance*. Ed. Cynthia Baron, Diane Carson, and Frank P. Tomasulo. Detroit: Wayne State UP, 2004. 173–91.
Casa de los Babys. Internet Movie Database. http://us.imdb.com/title/tt0303830/business. 20 January 2004.
Christensen, Terry. *Reel Politics: American Political Movies from Birth of a Nation to Platoon*. New York: Basil Blackwell, 1987.
Cohn, Lawrence. "Champs among Bantamweights." *Daily Variety*, 27 June 1990: 24–27.
———. "Champs among Bantamweights." *Daily Variety*, 26 June 1991: 66–74.
Combs, James E., and Sara T. Combs. *Film Propaganda and American Politics*. New York: Garland, 1994.
Cook, David A. *A History of Narrative Film*. 4th ed. New York: Norton, 2004.
Corliss, Richard. "Return of the Secaucus Seven." *Time*, 15 September 1980: 101.
Cox, Dan. "Studios Woo New Indies." *Variety*, 19–25 January 1998: 1, 102.
D'Alessandro, Anthony. "The Top 250 of 1999." *Variety*, 10–16 January 2000: 20–22.
———. "The Top 250 of 2000." *Variety*, 8–14 January 2001: 20–21.
DeKoven, Marianne. "To Bury and to Praise: John Sayles on the Death of the Sixties." *Minnesota Review* 30/31 (Spring/Fall 1988): 129–47.
Demeter, John. "Independent Film and Working-Class History: A Review of *Northern Lights* and *The Wobblies*." *Celluloid Power: Social Film Criticism from* The Birth of a Nation *to* Judgment at Nuremberg. Ed. David Platt. Metuchen, NJ: Scarecrow, 1992. 545–57.
Denby, David. "*Baby It's You*." *New York*, 11 April 1983: 72.
Ferncase, Richard. *Outsider Features: American Independent Films of the 1980s*. Westport, CT: Greenwood, 1996.
Foner, Philip S. "A Martyr to His Cause: The Scenario of the First Labor Film in the United States." *Labor History* 24.1 (1983): 103–11.
Garafola, Lynn. "Hollywood and the Myth of the Working Class." *Celluloid Power: Social Film Criticism from* The Birth of a Nation *to* Judgment at Nuremberg. Ed. David Platt. Metuchen, NJ: Scarecrow, 1992. 535–44.
Gianos, Phillip L. *Politics and Politicians in American Film*. Westport, CT: Praeger, 1998.
Glauberman, Naomi, and Claudia Fonda-Bonardi. "Return of the Secaucus Seven." *Cineaste* (Fall 1980): 32.

Hoberman, J. "Back on the Wild Side." *Premiere* (August 1992): 31.

Horne, Gerald. *Class Struggle in Hollywood, 1930–1950*. Austin: U of Texas P, 2001.

Jansen, Sue Curry. *Censorship: The Knot That Binds Power and Knowledge*. New York: Oxford UP, 1988.

Jones, Dorothy. "Communism and the Movies: A Study in Film Content." *Report on Blacklisting: I. The Movies*. Ed. John Cogley. New York: Fund for the New Republic, 1956. 196-233.

Kemp, Philip. *"Limbo." American Independent Cinema: A Sight and Sound Reader*. Ed. Jim Hillier. London: British Film Institute, 2001. 222-24.

Kephart, Edwin. "Return of the Secaucus Seven." *Films in Review* (November 1980): 566.

Kipen, David. "Picking Oscar's Brain." *Variety*, 8-14 January 1996: 43-46.

Klady, Leonard. "B.O. Performance of Films in 1995." *Variety*, 8-14 January 1996: 38-40.

———. "B.O. Performance Hits High in 1996." *Variety*, 13-19 January 1997: 19-25.

———. "The Lowdown on '94's Record Box Office Heights." *Variety*, 30 January-5 February 1995: 17-20.

———. "Top 250 of 1997." *Variety*, 26 January-1 February 1998: 17-18.

———. "The Top 250 of 1998." *Variety*, 11-17 January 1999: 33-34.

———."WB Grabs Top Share of 1993." *Variety*, 24-30 January 1994: 7, 14, 21.

Leff, Leonard L., and Jerold L. Simmons. *The Dame in the Kimono*. 2nd ed. Lexington: UP of Kentucky, 2001.

Levy, Emanuel. *Cinema of Outsiders: The Rise of American Independent Film*. New York: New York UP, 1999.

Lewis, Jon. *Hollywood v Hardcore: How the Struggle over Censorship Saved the Modern Film Industry*. New York: New York UP, 2000.

———, ed. *The New American Cinema*. Durham: Duke UP, 1998.

Lipsitz, George. "Academic Politics and Social Change." *Cultural Studies & Political Theory*. Ithaca: Cornell UP, 2000. 80-92.

———. *American Studies in a Moment of Danger*. Minneapolis: U of Minnesota P, 2001.

———. *Rainbow at Midnight: Labor and Culture in the 1940s*. Urbana: U of Illinois P, 1994.

Lyons, Charles. *The New Censors: Movies and the Culture Wars*. Philadelphia: Temple UP, 1997.

Maltby, Richard. *Hollywood Cinema*. 2nd ed. Oxford: Blackwell, 2003.

Merritt, Greg. *Celluloid Mavericks: A History of American Independent Film*. New York: Thunder's Mouth, 2000.

Meyer, David S., and William Hoynes. "*Shannon's Deal:* Competing Images of the Legal System on Primetime Television." *Journal of Popular Culture* 27.4 (1994): 31-41.

Miller, Frank. *Censored Hollywood: Sex, Sin and Violence on Screen*. Atlanta: Turner, 1994.

Molyneaux, Gerard. *John Sayles*. Los Angeles: Renaissance, 2000.
Neve, Brian. *Film and Politics in America: A Social Tradition*. London: Routledge, 1992.
Nichols, John. "Super Censorship Bowl." *The Nation*, 16 February 2004: 8.
Packer, George. "Decency and Muck: The Visions of John Sayles and Oliver Stone." *Dissent* (Summer 1997): 105–9.
Phipps, Keith. "John Sayles." The Onion A.V. Club. http://www.theavclub.com/avclub3310/vafeature3310.html. 17 February 2005.
Pierson, John. *Spike Mike Reloaded*. New York: Hyperion, 2003.
Pribram, E. Deidre. *Cinema and Culture: Independent Film in the United States, 1980–2001*. New York: Peter Lang, 2002.
Puette, William J. *Through Jaundiced Eyes: How the Media View Organized Labor*. Ithaca: ILR, 1992.
Roffman, Peter, and Jim Purdy. *The Hollywood Social Problem Film*. Bloomington: Indiana UP, 1981.
Rogin, Michael Paul. *Ronald Reagan, the Movie and Other Episodes in Political Demonology*. Berkeley: U of California P, 1987.
Roman, Monica. "Star-Powered Pix, Indie Style." *Variety*, 5–11 January 1998: 11, 22.
Rosen, David, with Peter Hamilton. *Off Hollywood: The Making and Marketing of Independent Films*. New York: Grove Weidenfeld, 1990.
Rosenbaum, Jonathan. *Movies as Politics*. Berkeley: U of California P, 1997.
———. *Movie Wars: How Hollywood and the Media Conspire to Limit What Films We Can See*. Chicago: A Cappella Books, 2000.
Ross, Steven J. *Working-Class Hollywood: Silent Film and the Shaping of Class in America*. Princeton: Princeton UP, 1998.
Ryan, Michael, and Douglas Kellner. *Camera Politica: The Politics and Ideology of Contemporary Hollywood Film*. Bloomington: Indiana UP, 1988.
Sarris, Andrew. "Return of the Secaucus Seven." *Village Voice*, 4–10 March 1981: 41.
"Save Our Films from the MPAA." http://angelfire.com/co3/freeourfilms. 26 November 2002.
Schamus, James. "To the Rear of the Back End: The Economics of Independent Cinema." *Contemporary Hollywood Cinema*. Ed. Steve Neale and Murray Smith. London: Routledge, 1998. 91–106.
Shull, Michael Slade. *Radicalism in American Silent Films, 1909–1929: A Filmography and History*. Jefferson, NC: McFarland, 2000.
Silver City. Internet Movie Database. http://www.imdb.com/title/tt0376890/business. 26 October 2004.
Simon, Ronald. "*Baby It's You*." *Films in Review* (May 1983): 302.
Smith, Gavin, ed. *Sayles on Sayles*. Boston: Faber and Faber, 1998.
Sunshine State. Internet Movie Database. http://us.imdb.com/title/tt0286179/business. 20 January 2003.
"Top Rental Films for 1992." *Daily Variety*, 11 January 1993: 22–24.

Vasey, Ruth. "Beyond Sex and Violence: 'Industry Policy' and the Regulation of Hollywood Movies, 1922–1939." *Controlling Hollywood: Censorship and Regulation in the Studio Era.* Ed. Matthew Bernstein. New Brunswick: Rutgers UP, 1999. 102–29.

———. *The World According to Hollywood, 1918–1939.* Madison: U of Wisconsin P, 1997.

Walsh, Francis R. "The Films We Never Saw: American Movies View Organized Labor, 1934–1954." *Labor History* 27.4 (1986): 564–80.

Wyatt, Justin. "The Formation of the 'Major Independent': Miramax, New Line and the New Hollywood." *Contemporary Hollywood Cinema.* Ed. Steve Neale and Murray Smith. London: Routledge, 1998. 74–90.

———. *High Concept: Movies and Marketing in Hollywood.* Austin: U of Texas P, 1994.

Zaniello, Tom. *Working Stiffs, Union Maids, Reds, and Riffraff: An Expanded Guide to Films and Labor.* Ithaca: ILR, 2003.

Zieger, Gay P., and Robert H. Zieger. "Unions on the Silver Screen: A Review Essay on *F.I.S.T., Blue Collar,* and *Norma Rae.*" *Labor History* 23.1 (1982): 67–78.

2

Breakups and Reunions: Late Realism in Early Sayles

Alex Woloch

> I'm totally uninterested in form for its own sake. But I am interested in story-telling technique.
> John Sayles

> I find that in this country there's a real suspicion of content. . . . [W]hat we treasure a film director . . . for is his ability to put his stamp on any material. The minute you're talking about that, you're automatically talking about *style*. On the other hand, there's a much smaller group of people who only care about content and whether you're politically correct or not.
> John Sayles

> Any theory of drama which . . . has as its starting-point not these facts of life, but problems of dramatic "stylization," of whatever kind, is inevitably side-tracked into formalism. Such theories do not recognize that the so-called "distance from life" of dramatic form is only a heightened and concentrated expression of certain tendencies in life itself. . . . But artistic form is never a simple mechanical image of social life. Admittedly, it arises as a reflection of social tendencies, but within this framework it has its own dynamic, its own direction which takes it towards or away from truthful representation.
> Georg Lukács

Realism and Nostalgia

The resonance between these comments by John Sayles and Georg Lukács points to a larger framework within which the complexity of Sayles's oeuvre might become more legible: as a subtle and ongoing negotiation with an aesthetics of realism that stands at the heart of one important tradition of left-wing literary theory. Sayles's films have often been compared to the nineteenth-century novel, and the terms of this comparison usually revolve around the same achievements that Lukács seeks to elucidate in nineteenth-century realism: the relation between private and public life, the depiction of a large, interconnected network of characters, the comprehension of a complicated social totality. But Sayles's adherence to the nineteenth-century novel—and even to realism itself—is deliberately anachronistic. He works in a mode of representation with a set of aesthetic principles that have little currency in contemporary culture or cultural theory. There has always been a notably Janus-like reception of Sayles's work. Long recognized as central to contemporary independent filmmaking, Sayles is also frequently diminished—if not dismissed—for precisely the lack of "style" that he, in turn, dismisses as irrelevant in these and other interviews. Indeed, Sayles's insistence that "story-telling" or "content" is more valuable than "form" or "style" deliberately plays into a critical response that has dogged him throughout his filmmaking career. For example, in his study of 1980s U.S. independent film, Emanuel Levy praises Sayles as "the uncrowned father of the new independent cinema" (82) but claims that the "refusal to employ a personal style results in the lack of visual signature or a distinctive Sayles trademark" (85). While Levy considers Sayles "thematically unpredictable," with a "diverse output" and an "assertive control over his work," he also argues that there is a "lack of visual flair," an "absence of visual distinction," "photographed scripts," and an "often . . . schematic construction" (85). Levy's mercurial comments are typical of the contradictory critical assessment that Sayles's work has elicited. How can the same filmmaker be unpredictable *and* schematic? With an "assertive control" but no "signature"? How is it possible, in short, to be an auteur *without style*?

This is a crucial question to ask of Sayles, and one that helps explain the curious ambiguities that have informed the reception of his films. It is as though there were a kind of intelligence at play in Sayles's films that is unrecognizable to prevalent modes of criticism and evaluation. Much of this, I would argue, reflects Sayles's explicit nostalgia for a form of representation that has come to be seen as outmoded, his interest in a tradition of social, and cinematic, realism, with few proponents today. But the nostalgia *for* realism should not be too quickly translated as a mere return *to* realism. It is the very nature of nostalgia to remain unsatisfied, and this kind of dissatisfaction is, in fact, one of Sayles's major concerns. I suggest that an aesthetic nostalgia—for that form of representation that seems to have been overwhelmed in the pursuit of style—is intertwined with the powerful thematics of nostalgia that pervade Sayles's films. Consider how often a longing for the past rests at the heart of his films: in the lost, youthful romances at the discovered epicenter of *Lone Star* (1996); in the aggrieved yearning of May Alice Culhane (Mary McDonnell) for her old, unwounded life in *Passion Fish* (1992); and, in the passion of Dr. Fuentes (Federico Luppi) in *Men With Guns* (1997) to relocate his old students and, through them, his own most-achieved social action from the past. In *Passion Fish*, a sudden and unbridgeable rupture between past and present structures this nostalgia, while in *Men With Guns* Fuentes's return to the past is marked by a painful and gradual unraveling (in a kind of reverse quest where each student he fails to find further disperses the history he is trying to recover). In *Passion Fish* the nostalgia is personal and based on a random tragedy, while in *Lone Star* and *Men With Guns* the nostalgia is charged with social and historical necessity. But in none of these cases can the past be simply grasped or re-presented: Sam Deeds (Chris Cooper) and Pilar Cruz (Elizabeth Peña), May Alice Culhane, and Dr. Fuentes all discover a fundamental temporal displacement at the very center of their experience, their hopes, and their often-acute grief.

This nostalgia is, indeed, already apparent in Sayles's earliest work, as *Return of the Secaucus Seven* (1980) revolves, ironically, around the experience of belatedness. While countless film debuts have a youthful subject—as though the story in the movie echoes the film's own improbable making—Sayles's first film centers on a backward-looking reunion. There is an animating tension between the prospective excitement of Sayles's cinematic arrival and the retrospective nature of the film's story. The nostalgia inherent within this reunion gives a structured and concrete form to that desire for the past that will run through Sayles's later films. Such nostalgia operates not only on the plane of the characters' desire but also in the very act of historic reminiscence that underlies many of Sayles's film projects. This is perhaps most notable in *Matewan* (1987), but it is also evident in the way history enters into *Lone Star* or *Sunshine State* (2002). These films do not merely seek to convey a sense of history but actively promote a sense of *historicity:* they are as much about the effort to comprehend or grasp history as they are fictional reenactments of historical events.[1] Often in Sayles, the presentation of a past is simultaneously a presentation of the search for the past, the partial recovery of history simultaneously a nostalgic encounter with history's loss.

This mixture of finding *and* losing history is again already apparent in *Return of the Secaucus Seven,* which organizes the characters' youthful nostalgia around a very specific historical axis: their nostalgia for the 1960s as a moment that has not just receded temporally but also politically. We can learn a lot about Sayles's aesthetic sense in his instinctive choice to begin his filmmaking career with this representation of history's representation rather than with the direct representation of a historical event. The choice grants the film an inevitably self-reflexive dimension: the sense of political and temporal loss depicted *in* the film is also shared *by* the film, and, indeed, we might argue that all of Sayles's work betrays a similar nostalgia for a political moment that is gone.

I want to suggest that the temporal displacement that structures the characters' nostalgic relationship to the 1960s in *Secaucus Seven* is paralleled by a subtle displacement within the very modality of Sayles's own realism: the activity of cinematic representation has been transformed, in other words, by the same political and temporal rupture that underlies the drama of looking back from 1980 to the 1960s. Consider this comment by David Cook in his authoritative account of American cinema in the 1970s: "After the late sixties, serious mimesis had become increasingly problematic in American cinema as a pervasive sense of irony about genre and representation descended on the mass audience by way of television. During the 1970s, genre was further destabilized by revision, parody and hybridization, until by the 1980s an aesthetics of serious representation had become virtually impossible in genre-coded films" (299). If Cook's encapsulation of this shift mirrors the temporal framework of *Secaucus Seven* (from the late 1960s to the end of the 1970s), the juxtaposition of "an aesthetics of serious representation" against "irony," "parody," and "hybridization" parallels Sayles's governing opposition between "content" and "style." Sayles's antipathy toward the cult of style is very much informed by this historical situation, as it produces a "problematic" nostalgia for "serious mimesis" that operates on the same political and temporal axis as the characters within *Secaucus Seven:* 1968/1980. It's in this sense that the decision not to look directly at the 1960s, but to look at characters who are looking back at the 1960s, provides an important keynote to Sayles's oeuvre. Sayles's nostalgic realism is intertwined with this restless—never fully successful—effort to "return," somewhat like the characters in *Secaucus Seven,* to a mode of representation that could directly, and coherently, comprehend our social and historical contexts.

Such a reading of Sayles's realism gives us a compelling vantage point to reassess the reputed lack of "style" in his films (and perhaps to move beyond an opposition between style and representation that fuels the devaluation of realist aesthetics in contemporary culture). It is, of course, quite possible to simply identify and bring out the "visual flair" within Sayles's films—to demonstrate that he is accomplished both at storytelling and at style. But we should not rush too quickly toward discerning this style, precisely as Sayles himself has made it clear that he is interested in a different *kind* of style from what would be most immediately apparent. As Sayles suggests, he is not uninterested in technique, but rather concerned with elaborating technique in a coherent relationship to a referential ground. A useful precedent for considering this problem of style is offered by André Bazin, the seminal theorist of the aesthetics of film realism. In his distinction between depth-of-field and montage-driven effects, Bazin frequently grapples with the paradoxes of a mode of representation that seeks to submerge itself within the plentitude of the referenced image. In his essay on William Wyler, for example, Bazin dwells at length on what he calls a "style without style" (1958, 161) suggesting that Wyler's artistry—based on the still camera silently registering reality—is "intentionally self-effacing" (150) and, because of this, demands a particular critical method. "If one tried to characterize [Wyler's] *mise en scène*," he notes, "starting from the 'form,' one would necessarily have to give a negative definition." Self-effacement—or the effort at self-effacement—is a particularly important quality in John Sayles's films, both in a biographical sense (the concealing of the director's own hand) and a formal one (the absorption of the camera into the story that is being conveyed). Compared to many other prominent American independent filmmakers—such as Martin Scorsese, Jim Jarmusch, Quentin Tarantino, and Spike Lee—it is harder to discern Sayles's directorial presence, and this kind of effacement is directly connected to Sayles's sense of the ideal relationship between form and content, story and discourse.[2]

We might guess that Sayles's "style" would emerge against, and at the borders of, this kind of self-effacement, marking the points where a directorial persona does become more legible. But in fact there are important ways that Sayles's style depends, as Bazin suggests, on the very modality of self-effacement. Consider the way that Levy highlights Sayles's tendency to be "thematically unpredictable" as a hallmark of his independence. As with most of Levy's terms, this is part of the conventional assessment of Sayles, echoed, for example, in both a careful overview of Sayles's career by Gavin Smith ("the sheer diversity of Sayles's cinematic output cannot be overstated" [xiv]) and in a 1984 newspaper article on *Matewan* that begins by summarizing Sayles's early films:

> No one can ever accuse director John Sayles of sticking to the safe and predictable road. In five feature films made over the past eight years, Sayles has portrayed: a gang of '60s activists (*Return of the Secaucus Seven*), a naive college professor's wife who turns gay (*Lianna*), a middle-class coed who falls for a working class hood (*Baby It's You*) and a speechless black extraterrestrial who visits Harlem (*The Brother from Another Planet*). Now, in his biggest, most ambitious film yet, Sayles has turned his lens to West Virginia coal miners and their efforts to unionize. (Carson 90)

Unpredictability, the very sign of Sayles's personality, is purchased here precisely by our inability to connect these different films to a single person in any immediate or direct way. Sayles's legible independence coalesces precisely as these films—in their difference from one another—escape from a clearly defined authorial ambit. To be "unpredictable" as a film director is to gain a kind of style by a lack of style. (And the newspaper instinctively depicts this in terms of "turn[ing the] lens" toward a new subject, that most essential metaphor for the realist camera.)

This relationship between Sayles's manifestation as an auteur and his concurrent self-effacement or disappearance is not only apparent in the eclectic or diverse qualities of his films (as though our sense of Sayles's coherent personality derives in the suggestive gaps between the different film projects as much as in the films themselves). We can find another version of this dialectical process in Sayles's memorable inscriptions of himself as an actor within his own films. Perhaps more than any other director, Sayles has perfected what we might call the anti-Hitchcockian cameo. Again under the paradoxical register of self-effacement, Sayles's very appearances ironically signal the director's fading from the film, rather than acting (like Hitchcock's) as a signature that points directly to the filmmaker's stylistic manifestation in, and control of, every single shot. Hitchcock's small cameos always serve to remind us that, in fact, the director is *everywhere* in the discourse. Sayles's more extended minor parts work in various ways to place him outside of a pivotal role within the filmed scenario. Sayles either casts himself as someone detached from, and perhaps an observer of, the central action (as in *Return of the Secaucus Seven*, *Lianna*, or *Eight Men Out*) or, more ostentatiously, takes on a clearly villainous—yet extraneous—role (in *The Brother from Another Planet*, *Matewan*, *City of Hope*). In both cases, Sayles puts himself within the world of the films only to displace himself from them, once again dramatizing the film's escape from his own hand as director.

For two of the most memorable roles—the bounty hunter in *The Brother from Another Planet* (1984) and the preacher in *Matewan*—Sayles takes on a comically terrible authority. If Sayles's minor figures are often noticeably detached from the central story, as the preacher and particularly as the bounty hunter, Sayles pits himself against the very characters he is interested, as director, in capturing on film. When Sayles plays a malevolent preacher or alien bounty hunter, it is hard not to see his problematic authority, as a character, subtly extending to his directorial authority, as the agent of representation or the filmic auteur. Indeed to "capture" reality is one shorthand for the realist project itself, and we might say that Sayles as bounty hunter is seeking to capture the Brother, within the story of the film, in much the same way as the director seeks to capture the story—and the character—onscreen. It is this sense of "capture," for example, that Harmon King (Leo Burmester), the bitter cannery worker in *Limbo* (1999), means when he imagines the entrepreneurs who are pushing out the factory workers framing the close of the plant itself as an attraction: "They'll be one of those floating nursing homes with five hundred sons of bitches with their cameras capturing the moment."

I want to dwell a little bit more on this dialectic between "capture" and "escape." As we have seen, Sayles's persona—"independent," "surprising," "unpredictable"—emerges only as the films avoid too strong a relationship between themselves, so that the very disunity of the films, which fly off in any number of directions, somehow produces the coherent personality that can contain them. In a similar way, Sayles's cameos position him outside of the stories that he, as director, is unfolding. If the realist style is wary of estranging itself too far from the referential ground, becoming merely "form for form's sake," it also is concerned with the danger of completely "capturing" the story—since any representation will always be only a mediated and partial version of reality itself. Sayles's inscription of himself into these roles suggests the way that the filmmaker has constantly posed realism as a formal *problem*. None of Sayles's films espouses a realism that confidently asserts itself as an absolute or direct translation of reality. Sayles gravitates toward a more open-ended version of realism, one that continually oscillates between the dynamics of capture and escape, as the commitment to representing social reality is always informed by, and shot through with, a sense that lived reality exceeds whatever aesthetic representation has been constructed.[3]

If Sayles's inscription of himself as someone detached from, and potentially hostile to, the characters in the film indicates his awareness of representation as intricate and precarious, we could argue that the great theorists of literary and cinematic realism—Auerbach, Lukács, Bazin—have always comprehended aesthetic representation in these terms, never settling for a static or inert comprehension of reality.[4] For instance, Lukács acknowledges the necessary incompleteness of representation in his very summation of aesthetic totality: "Tragedy and great epic thus both lay claim to portraying the totality of the life-process. It is obvious in both cases that this can only be a result of artistic structure, of formal concentration in the artistic reflection of the most important features of objective reality. For obviously the real, substantial, infinite and extensive totality of life can only be reproduced mentally in a relative form" (91). And similarly, Bazin's discussion of "self-effacing" cinema, which strives to "reveal" rather than "add to" reality, offers a number of different configurations of the relationship between screen and image: from respectful expression and even resurrection to capture or forced confession.[5]

But Sayles's sense of representation, coming, as we have suggested, so self-consciously after the realist moment has passed, is particularly aware of, and takes particular advantage of, these kinds of limits. In a brief 1997 essay appearing in *Dissent*, George Packer has situated Sayles's films in just this kind of belated relation to the politics—and aesthetics—that animate them. In one sense, Packer's essay—a comparison of Sayles and Oliver Stone—repeats the conventional reading of Sayles's virtues and flaws. Packer identifies Stone as a hyperformal director, deeply reliant on montage and camera movement, while reading Sayles as essentially aformal, with an "understated" style, "slow" pace, and "simple" cinematography (106). For Packer, Stone and Sayles are the two most important political filmmakers in the United States, and they present a stark trade-off: we can have either a "quiet" decency and "cinematic plainness," which fails to attract much attention and can be "slow," "earnest," and "didactic," or a "loud" confusion, full of "excitement," with "technical skill," and "visually inventive," but dependent "more and more on the editing room—on confusion—for [their] effect" (107–8). This reading of Sayles, as we have seen, is not original in its focus on "quietness," against cinematic loudness—an opposition that almost inevitably becomes one of content against form as well.[6] But Packer offers a suggestive political, and historical, context for his stylistic comparison, comprehending both Sayles's and Stone's temperaments as filmmakers in the wake of the 1960s, as though each filmmaker is able to grasp, and hold onto, one remnant of this political moment. Their technical contrast, Packer argues, "is deeper and more interesting" than simply a difference in style, "and in a way it goes back to the sixties. It's the difference between . . . collective hope and individual excess, the Port Huron Statement and Mark Rudd" (106). By reading both Stone and Sayles as post-1960s auteurs, he deftly connects their divergent formal tendencies back to a shared political and historical crisis: the stylistic trade-off is actually a consequence of the political trade-offs that necessarily follow the fragmentation and implosion of the active Left in the late 1960s (from SDS to the Weathermen) and the ascendancy of the New Right from Nixon to Reagan. The implication of Packer's argument—and his crucial insight about Sayles—is that after the crisis of the late 1960s no political aesthetic, or system of cinematic style, can have it all. In the transition between his 1977 novel *Union Dues* (set in 1969) and the 1980 *Return of the Secaucus Seven* (set in the mid-1970s but looking back to the late 1960s), Sayles's shift from novel into film seems to mark exactly this moment that Packer is discussing. Sayles's bitterness toward what we would have to call the Late New Left in *Union Dues*—his insistence on embedding the *sectarian* fragmentation that defines the characters in the Third Way collective within the social fragmentation registered by the novel's wider character-system—is transmuted into the loose nostalgia of *Secaucus Seven:* what is being destroyed in *Union Dues* is now already lost.

I want to further consider how Sayles's nostalgia for realism, embedded in this richly specific historical and political context, gives him a particular purchase on a nostalgia that is intrinsic to realism, to the very act of representing. Seeking unsuccessfully to "return" to an idealized mode of social representation (which would also mark a return to the lost political moment—and possibilities—of the 1960s), Sayles makes the tension between convergence and displacement, which underlies this effort, work to reanimate and widen representation itself. If Lukács is the great elaborator of the social realist aesthetic, he also is a notorious apologist for twentieth-century socialist realism, the disastrous limit of that "political correctness" Sayles understands as the unhappy antithesis to "form for form's sake." In his shift from the subtle analysis of the nineteenth-century novel to the polemics for Soviet state literature, Lukács disastrously closes realist discourse off, sealing it to a false apotheosis, both political and aesthetic. Sayles's nostalgia for the comprehensive mode of representation offered by the realist aesthetic is embedded within a much deeper longing that colors the experience of the U.S. Left under Reagan and after. Under the spell of this longing, Sayles's realism never asserts itself as an absolute or direct encoding of reality. Instead, Sayles brilliantly harnesses both a negative and a positive motive for incomplete representation: an adequate picture of the social world is not possible because of the blinding ideology specific to Reagan's America (and Hollywood film culture) and because the dignity and experience of ordinary human life will always be somewhat greater than what is captured on the discursive plane. In this sense, most of Sayles's films act simultaneously as dirge and critique, brilliantly holding the line against either sentimentalism (which too quickly conjures up simplified versions of our social world) or implosive despair (which gives up on the project of social representation altogether). Sayles's movies — from the 1980 *Return of the Secaucus Seven* to the PATCO-era *Matewan* to *Lone Star* and *Men With Guns*—might present the most accomplished rewriting of Reagan's America offered by any filmmaker, and this rewriting is necessarily twofold: not simply devising numerous strategies to comprehend a largely invisible social reality but also—through its intricate formal circumspection—conveying the sense of a reality which has been elided and still awaits recognition.

The complicated effort to register reality as it has been missed informs multiple registers of Sayles's films, from the structure of a single image to intricate patternings of discovery and plot. Sayles is pervasively aware of the problem of misrepresentation, whether in terms of an entire history that is distorted or a detail, action, or person overlooked. An important example of this, alluded to above, is *Limbo*'s depiction of the tourist industry as a mechanism of representation seeking to "capture" the Alaskan experience. Here different kinds of misrepresentation—historical, aesthetic, social—are powerfully fused, and set against the very concentration on place or locale that becomes an emblem of Sayles's mature filmmaking. In fact most of the settings of Sayles's later films—Alaska, Texas, and Florida—are subject to contested representations within the story, and such scenes (as when different factions argue about the most accurate representation of Texas history in *Lone Star*) inevitably reflect on the mimetic ambition of the films themselves. Both the real-estate speculators in *Limbo*'s story and Sayles himself, as the organizer of the discourse, are interested in framing, or representing, the totality of this Alaskan community. The projected transformation of Alaska into a kind of theme park is an event represented within the film and an act of representation itself—and the distorted picture that such a framework offers of Alaska is contested both *in* the story (as the working-class characters are pitted against these businessmen) and *by* the discourse (as Sayles's film itself strives in various ways to reimagine and represent the conjunction of wilderness and society in Alaska). *Limbo*, in fact, demonstrates the intrinsically *formal* dimensions of Sayles's realism as it engages the problem of misrepresentation. Beginning with a familiar Saylesean depiction of a polycentric and embattled community, comprising several individuals set within a larger, dynamically articulated social totality, *Limbo* suddenly morphs into a dysphoric and troubling adventure film, as the lead characters, Donna De Angelo (Mary Elizabeth Mastrantonio), her daughter Noelle (Vanessa Martinez), and Joe Gastineau (David Strathairn) are abruptly stranded on a remote island, threatened both by poor weather and criminals of whom they have inadvertently run afoul. Sayles intends this surprising and sudden shift to disrupt both the characters and the audience, as the collision between two different kinds of story—and two different genres of film—provokes a necessary awareness of the mediation between discourse and story. Like many more overtly stylistic or self-reflexive films, *Limbo* thus deploys this formal rupture not merely to represent Alaska's rugged coastline more realistically, but to unsettle our embedded and generically coded expectations about film representation itself. In this sense, the terrific ending—or nonending—of the film is not a betrayal but something built into and motivated by the film as a whole. It is also one of the most literal examples of consciously partial representation in Sayles's work, providing clear evidence of how a formal principle of withholding seems built into the very enterprise of Sayles's realism.

Limbo, in this sense, is a model for (and a modeling of) Sayles's complicated meditation on the relation between realism, genre, and form. Many of Sayles's films battle various forms of generic distortion, working out toward an achieved but always partial representation constructed vis-à-vis the continual negation of misrepresentations. The coming-of-age film in *Baby It's You* (to be discussed below); science fiction in *The Brother from Another Planet*; the western in *Lone Star*; the adventure film in *Limbo*; the poetics of cinematic violence in *Men With Guns*: each of these dominant ideological genres is transformed in its confrontation with Sayles's social realism. This dynamic engagement with genre resembles Lukács's advocacy of a "critical realism" that, rather than offering a direct or complete representation of social reality, aims at engaging with, and shattering, *other* literary forms that misrepresent reality. Ultimately, critical realism sees any achieved representation and the negative engagement with misrepresentation as necessarily conjoined. In this way (to take another clear example) Sayles's decision to use almost all Spanish in *Men With Guns* is designed not merely to be realistic but also precisely to estrange the English-speaking audience from the referenced world of the film.[7] If the language in *Men With Guns* signifies in part through the way that it does not directly communicate to the audience, we might also consider the "silence" or "quiet" that has always been associated both (positively) with Sayles's realism and (negatively) with his lack of style. As Sayles suggests in his DVD commentary on *Limbo*, "A lot of times my favorite scenes in movies, in my own movies, are ones where there's no dialogue, where it's just about rhythm and something where you just get a break from everybody else and sit with a character." This poetics of silence flows into the repudiation of any style that works to separate the camera's organization of the image from the image itself. The mimetic stakes of this commitment to silence are suggested in the figuration of the camera as pausing and "sitting with a character," as though striving to eliminate any mediation in order to grasp, or recognize, the person in all of his or her fullness. In this sense, silence goes together with Sayles's tendency to privilege the still camera and the long take, which in combination work to linger on the transposed reality, and, most particularly, on the human beings who populate this referenced world. But once again silently "sitting with" or "lingering on" can actually make us conscious of an implied fullness that cannot be adequately accounted for or completely represented.

"Silence" in Sayles's films is both expressive and elliptical, the degree zero of a complicated referential logic. The double logic is perhaps most evident in the absolute (and thus formal) silencing of Joe Morton in the lead role in *The Brother from Another Planet*, which subtly operates in two distinct ways. On the one hand, Morton's silence radically curtails the Brother's ability to communicate, cuts him off, reinforces his profound and inescapable imprisonment within himself. But, on the other hand, this silence paradoxically gives the audience a more complete sense of the character's subjective comprehension of his experience, facilitating a mode of representation that takes advantage of the achieved distance between character and viewer. Would the scream that the Brother emits near the beginning of the film be so piercing if it were not silent? This character's silence is—perhaps like the nonending of *Limbo*—both a bounded horizon and a powerful demonstration of Sayles's realism: an obvious constraint, the muteness also adds to our sense of the Brother's predicament in its very withholding.[8] (In this sense, the Brother's formalized muteness resonates with the generic ambiguity of the film as a whole, which oscillates between B-movie science fiction and cinema verité in pursuing a fugitive African American experience.)[9] Suggestive and detached, realist and nonrealistic, the Brother's silence is ultimately an inscribed emblem of Sayles's aesthetic stance.

Return of the Secaucus Seven and Baby It's You

Joe Morton's silence; the deliberate (and costly) "foreignness" of *Men With Guns*; the memorable withholding of the story at the end of *Limbo:* these are some of the more evident ways in which Sayles's realism relies on the puncturing as well as the elaboration of representation. As I have suggested, this formal doubleness is already imbued with political and historical significance in *Return of the Secaucus Seven*—a film that is both the representation of a 1960s story and a story about the representation of the 1960s. It is no coincidence that Sayles's efforts as a filmmaker not only start at the moment of the New Right's (long) ascendancy but also that his entrance into independent film revolves around the experience of this ascendancy as a temporal disjunction. In this sense, it is crucial that Sayles, who is arguably the leading American realist, enters into film with the quintessential post-leftist film: a film that is not a direct immersion into ideology but, on the contrary, an ironic representation of a nostalgic, or differentiated, encounter with ideology. This nostalgic irony is most ostentatiously realized in the characters' reenactment of a scene from *Salt of the Earth* (Biberman, 1954), when they are arrested at the end of a very long Saturday and unfold the history behind the film's title. When Maura (Karen Trott), Irene (Jean Passanante), and Katie (Maggie Renzi) chant, "We want the formula!" the scene offers us a double set of displaced imitations, both temporal and discursive. As the audience watches the characters imitating their own *previous* 1960s imitation of this McCarthy-era film, the differentiated temporal relationship between the two arrests becomes, momentarily, equivalent to the differentiated relationship between Sayles's own unfolding film and this icon of left-wing agitprop.

This explicitly self-reflexive moment suggests a larger blurring of story and discourse, a blurring facilitated above all by the structure of the reunion itself, the central device *and* concern of the film. Subject to scrutiny and elaboration, the reunion is also a technique of representation that comprehends history and simultaneously conveys a sense of historical loss. The reunion creates a kind of double space where all events are at once inconsequential (as merely part of the weekend's fleeting activities) and significant (as a refraction—nostalgic and imperfect—of the friends' larger history). As a series of activities, the reunion is the object of filmic representation—a plotted sequence of events that takes place within the discourse. In fact, Sayles deliberately oversaturates the film with a sequence of story "arcs": Frances (Maggie Cousineau) getting together with Ron (David Strathairn); Irene's boyfriend, Chip (Gordon Clapp), getting accepted into the group of friends; the love triangle between Maura, J. T. (Adam Le Fevre), and Jeff (Mark Arnott). At the same time, and just as consistently, the reunion is a strategy or method of representation. Here, an embedded story—the original lives of these characters, the long history of their friendship, and, finally, the experience of the 1960s itself—is only partially grasped. Sayles brilliantly elaborates the reunion's formal division between event and representation by making the central event that occurs within the reunion the breakup of Maura and Jeff. The film brings together the seven friends only to focus on the way that two of them are leaving each other. This nesting of a breakup *within* a reunion thematically underscores the way that throughout the weekend all the characters confront the distance of the past and, more specifically, the distance of the political idealism and confidence of the 1960s.

Politics, in the world of *Return of the Secaucus Seven*, is very much the art of imperfect action: all the characters are faced with dilemmas that present a range of choices, none of which will be fully sufficient. In this sense, the friends' inevitable drift away from one another is not merely personal, or vocational, but embedded within a larger dispersion of the very ideals of the 1960s. The film makes sure to contextualize each of the different choices—whether working in a methadone clinic, teaching high school, pursuing music, becoming a doctor or, in the case of Irene, working for an unnamed senator—or, more precisely, to catch each of them within a balance, to present them as radically delimited effectuations of 1960s ideals. This is, in fact, necessarily the case: no character, whatever the purity or intensity of his or her personality, would be able to transcend the imperfections ushered in by the very collapse of the New Left as a political movement. Instead, everyone is caught in a recoil effect, not merely facing a series of choices on the level of action (pragmatism against detached idealism, art against politics) but also a series of possible consequences to these choices, on the level of character (becoming too bitter, too condescending, too instrumental, too marginal, and so on). In this way, for example, Jeff's activism is mistakenly reduced by a minor character to merely "working with junkies," even as the film suggests that his own behavior has, in fact, become too affected by the wounded persons he treats. This imperfection is summed up in Irene's deceptively simple speech about working for the unnamed senator: "I know people in state agencies, a lot of them came out of V.I.S.T.A. like Mike, and Jeff and Maura, and they're doing good stuff, housing, sex education, all kinds of stuff. They're using the money the state has provided. And these people tell me if the senator was defeated they'd be out of business. . . . I have a very limited, very subtle kind of power. . . . I'm able to divert a little bit of the state's power off to the people who really need it."

One of the key accomplishments of Sayles's first film is to connect this sense of political imperfection—as it emerges out of the historical recession of the 1960s—with both the imperfection of the reunion and the filming of the reunion itself. The quick passage of time; the tenderness of the friends' meetings and departures; the sense that the weekend only inadequately revives their old friendships: all of the compromises intrinsic to the reunion serve to reiterate, in the microcosm and deflation of the weekend, the political compromises faced by the friends.[10] These compromises—the wistful conjuring of the past, the melancholy of the breakup at the heart of the reunion—are ultimately ones of representation and, as such, are further mirrored by the film's own imperfect effort to represent the reunion. Rarely have the constraints of a low-budget film served the vehicle more effectively. The imperfection of the reunion—given thematic amplification by the breakup at the center of the plot—is continually mirrored, and elaborated, in the filming process, with its low production value that saturates the dynamics of mise-en-scène, editing, camera movement, and so on. Perhaps this is most explicit in the game of charades. Here the various framing strategies and editing choices deployed to capture the crowded room with a single camera are subtly resonant with the activity taking place in the crowded room—which is, of course, nothing other than a game of highly bounded, constrained representation. This kind of delimitation extends from the formal dynamics of individual shots to the equally fascinating interplay of revelation and constraint on the level of plot. *Return of the Secaucus Seven* has a pervasive slightness to it, engaging plotlines and character-arcs only to drift subtly away from them. The film strikes a careful balance between linear development and episodic digression, between the dramatic revelation and the transient sketch. We can see this, for example, in the approach to characterization, as the film casually suggests the nature of each character who falls into its ambit without insisting on, or aggressively demonstrating, its own revelatory powers. For instance, while the breakup of Jeff and Maura (the most melodramatic plot element in the film) hints at a kind of stubborn unchangingness within Jeff's character, the film, despite the obvious political resonance of this kind of stubbornness, does not lock the character into these qualities. In fact, it resists the implicit climax within this kind of character portrayal (where the narrative is driven toward a kind of implacable, and essential, truth about each of the central characters, revealed through a dramatic conflict) in much the same way as it juxtaposes the loose temporality of the reunion against a grander sense of historical conflict. At the same time, however, we cannot see *Return of the Secaucus Seven* as merely a slice of life or a series of episodic sketches. At almost all points, the film does suggest a pressing exigency, conveying the conflict between the characters' political ideals and the world around them. The lodging of a breakup within a reunion, a falling apart within a coming together, is merely the most structurally evident example of this. ("What's a reunion without a little drama?" Maura asks, when her friends first learn about the news of her breakup with Jeff.)

These terms of breakup and reunion—like the dialectic between "capture" and "escape"—have a resonance for the act of representation itself, as though any artistic representation is balanced between two simultaneous processes: "the reunion," which melds together form and content, conveying the plentitude of the referenced object, and "the breakup," which acknowledges the necessary separateness of content and form, story and style.[11] *Return of the Secaucus Seven*, from the title on, actually dramatizes this process, showing how the characters themselves come to terms with these vicissitudes of representation and embedding this within a charged and meaningful political context. Perhaps the most explicit signaling of this appears in the way the film is framed by less complete forms of visual representation: the sketches (of the seven characters' faces) that roll underneath the opening title sequence, and the still photographs (taken from scenes *during* the weekend) that roll underneath the closing credits. These two sequences enact the nostalgic loss depicted within the story, now on the level of discourse itself: they move us away from the more complete representation that they frame, even while reminding us that this representation is, also, an incomplete, heavily mediated depiction of the past. The drawings and still photographs serve as a reminder of "breaking up" (in their very status as partial representations), and they also underscore the idea of reunion. The opening series of sketches—presumably the mug shots taken of the characters during their initial arrest—are, more than any other moment in the film, rooted in the event that ironically forms the locus of the characters' collective memory. The closing series of photographs, meanwhile, plunges us back into the film we have just viewed. Accompanied by J. T.'s own plaintive musical performance at the very center of the weekend, these pictures reenact frozen moments from the film that has passed. The end credits thus clinch the self-reflexivity of Sayles's first film—placing the audience in the same relationship to the represented events we have just witnessed as the characters themselves bear to the events of their past. In this sense, the end of Sayles's film is deliberately poised on the cross-currents of the breakup and the reunion: the still photographs simultaneously return us to and sever us from the content of the film, as the audience's formal relationship to the story converges on the characters' nostalgic relationship to—and representation of—the 1960s.

At first glance, it is difficult to see any continuity between *Baby It's You* and *Return of the Secaucus Seven*. They seem to stare at each other across the divide of Saylesean "unpredictability." Yet the two films share a number of features that we have already identified: both are nostalgic; both concern the 1960s; and both revolve around a breakup. In *Return of the Secaucus Seven*, as we have seen, nostalgia is inscribed within the story; in *Baby It's You* (beginning with the title), nostalgia is the operative mode of the filmic discourse itself. The two films move in opposite directions: *Baby It's You* begins as a projected recovery of the past (in the Hollywood mode) and then, within the story, subtly inscribes a temporal difference that shatters this framework of representation. The ironic realism and progressive politics of *Return to Secaucus Seven* was swallowed up in the Hollywood patina of *The Big Chill* (1983), and Sayles's third feature, *Baby It's You*, returns the favor. The realism of *Baby It's You* is, like *The Brother from Another Planet*, intrinsically negative, intent on shattering the frame of a projected misrepresentation. The film is a deliberate engagement with *Hollywood* nostalgia, which, by the end of the 1970s was, as David Cook suggests, nothing if not antirealist. *Baby It's You*, indeed, is set against one of the formative blockbusters of the 1970s—George Lucas's *American Graffiti* (1973), a "nostalgic re-creation of early 60s adolescence" as Cook puts it (138), which, in its very insouciant shift from 1973 back to 1962, enacts the exact political occlusion at the center of Sayles's interest. In this sense, *The Big Chill*—made by Lawrence Kasdan, the screenwriter of Lucas's *The Empire Strikes Back* (1980)—and *American Graffiti* bear a certain symbiotic relationship to each other: representing the political history, and constituting the cinematic history, which Sayles's work is set against.

In his one studio production, Sayles himself seems to have experienced the kinds of imperfect choices that confront the characters in *Return of Secaucus Seven*, nearly walking away from the film and taking his name off of the project because of a creative clash with the studio. The step away from independent production clearly did not serve Sayles well, but it is not so clear that it served the film poorly. As Sayles replies when asked whether the film has "survived" the studio system, "I'm very happy with it. I nearly didn't survive, but the movie did" (Carson 75). In fact, we might even make a stronger case and consider Sayles's difficult "breakup" with the studio as an important part of the film. As Sayles makes clear, this actual rupture, between the independent filmmaker and the studio system, finds a location in a very specific rupture within the film itself. "It was Sayles's insistence on having the story explore the characters' lives after high school—a daring concept for a teen movie in Hollywood these days—that got the project into a bit of trouble." Sayles further attests:

> It follows these characters over two big hills. . . . One is from 1966 in Trenton, New Jersey, to 1967 at Sarah Lawrence, which was a high jump in what was expected of somebody who was young. . . . The other big jump is from high school, which is the last bastion of true democracy in our society, where you have classes and eat lunch with the guy who's going to be picking up your garbage later in life, to the year after, when she goes to college and he runs into the fact that he's going nowhere. *It's about class in America, and where the divisions are.* It's about how certain things are possible in high school, but when people enter the real world, they become impossible. (Carson 33, emphasis added)

Both of these "jumps," in fact, occur at the same moment—or within the same gap—in the film: the shift from high school to college, a temporal division, coincides with what Sayles seamlessly shifts toward, a class division. These two kinds of division underlie the most important formal feature of the film, its break into two separate, and jarring, acts: a break signaled formally by an extended fade-out that marks the division between Trenton and Sarah Lawrence College. It was precisely this division, in turn, that provoked Sayles's own division with the studio: "After viewing a rough cut, Paramount reportedly asked for changes in the second half of the film. Sayles balked. 'It gets interesting and complex in the second half,' he said after the screening, adding with a sting, 'which is why Paramount doesn't like it'" (Carson 33).

We are dealing here with a series of embedded ruptures: in the production of the film (between director and studio); in the form and genre of the film (between the first and second halves); in the plot of the film (between high school and college); and finally in the romantic rift between the two lovers that rests at the heart of the film's imagined story. The shift between high school and college is so important because it works to open up the gap that nostalgia closes from within the film itself. While the "nostalgic re-creation" seeks to seal present and past together on the level of *form*, we confront in *Baby It's You* a story that reasserts the difference between past and present. But this temporal split—high school and after—is not simply chronological, just as the difference between the 1960s and the 1970s is not simply chronological. *Baby It's You*'s main accomplishment is to comprehend the characters' differentiation from their past in terms of a breakup that finally revolves, as Sayles's comment suggests, around class division. If the starting point of *Baby It's You* is nostalgia, its end point is class division. In fact, the film moves inexorably toward this—through nostalgia, through temporal difference, through the romantic breakup to the stark inequality of the two characters. In this sense, *Baby It's You* is not a realistic film, but suggestively opens out onto a reality: once again, the very reality of class division that is elided in the early 1980s. What is exemplary about the film, in other words, is not its mimetic replication of reality but the movement away from nostalgia toward the recognition of division—a movement that forms the animating impulse and trajectory of the film. And this trajectory suggests the place of this work within Sayles's diverse and eclectic oeuvre. (Consider, in this sense, the strange affinity of *Baby It's You* with the much more mature *Limbo*, which, as we have seen, also revolves around a rupture, in both story and discourse, that makes the realist effect much more intricate.)

The subtle imbrication of class division and nostalgia is made evident toward the end of the film, when Jill (Rosanna Arquette) goes to Florida and discovers that Sheik (Vincent Spano) has taken a low-paying job lip-synching Frank Sinatra and other nostalgic lounge acts. Sayles has carefully inscribed the recirculation of culture into both the film's discourse (most clearly through the aggressive diegetic and extradiegetic soundtrack) and in the referenced story (all the characters seem to continually imitate speech, mannerisms, and desires that they have culled from popular films and songs). The suggestion that nostalgia might be nothing other *than* recycling is summed up in the painful depiction of Sheik's lip-synching gig in Florida, calling into question the very project of "nostalgic re-creation." The representation of lip-synching, in this sense, demonstrates how the film shatters this ideology of nostalgia from the inside out: a more poignant realism is purchased in the grim exposure of the mechanism that underlies nostalgia.

While this is the most extreme and acutely realized example, the film has been trafficking in both nostalgia and recycling from the very beginning, and in both the story and the discourse. The first scene gives a remarkable summary of this process, subtly integrating the dynamics of class and nostalgia. The film opens with the ring of a bell that cuts into and is laid over the opening credits' song, the two sounds together suggesting that we are witnessing an act of memory, that the film is plunging us back into a collectively remembered past. Against this working of memory the film will juxtapose Sheik's melancholy investment in the present. This character conveys a sense of urgency, of time fleeing, that is registered in his first speech ("I can tell a lot about a person in five minutes"); finds its most poignant balance in the day spent at the beach; and reaches an angry pitch of intensity in the film's final scenes. Sheik's desire, in other words, speaks expressively against—even as it is partially captured within—the projected representation of the screen: Sheik is not merely at odds with the authorities in the film, but against the very unfolding of the film itself, the nostalgic superstructure of which seems guaranteed, in the end, to offer him simply one more raw deal. "Promises, promises," Sheik repeats bitterly to his father and to the school principal, the two represented sources of authority—it is the phrase that would probably encapsulate his relationship to Jill, and it might as well be spoken to the camera itself, which, however much attention it registers on Sheik, never loses its central focus on Jill.

This disparity between the two lovers is carefully established in the first scene, where the camera, indeed, does almost all the work in positioning the relationship of the two characters—in a way that manages to tell the entire story before it has begun. The camera inscribes an excess into their relationship, something beyond either character's grasp or control. In his commentary on *Sunshine State,* Sayles talks about the challenge of introducing each character within the framework of the screen:[12] a formal problem that is thematized in the case of each of the coprotagonists in *Baby It's You*. It is crucial that Jill comes first. She is established emerging against a crowd; he is established only in relation to her—as what she comes up against. But Jill's foregrounding does not assure her much of a privilege; on the contrary, Jill emerges within a teeming crowd of students, threatened to be lost in exactly the "democratic" context that Sayles invokes in his interview. Furthermore, it is Jill who first begins to "recycle," as Sheik enters not just a preexisting visual structure but also a preexisting chain of mediated desire. As soon as Sheik passes, Jill's friend asks, "Do you know *him*?" comparing the stranger to another boy who had just passed Jill seconds earlier in the hall; and this first character, who also catches Jill's attention, is preceded by the girls' discussion of a film character, who is himself taken from a play. The alacrity with which these displacements take place establishes the way the film, in general, seems to propel these two characters into the plot, without ever giving either of them enough control.

This mediated chain ensures that any object of desire is only represented partially (not seen in-and-of-itself but only in relation to the circulating images of other people, movies, characters, songs, and so on), and the film reinforces this through its own visual comprehension of Sheik. The camera, starting with a crowd of students pouring into the empty hallway (over the sounds of the bell and the song) begins to focus on Jill and, more peripherally, her friends, slowly tracking back and around the corner of the hallway. We first see Sheik's back imposing in the foreground, then he collides into Jill; the camera, still tracking slowly backward, tilts up for a close-up of Sheik's face as he turns to look at Jill. The only cuts of the opening scene are a quick matching cut to Jill and then a cut to Jill's friend, who is looking at her (looking at him). The camera pulls back to frame the four friends once again, follows them down the hall and into their classrooms. But the deep focus continues to inscribe Sheik—who now stands like a statue, staring at the departing girls. We see him only indirectly, blocked from view as the four girls hover, in the foreground, outside the classroom. In other words, as Sheik is dropped into the background, left behind by the girls, Sayles makes sure that we *see* him being left behind—but this includes seeing him, as it were, getting thrust out of view. This process is concluded with the striking deep-focus shot of Sheik slowly emerging from background into foreground once everyone else has cleared out of the hallway. The effect is not so much to foreground Sheik as to foreground our very sense of background itself—Sheik is still forgotten, abandoned, left behind by all but the camera (in precisely the way that a delinquent student might be "left back").[13]

This scene works to inscribe Sheik as he is overlooked, and we might juxtapose it with a later shot of Jill that, on the contrary, suggests a fullness of experience that is not registered directly by the camera. In this scene, the camera focuses silently on Jill as she discovers that she has been cast as the lead role in her high school play. Jill's acting is, of course, another extreme of cultural recycling—her own upward mobility is formed in relation to playing these parts much as Sheik's downward mobility is encapsulated in his lip-synching in Miami. ("Forget everything you've learned in high school," is the first advice of Jill's drama professor.) At the same time, the camera confers attention onto Jill herself in the scene, lingering on the character as she discovers she has been cast as Kitty Duval in *The Time of Your Life*. The inert camera, positioned behind the glass, would seem to exemplify that absence of "visual flair" that critics note in Sayles, a lack of style associated with the intention to directly present the story or referential content of the film. The scene is typically Saylsean, however, in the way it stays fixed on Jill, as though trying to grasp, through this still attention, her own sense of emotion when she discovers her role in the play. Jill looks at the casting sheet (and thus directly at the camera) and then she turns while the camera stays still, and turns around again, to look. This turning serves to separate her from the camera, and yet it is clearly in this movement (as her back faces the audience) that her emotion is "captured"—but precisely in being captured, this emotion remains something that belongs to the character herself and is not directly legible to the film, camera, or audience.

These two scenes might suggest the way that Sayles's very recording of the two characters is organized around the same dialectic between "breakup" and "reunion" that is so thematically central to this film as well as to *Return of the Secaucus Seven*. *Baby It's You*'s final scene offers an acute balance between these two processes: the film ends with Sheik and Jill both together and apart, reuniting in a dance that brings them physically together while in no way suggesting that they have not broken up. But, as we have seen, this subtle ending to their fraught relationship resembles the doubleness of representation in the film as a whole, encapsulated in the way that the camera can both register what has been excluded (when Sheik moves from background to foreground) and exclude what has been registered (as when it suggests Jill's emotions by the very manner in which she turns away). The "breakup" and the "reunion"—which sketch the double movement of nostalgia—are central to Sayles's filmmaking techniques and thematic concerns. In *Return of the Secaucus Seven*, they provide a thematic vocabulary to understand formal processes. And as both theme and form the dialectic between breakup and reunion is embedded in a specific political and historical context, registering the collective loss that underlies the temporal pathos of the film (in the shift from 1967 to 1975). *Baby It's You*, in turn, seeks to rewrite the very genre of Hollywood nostalgia itself, reworking this "antimimetic" form from the inside out, using a breakup, once again, to expose the ideological constraints of the coming-of-age film and open out onto social division. The two films, along with *Lianna* and *The Brother from Another Planet*, constitute the first phase of Sayles's film career. They work—together and apart—as a prism that offers numerous (potentially endless) refractions of social reality while registering the loss of reality implicit in contemporary U.S. politics. The later films, with more ambitious historical and social frames, build on this pluralistic and democratic basis to suggest—against all political odds—a sense of totality within American life.

NOTES

For helpful responses to this essay, I would like to thank Natalka Freeland, Robert Kaufman, D. A. Miller, Sianne Ngai, and Robert Polhemus, as well as the editors of this volume. Special thanks to Karla Oeler for her engagement and expertise.

The epigraphs to this chapter are drawn from: Gavin Smith, *Sayles on Sayles* (100); Diane Carson, *John Sayles: Interviews* (41); and Georg Lukács, *The Historical Novel* (105).

1. In *Lone Star*, most famously, the history we can discover is profoundly intertwined with the effacement of history, as the comprehension of the past (by Sam and Pilar) turns out to hinge on discovering the way an even more remote past has been concealed. "Forget the Alamo" is the most famous ending of Sayles's films and conjures up this intricate process most concisely: by "forget the Alamo," Pilar Cruz really means forget the forgetfulness that has been organized under the rubric of "remembering the Alamo," or in the more specific terms of *Lone Star*'s plot, forget the legacy of forgetfulness they have been embedded within. In this ending, then, forgetting and remembering are intimately, and intricately, conjoined. *Matewan* might appear to be Sayles's most direct enactment of history—and it is sometimes faulted for this—but, in the context of the 1980s, this explicitly nostalgic reenactment is infused with an awareness that its story not only has been—but also is actively being—forgotten.

2. See, for example, Robert Kolker's study of American auteurship in the 1970s, *A Cinema of Loneliness*, which, from the title on, emphasizes the way the thematic concerns of independent filmmakers (loneliness, alienation, subjectivity) continually motivate formal strategies that work to separate the filmic signifier from a direct or instant absorption into story.

"Loneliness," operates, for Kolker, across story and style, much as I argue that the "breakup" and the "reunion" are both thematically and formally central to Sayles. In Kolker's study, Martin Scorsese's *Taxi Driver* (which, like *Return of the Secaucus Seven*, is a post-Vietnam, post-1960s film) is the emblematic example of how "loneliness" travels from being an object of representation to inform the modalities of representation itself.

3. This idea of representation runs directly counter to a received notion of realism as naïve, ideologically aggressive, and, most importantly, antiformal. As Christopher Prendergast writes in a summary of this simplistic but quite pervasive devaluation of realism: "Mimetic or representational notions have been exposed as an 'illusion,' in the sense of a rhetorical trick designed to mask the arbitrary character of the literary sign, and similarly contaminated by an ideology whose effort is to convince us of an enduring (human) Nature beyond the changing and heterogeneous forms of culture and history. . . . The authoritarian gesture of mimesis is to imprison us in a world which, by virtue of its familiarity, is closed to analysis and criticism. . . . Whence the tendency in 'modernist' aesthetics to construe what is most vital in literary texts in terms of an impulse to question and rebel against the order of mimesis" (2, 6). This rebellion inevitably revolves around the separation of the signifying plane from its referential ground, even as the ideological "illusion" that Prendergast identifies hinges on the projected union between text and referent.

4. Auerbach's *Mimesis*, with its twenty chapters that detail the dynamics of social representation in texts from twenty distinct moments in European cultural history, offers the most capacious history yet written of social realism. In Auerbach's account, each achieved form of representation, fully elaborated in a specific section of the book, is ironically revealed as partial in relation to the forms that follow (and are often motivated by) it. In this way, the progressive accomplishment of mimesis is increasingly shadowed by a negation implicit in Auerbach's philological approach.

5. If Bazin calls the cinematic image "the preservation of life by a representation of life" (1967, 10) he also describes Stroheim's *Greed* as laying reality "bare like a suspect confessing under the relentless examination of the commissioner of police" (1967, 27). And, again, explicitly playing with the idea of capture as it spans across story and discourse, he writes, "If slapstick comedy succeeded before the days of Griffith and montage, it is because most of its gags derived from a comedy of space. . . . In *The Circus* Chaplin is truly in the lion's cage and both are enclosed within the framework of the screen" (1958, 52).

6. Packer's distinction between "cinematic plainness" and a "technical skill" that emerges in the "editing room" suggestively resembles Bazin's foundational distinction between the rapid editing of montage-driven cinema and the still camera that underlies the depth of field associated with realist cinema.

7. Sayles highlights this through the shrewd inscription of the American audience with the brief appearance of Harriet (Kathryn Grody) and An-

drew (Mandy Patinkin). This self-reflexive gesture—which cunningly renders the Americans' English as foreign—once again, as with *Limbo*, uses tourism as a form of misrepresentation that is placed in dialogue with the intricate aesthetics of representation in Sayles's own film.

8. In the story itself the Brother's forced silence ironically tends to motivate more interactions with other characters and, indeed, becomes a major vehicle in advancing the plot. I want to suggest that the way silence connects the Brother with these characters (against our expectations) mirrors the way silence advances the film's own achieved representation.

9. Sayles's film manipulates the essential artifice of science fiction to construct a method of indirect presentation that comments both on the actual nature of race (and racial segregation) in the United States and, simultaneously, on the effacement of blacks in Hollywood representation. Racial inequality is not grasped directly by the film, but in the parodic deflation of the sci-fi genre the reality—and historical consequence—of enslavement poignantly emerges more powerful because of its elliptical comprehension.

10. Every moment in *Secaucus Seven* thus has two simultaneous frames of reference: a weekend and a decade. Throughout the film, Sayles breaks the reunion down into discrete, bounded activities, most notably in the many games the characters play (basketball, charades, even Clue) and also in the different combinations of characters performing chores. Each of these games is presented as a bounded activity that, ultimately, has reference to a larger context. (In this way, for example, the game of charades becomes an opportunity to test and welcome Chip, the basketball game turns into an argument between J. T. and Jeff, etc.) In other words, the characters are not playing these games for the love of the games, but rather as a medium—within the delimited context of the weekend—for indirectly expressing something else. And in just the same way the reunion as a whole is a bounded and ultimately formalized expression of history: the weekend as a totality, full of necessary compromises, bears a similar relationship to the characters' shared past as each game does to the sustained friendships that contextualize and animate them.

11. Perhaps the most succinct formal rendering of this occurs in the scene at the end of the reunion where Jeff is chopping wood, a scene that is clearly integrated into the fragmentation intrinsic both to his breakup with Maura and the dispersion at the end of the weekend. This sense of breaking up creates a parallel between each piece of wood that Jeff splits and the alternating montage between his isolated activity and the other friends' departure. But, within the scene itself, Sayles also creates an oscillation: ending not with the rapid cuts (of Jeff cutting) but with a still and quiet shot of Jeff sitting on the stump of wood, with all the fragments of his labor splayed around him. Formally, this shot works to literally encapsulate the frenetic montage (linked metonymically with these shards of wood) within a classically "realist" image.

12. Sayles comments, "I'm about to introduce a character, Flash Philips. One of the things you often think about when you're screenwriting is

how you introduce a character, what's the first time we see him, does it tell you something about who he is."

13. We might consider the introduction of J. T. as a parallel scene near the beginning of *Return of the Secaucus Seven*. The camera views him trying to hitch a ride, passed by car after car; in other words, he is first seen as he is being overlooked. In ironic counterpoint to this storied situation the camera makes a series of rapid cuts in toward his face, so that he comes into increasing focus, within the filmed space, as the cars pass him by unseen.

WORKS CITED

Auerbach, Erich. *Mimesis: The Representation of Reality in Western Literature*. Trans. Willard R. Trask. Princeton: Princeton UP, 1953.

Bazin, André. *What Is Cinema?* Vol. 1. Trans. Hugh Gray. Berkeley: U of California P, 1967.

———. *Qu'est-ce que c'est le cinema? Ontologie et langage*. Paris: Editions du Serf, 1958.

Carson, Diane, ed. *John Sayles: Interviews*. Jackson: UP of Mississippi, 1999.

Cook, David. *Lost Illusions: American Cinema in the Shadow of Watergate and Vietnam, 1970–1979*. New York: Scribner, 2000.

Kolker, Robert. *A Cinema of Loneliness*. 3rd ed. Oxford: Oxford UP, 2000.

Levy, Emanuel. *A Cinema of Outsiders: The Rise of American Independent Film*. New York: New York UP, 1999.

Limbo. Directed by John Sayles. Sony Pictures' Screen Gems, 1999. DVD.

Lukács, Georg. *The Historical Novel*. Trans. Hannah and Stanley Mitchell. Lincoln: U of Nebraska P, 1983.

Packer, George. "Decency and Muck: The Visions of John Sayles and Oliver Stone." *Dissent* 44.3 (1997): 105–10.

Prendergast, Christopher. *The Order of Mimesis: Balzac, Stendhal, Nerval and Flaubert*. Cambridge: Cambridge UP, 1986.

Smith, Gavin. *Sayles on Sayles*. Boston: Faber and Faber, 1998.

Sunshine State. Directed by John Sayles. Sony Pictures Classics, 2002. DVD.

3

The False Salvation of the Here and Now:

Aliens, Images, and the Commodification of Desire in *The Brother from Another Planet*

Mark Bould

In *The Brother from Another Planet* (1984) Sayles returns to science fiction, the genre in which he obtained his first screenwriting work with *Piranha* (Dante 1978) and *Alligator* (Teague 1980). Within a couple of years of its release, it received the distinction of being selected by Vivian Sobchack in the groundbreaking final chapter of her Fredric Jameson–inspired revised edition of *Screening Space* as one of a small number of "postfuturist" science-fiction movies exemplifying "the radical alteration of our culture's temporal and spatial consciousness" (223) brought about by the spread of electronic and digital media. More specifically, she related it to other "[m]arginal and postmodern SF" movies that similarly

> suggest there is no original model for being, and that (as Foucault notes) the similarity we see across difference "develops in series that have neither beginning nor end," representing the circulation "of the simulacrum as an indefinite and reversible relation of the similar to the similar" propagated nonhierarchically from "small differences among small differences." Margaret, the androgynous new-wave model of *Liquid Sky* [Tsukerman 1983], and her spaced-out friends, or Otto and his myriad bizarre acquaintances in *Repo Man* [Cox 1984] are as slightly different from each other as they are different from the marked "aliens" and yet they are as similarly alien-ated as are any of

the aliens. Similarly the same and different, the Brother from
another planet is as human and alien as any alien-ated human
extraterrestrialized in New York's Harlem. (297; quoting Foucault 44)

The more obvious comparison is, of course, with *Blade Runner*
(Scott 1982), a movie whose premises *The Brother from Another
Planet* inverts, telling the story from the point of view of the
alien/replicant rather than the Men in Black/blade runner. *Blade
Runner* has often been interpreted in terms of race—the replicants are runaway slaves, and the police fly over Los Angeles,
deciding who is human—and in such readings the interplay of
similarity and difference is exemplified by the claim that Roy
Batty (Rutger Hauer) is some kind of ironic Aryan.[1]

Sobchack's treatment of *The Brother from Another Planet*
neglects the ways in which the only science-fiction movie written and directed by Sayles[2] expands upon the potential for social
commentary and political allegory evident in his earlier forays
into the genre. This is in part a consequence of her importation
of Jameson's disinclination to moralize, evident in the failure of
his "intellectually cool and aesthetically distanced" essay "Postmodernism, or the Cultural Logic of Late Capitalism" to "convey any real sense of shock or horror about postmodern culture
or about the economic relations which it supposedly represents"
(Gordon 390).

In order to explore this critical—and, indeed, moralizing—
dimension of the movie, I start this essay by discussing the function of the alien in science fiction so as to better understand what
is at stake in *The Brother from Another Planet*'s representation
of the alien, beginning with a consideration of the opening sequences of *The Brother from Another Planet* and *Men in Black*
(Sonnenfeld 1997), both of which, despite being made thirteen
years apart, are concerned with extraterrestrials as immigrants
and assign significant, if contrasting, roles to Men in Black. I
then discuss *The Brother from Another Planet*'s critique of an
alienating culture of commodity consumption. As Sobchack's
reading of late capitalism's postfuturist science-fiction movies
suggests, the image plays a central role in that culture, and consequently I discuss in some detail two of the images of women to
which the movie draws particular attention: those of the singer
Malverne Davis (Dee Dee Bridgewater) and of the Statue of Lib-

Commodification of Desire in *Brother from Another Planet*

The Brother (Joe Morton) stands up, emphatically entering America, with the Statue of Liberty now in focus behind him.

erty. Previous readings of *The Brother from Another Planet* have emphasized the final shot of the movie, typically misdescribing and thus misinterpreting it; therefore, I will close this essay by offering a corrective to a pair of such misreadings.

The Brother from Another Planet: after crashing his fleetingly evoked spaceship into the stretch of water between Bedloe Island, home of the Statue of Liberty, and Ellis Island, home of the immigrants' Detention Center, the Brother (Joe Morton) levers himself out of the water and half-crawls, half-flops onto dry land. It is nighttime, and the Statue of Liberty is an out-of-focus but nonetheless recognizable vertical smudge behind him. There is a cut, and the Brother stands up into the new shot, intruding into the frame and thus emphatically entering America. Now the Statue of Liberty is in focus behind him, but still he does not see it, and then the focus changes and it becomes a smudge once more. He turns to his right. Now in profile, his eyeline is on the same level as the yellow lozenge of light at the top of the Statue's torch; but still he does not see it. The camera reframes his body so as to reveal that instead of a foot his right leg terminates in a bloody stump. It is a fresh injury from which blood is still pouring. Either he has lost his foot in the crash or, as his later comparison of himself to a picture of a runaway slave implies, he has severed it in order to remove a shackle. When he reaches down to touch the wound, his hand glows with a healing orange light.

He hops toward the Detention Center. Inside is a vast and empty space. Every noise echoes. He rests a hand on a wall to support himself, and in response to his touch a disembodied voice calls out. Startled, he lets go of the wall, then tentatively touches it again. More voices reverberate around the hall. He hops away into the middle of the deserted space, but when he sits down on a bench the voices start up again. He hops away, and as he looks around at the arched roof a disorienting babble of voices erupts from nowhere. The Brother lets out a silent scream and collapses to the floor.

The opening credits follow, and then the movie cuts to the following morning. The camera pans across the Manhattan skyline, starting with the twin towers of the World Trade Center and ending on the Brother as he looks across at the city, the Statue of Liberty an out-of-focus smudge behind him. A boat's siren causes him to turn toward the Statue, and the Brother's point-of-view shot of the boat is followed by a close-up of his face in which the direction of his gaze seems to change slightly. It is initially implied that the following in-focus shot of the Statue is also his point-of-view shot. However, he then steps into the frame and the Statue goes out of focus, retrospectively placing the shot's apparent origin *sous rature* and returning the Brother to the same visual field as the Statue. This recurrent failure of the Brother to see the Statue of Liberty, and the persistence with which it is made visible to the audience before being eased out of focus or otherwise denied to the Brother's gaze, is a nagging feature of the opening sequence to which I return below.

Men in Black: a CGI bug, which has soared and swooped over the desert during the opening credits, is splattered across the windshield of a van that is smuggling a dozen illegal immigrants into the United States. Stopped by the Border Patrol, the driver claims that he has merely been fishing across the border in Mexico. When INS agent Janus (Fredric Lane) opens the van and discovers the immigrants, he says that he would have thrown them back. Just then, a black car pulls up and two Men in Black step out. Claiming to be from Division 6, they take command.

Kay (Tommy Lee Jones) questions the immigrants. Having picked out the most stereotypical Mexican—he is dressed in a shapeless blanketlike poncho over an equally shapeless gown, with a lank and greasy mass of hair and a scruffy moustache and beard—Kay tells the others to continue on their way. Kay and Dee (Richard Hamilton) march their prisoner off into the desert. Away from the Border Patrol, Kay pulls a knife on the Mexican and cuts open his disguise, revealing the extraterrestrial Mikey (John Alexander). The most Mexican of the Mexicans is, it seems, truly alien. Kay and Dee scoff at Mikey's claim to be a political refugee, and point out that his very presence has broken seven treaties. Suddenly, Mikey spots Agent Janus, who has witnessed the end of this exchange, and charges at him. Kay shoots Mikey with a futuristic silver handgun. Mikey explodes in a cloud of blue alien gloop that drenches Janus and much of the surrounding area. Kay then uses a Neuralyzer, a device given to the Men in Black by some friends "from out of town," to erase the Border Patrol officers' memories of the night's events.

In order to comprehend the significance of these two sequences and the narratives that develop from them, it is necessary to consider briefly the role of the alien in science fiction. In his recent essay on the peculiar relative absence of the nation, nationality, and nationalism from science fiction's future visions, Istvan Csicsery-Ronay Jr. identifies several major strategies by which the genre expunges "nations as agents or subjects of future history and national cultures as historical forces," including, of greatest relevance in this context, that of *"biological displacement"* (223; italics in original). By abjuring national identity in this way, science fiction is able to elide "the distinction between national culture and race" and to let the "political-cultural problems of nationality and ethnicity . . . slip into the context of racial difference." The main device science fiction uses to achieve this is the figure of the alien, and because this figure is "ontologically other only by virtue of its being biologically Other," its depiction is typically built upon a "fundamental ambivalence." According to Csicsery-Ronay Jr., science fiction tends to imagine "alien-human difference as analogous to terrestrial racial difference," depicting alien-human "biological relations . . . as a nebulous kind of species difference" and thus permitting "much the same imaginary sleight-of-hand as the concept of race." This allows the dominant members of a culture to see aspects of themselves objectified in Others while also disavowing them, by placing the Others beyond a nonnegotiable *essential* line of separation. As a result, human national-political, ethnic, class, and gender differences are distanced beyond mediating human institutions. Rapprochement is only possible accompanied by the anxiety that differences may prove to be intractable and even dangerous; or at the risk of violating a taboo about which the central protagonists are deeply ambivalent and the audience is ontologically confused. . . . Race insinuates the model of species difference into relations among members of the human species. It purports to name qualities deeper than expression, and consequently deeper than culture and politics. Race implies forces that cannot be examined in oneself and yet that may manifest themselves at any time. The insidiousness of race lies precisely in this precondition for its being imagined at all, lying beneath all conscious articulations, all sharing of premises, all decisions. When race is in play, it implies that nature supersedes culture. (228; italics in original)

The encounter with the alien has been a staple of science fiction since the origins of the modern genre in H. G. Wells's work of the 1890s. Ziauddin Sardar has traced the dominant imagery of this encounter back to the origins of European identity in the fight against Islam in the eighth century. "This war of the worlds," he writes, "began with the battle of Tours in October AD 732 near Poitiers in western France," (7) and in it we see again "the armies of Charles Martel turning the tide, . . . Charlemagne and his paladins at Roncesvalle mustering for the first time a common sense of European identity, gathering the armies of Western Christendom to confront the Muslim hordes" (6). Evidence for Sardar's claim can be found in the "alien" invader of Richard Marsh's *The Beetle* (1897), a monstrous threat to Imperial Britain that has much in common with Bram Stoker's eponymous *Dracula* (1897) and the Martians of Wells's *The War of the Worlds* (1898). As Rhys Garnett observes, Marsh's

alien intruder is variously described as an Algerian, an "arab of the Soudan," an "unbaptised Mohammedan," and "Egypto-Arabian" and, later, as "Oriental to his finger-tips" yet "hardly an Arab . . . not a fellah," perhaps "not a Mohammedan at all" and, because of his "thick and shapeless lips," as having "more than a streak of negro blood." . . . Because he is none of these things specifically, he is all of them approximately. (34–35)

Alongside the alien monstrosity, literary science fiction has also, from the start, offered positive views of the alien, such as the angelic visitor of Wells's *The Wonderful Visit* (1895), the sympathetic alien Tweel in Stanley G. Weinbaum's "A Martian Odyssey" (1934), and Raymond Z. Gallun's Martian "Old Faithful" (1934). The most sustained example of the potentially positive ambiguity of the alien Other can be found in Gwyneth Jones's remarkable *White Queen* (1991). Jones recalls,

> I planned to give my alien conquerors the characteristics, all the supposed deficiencies, that Europeans came to see in their subject races in darkest Africa and the mystic East—"animal" nature, irrationality, intuition; mechanical incompetence, indifference to time, helpless aversion to theory and measurement; and I planned to have them win the territorial battle this time. It was no coincidence, for my purposes, that the same list of qualities or deficiencies—a nature closer to the animal, intuitive communication skills and all the rest of it—were and still are routinely awarded to *women*, the defeated natives, supplanted rulers of men, in cultures north and south, west and east, white and non-white, the human world over. (110; italics in original)

However, cinematic science fiction has more typically focused on the alien as threat. This is particularly evident in 1950s movies such as *The Thing* (Nyby 1951), *Invaders from Mars* (Menzies 1953), *The War of the Worlds* (Haskin 1953), *Earth vs. The Flying Saucers* (Sears 1956), and the *Quatermass* trilogy (Guest 1956 and 1957; Baker 1968). Even when the aliens were only ambiguously threatening, as in *The Day the Earth Stood Still* (Wise 1951) or *It Came from Outer Space* (Arnold 1953), they were nonetheless treated as a threat by most terrestrial characters and institutions. Perhaps the most instructive example is provided by the pod people, those unfeeling alien simulacra of humans from *Invasion of the Body Snatchers* (Siegel 1956). Often taken to represent the threat of communist infiltration, they are rather more convincing as metaphors for the enervating conformism of Eisenhower's placid decade. As always, these aliens tell us rather more about ourselves than about some Other that they are supposed to represent.

As Csicsery-Ronay Jr. suggests, imagining Otherness in terms of racialized difference has long been a major strategy of both literary and cinematic science fiction, although it is perhaps more prevalent and less well-thought-through in nonliterary science fiction, which depends more heavily upon the immediacy of the visual image. This has long been characteristic of the *Star Trek* franchise,[3] and among the more egregious recent examples from movies are the "violent, sexually predatory libel on black manhood" (Roberts 26) that stalks the Aryan Robinson family in *Lost in Space* (Hopkins 1998) and the justly maligned racial stereotyping of *Star Wars Episode 1: The Phantom Menace* (Lucas 1999).

Although *The Brother from Another Planet* invites comparison with a number of contemporaneous science-fiction movies, including *E.T. the Extra-Terrestrial* (Spielberg 1982), which it openly spoofs, and *Starman* (Carpenter 1984), I am here more interested in considering it alongside other science-fiction movies overtly concerned with the supposed threat to American society posed by the immigration of nonwhite illegal aliens. For example, *Independence Day* (Emmerich 1996), like *Men in Black*, is a NAFTA-era film with important scenes set closer to Mexico than Canada. In *Independence Day*, the U.S. president James Whitmore (Bill Pullman), a combat veteran of the Gulf War, organizes global war against the aliens because he has received the awful revelation that the aliens are migrant laborers—paranoia about immigration from Latin America has often been paralleled by anxiety about the northward progress of foreign and potentially devastating species of insects—and therefore they must be destroyed: "I saw its thoughts. I saw what they're planning to do. They're like locusts. They're moving from planet to planet, their whole civilization. After they've consumed every natural resource they move one. And we're next. Nuke 'em. Let's nuke the bastards." The assertions that it is migrant labor—rather than migrant capital—that destroys environments, communities, and the more positive aspects of civil society, and that only the labor embodied in commodities and the surplus value (profit) produced by labor have the right to cross national boundaries, are vital components of the neoliberal ideology *Independence Day* and *Men in Black* replicate.

As indicated at the start of this essay, *Men in Black* deserves closer attention as the gaps and contradictions in its ideologically complex opening sequence are often revelatory. Although Janus's response to Nick's lie about fishing is intended merely to be jokey, taken alongside Kay's reference to out-of-town friends it suggests a lot about contemporary Western immigration policies that often claim not to be racist, but which nonetheless distinguish between unskilled "economic migrants" from the "developing" world and skilled "immigrants" from the "developed" world. Considering that immigration is a discourse riven with euphemisms, Mikey may indeed be a political refugee, despite the skepticism with which his claim is met. That he has broken a number of treaties may criminalize him—in a telling ambiguity, it is unclear whether it is his presence on Earth or in America that is the problem—but there is absolutely no reason to suppose secret treaties enforced by a covert paramilitary organization are just. In this context, it is significant that in order for the Men in Black to be presented as heroes, Kay is shown to be unconcerned about the illegal immigrants he only ironically describes as "the dangerous aliens."[4]

By dismissing the other immigrants and focusing on Mikey, *Men in Black* performs precisely the disavowal Csicsery-Ronay Jr. describes. National culture and "the political-cultural problems of nationality and ethnicity" have been transformed into an image of racial difference imagined as species difference. That the rest of the film should be so concerned with the recruitment, training, and first mission of Kay's new partner, the African American Jay (Will Smith), is indicative of the extent of the movie's disavowal mechanisms.[5]

The expensive computer-generated effects that dominate *Men in Black* could not be more different from the very cheap—and scarce—special effects in *The Brother from Another Planet*. The latter's cheerfully low-budget opening effects sequence—in which the Brother's spaceship falls out of the sky—constitutes a declaration that the movie is unconcerned with the hegemonic aesthetic of post–*Star Wars* (Lucas 1977) blockbuster science fiction, an aesthetic so dominated by spectacle that science-fiction movies now often seem to be merely tediously extended advertisements for cutting-edge cinema technologies.[6] Moreover, this retreat from special effects is accompanied by a rejection of the frequently unreflexive imagery of cinematic science fiction. As the title of this movie, its opening Afro-Caribbean music, and our first glimpse of the Brother tell us, race will not be displaced onto the figure of the alien. Racial difference will not be imagined as species difference but species difference as racial difference. In stark contrast to *Blade Runner*, the alien will have the appearance of the Other it is supposed to displace. This makes the significance of the opening sequence clear. For a black person to enter the United States via the traditional route of European immigration is rare enough—and this is emphasized by the babble of European tongues the Brother "hears" inside the deserted Detention Center—but in a society still divided on racial grounds (among others) it is a fitting irony that he should repeatedly and so insistently not even see the symbol of freedom intended to welcome the "huddled masses."[7]

Toward the end of *Baby It's You*, as Sheik (Vincent Spano) rushes back from Florida to see Jill (Rosanna Arquette), he drives into New York, and for a brief moment we get a fleeting and atypical glimpse of the Statue of Liberty, seen through a gap between houses. In a movie concerned with the unattainability of images (Sheik's desire to be like Frank Sinatra; Jill's desire to become a star, an image), this momentary sighting of that quintessentially American icon does more than just function as a shorthand signifier of Sheik's location. It ties the protagonists' thwarted desires and ambitions into American ideology and suggests that the image of America is as illusory and unattainable as those things for which Jill and Sheik yearn. In the opening scenes of *The Brother from Another Planet*, the Statue of Liberty is heavily ironized in a similar manner, extending the preceding movie's critique of the falsely utopian ideology of commodity culture.

The scene of the Brother's collapse in the Detention Center is the first of several occasions in the movie in which history—often racial or class history—is inscribed in the physical structures and spaces of the city. This is exemplified in the scene on the subway in which the Card Trickster (Fisher Stevens), who has just shown the Brother an elaborate trick, offers to perform a rather more impressive piece of conjuring: making all the white people disappear. This is achieved simply by pulling into a station; and, sure enough, all the white people debark before the train continues on into Harlem.

However, we do see some white people in Harlem. Two guys from Indiana in town for a "Self-Actualization conference" suddenly find they have wandered by mistake into this predominantly nonwhite part of the city. A white cop on his first day in the precinct sits down next to the Brother and tells him about the cannibalistic horror stories with which his partner has been tormenting him. These white guys in Harlem have a vital function in the movie's analysis of oppression and exploitation inasmuch as their comments can be easily identified as being racist; however, as characters, even ones so briefly sketched in, they are rather more complex. Clearly, their racism is not malicious: they are naïve characters, insensitive—ignorant, even—but their racism is unintended. By deploying such characters, *The Brother from Another Planet* is able to demonstrate the pervasiveness of racism in American society without making it the sole explanation for oppression. Rather, the major root of that oppression is located in American ideology as an articulation of capitalist social relations and commodity culture. Virgil (Sidney Sheriff Jr.) instructs the Brother on their nocturnal tour of Harlem: "Children withering away up here, brother, worshipping the idol of capital, lusting after the false salvation of the here and now. Black brother and sister perishing up here, man, waiting for scraps from oppressor's table. Oppressor got us a ho's bed, doing tricks to get reward. Oppressor need a slave, him find it here. Oppressor need a harlot, him find it here." This key speech, which utilizes the imagery of racial and sexual oppression, locates the source of oppression outside of specifically racial and sexual contexts by personifying capital itself as the "oppressor" (while retaining the sense that the oppressors within the system are, to the extent that they can be individualized, almost certainly white and male). Just as the runaway slaves recalled in the scene at the Harriet Tubman exhibition sought freedom in Harlem—the "Promised Land" ironically invoked in the film's closing moments by the African American spiritual of that name (and as its lyrics continue, "still not there")—so various characters in the movie seek the Promised Land promised but not delivered by commodity consumption. As Tom Moylan notes of the muting of utopian discourse in the twentieth century, "utopia has been absorbed into the affirmative ideologies of the totalizing systems of Stalinist Russia, Nazi Germany, and the corporate United States. Each of these formations has contained and co-opted utopia into the maintenance of the given system. Stimulated but unfulfilled desires are effaced and channelled into the service of the state or the consumer paradise" (8).

The main group of such characters are the regulars at Odell's bar. Tolerant acquaintances rather than friends, there is little in their interactions to suggest genuine human solidarity. They seem to meet as much by chance as desire for contact, although the bar itself offers them an important haven from the world. That the promised land their ancestors sought should be reduced to a bar is a painful irony that suggests that to whatever extent African Americans are still excluded from aspects of American life, consumption is not one of them (as long as, like everyone else, they have the ability to pay). The strength of this critique lies in the fact that it does not condemn the habitués of Odell's bar—in fact, it treats them affectionately as figures of community, however diminished—and it is careful to situate alcohol within a context of other "drugs," including the narcotics for which the junkies fight and die and the stimulus and near-orgasmic pleasure sought by the perpetually bored Ace (Liane Curtis) in the video games arcade. What each of the "drugs" has in common is the commodification of desire, something to which the Brother himself succumbs.[8]

Almost an hour into the movie, the Brother, who has been making a meager living squeegeeing windshields, wanders down a city street munching on an apple and a cabbage. The camera tracks away from him, keeping him in long shot. He is briefly surprised by a woman wearing deelyboppers. He sets free a dog someone has chained up. Suddenly, he notices something off to his right, and the camera pans to follow him, still tracking back as he passes from a long medium shot to a closer medium shot. He stops in front of a wall covered in (at least sixty-four) posters advertising a new album by Malverne Davis. There is a medium shot of him facing the wall, a background composed of nothing but the replicated image of Malverne. Cut to a medium shot of the Brother, the camera slowly tracking into his face; cut to a reverse shot, the camera slowly tracking in on one poster. The camera tracks in closer to the Brother, and then to the poster, and again, getting closer to both the Brother and the poster. The Brother blinks, a faint smile growing on his face. On the soundtrack, we hear "Two People in the World" by Little Anthony and the Imperials. After the final reverse shot of the poster of Malverne, there is a fifteen-shot montage sequence of the Brother beginning to notice the sexualized—and sexist—images of women that fill the city: advertisements for beer and Jamaican holidays, strippers, pornographic films and magazines, fashion and lifestyle magazines, and several more images of Malverne. (To quote Moylan again, "In western industrial societies, utopian longing can be discovered as the underlying stimulus to the machinery of ad-

The Brother (Joe Morton) stops in front of a wall with numerous posters signaling the commodification of desire to which he succumbs.

vertising" [8].) Finding Malverne's new album displayed in a record-shop window, the Brother buys a copy. He extracts the record, touches it, and then discards it along with the polyethylene wrapper. He walks down the street, the album sleeve held high, admiring her image.

This sequence represents a turning point in the movie: suddenly the Brother begins to care about his appearance and express strong emotions, such as his desire to see Malverne and subsequent frustration when the doorman will not let him into the club where she is performing. It is also after this that he finds the dead junkie, shoots up, is taken on a night tour of Harlem by Virgil, and smokes a joint. After the trip to the Harriet Tubman exhibition with Little Earl (Herbert Newsome), the Brother becomes a rather more active figure, first meeting and sleeping with Malverne and then tracing the drugs plaguing his neighborhood back to Mr. Vance (Edward Baran).

The liaison between the Brother and Malverne is worth considering in some detail as it is simultaneously the movie's most successful attempt at depicting genuine human contact and, because of its transitoriness, a doleful indictment of the commodification to which capital subjects us. The neatly turned-out

Brother sits alone in the club, not drinking his drink, but content to watch Malverne as she sings. Presumably intended to evoke a Diana Ross figure, yet one whose success faded after splitting from her group, The Rubies, Malverne is attempting to make some kind of comeback or, at the very least, to continue to make a living singing. After her opening set, she joins the Brother at his table and recruits him into the fiction that he is her gentleman friend Lewis from Philadelphia so as to ward off the advances of the club owner, Mr. Price (Carl Gordon). When the rather sleazy Mr. Price joins them, he is dismissive of the mute Brother, and attempts to use his position to proposition Malverne, reminding her that she is no longer "flying high." Because he now owns the club and she now works for him, he seems to feel he in some way now owns her, and it signifies something of her status in his eyes that she is not alone when she complains that he has "been on my ass"; both the bouncer (Randy Frazier) and the waitress (Dwania Kyles) use exactly the same expression to describe his treatment of them. Malverne tells Mr. Price that she and Lewis have already made plans for the evening, and as he leaves, Malverne reasserts the independence that has characterized her thus far, saying, "I will never tumble down that low." She is not without a trace of vanity, however, and her pleasure in the fact that the Brother really likes her singing seems genuine and further humanizes her.

The scene cuts to a bathroom in which Malverne, dressed in a negligee, peels off her fake eyelashes and hair extensions. When she enters the bedroom and asks the Brother whether he is still interested, he applauds this stripping away of the image. As they begin to kiss, Malverne says, "Let's forget about that woman you saw on stage. It's just you and me, okay?"

Aware of the way her image has been commodified, Malverne insists that both she and the Brother remember that she is not that image. We do not see their lovemaking; the movie excises it from the visual field, refusing to reduce this potentially utopian moment to a consumable image, merely hinting in the following scene at its passionate nature (Malverne tells the Brother he will have to do something about his toenails) and, through the physical proximity of Malverne and the Brother as they sit alongside each other on the end of the bed, at the intimacy it has engendered between them.

Ultimately, though, Malverne is unable to escape her commodity status for any longer than their night together. She is a commodity in the sense that capital reduces all workers to that status. As Marx and Engels argued, "The bourgeoisie, wherever it has got the upper hand . . . has left remaining no other nexus between man and man than naked self-interest, than callous 'cash payment.' . . . It has resolved personal worth into exchange value" (486–87). Moreover, the "modern working class, . . . who live only so long as they find work, and who find work only so long as their labour increases capital . . . who must sell themselves piecemeal, are a commodity, like every other article of commerce, and are consequently exposed to all the vicissitudes of competition, to all the fluctuations of the market" (490–91).[9] Like all commodities, she is unable to provide more than a fleeting satisfaction of the Brother's desire because her job requires her to leave the next day, and as she has no more bookings lined up she has no idea when she will be back in New York. Just as the Brother's desire for her was prompted by her commodification, so she too is subject to her status as commodity.

And, ultimately, it is rage against the commodity form—particularly when it proves fatal—that drives the Brother to seek out and kill the drug kingpin, Mr. Vance. That it is possible to generalize out from narcotics to the commodity form is not only supported by the montage sequence described above, but also by one particular shot when the Brother is following the trail of the drugs. On an empty lot outside the city he watches a deal in progress. In the background, in focus and clearly visible, are the twin towers of the World Trade Center, a more convincing emblem, perhaps, of the society in which the Brother finds himself than the Statue of Liberty.

My description of the opening sequence of *The Brother from Another Planet* at the start of this essay dwelt upon the way in which the movie toys with the audience, teasing us with glimpses of the Statue of Liberty that the Brother himself fails to see. This interplay of clarity and obscurity as the Statue slips in and out of focus, of visibility for the extradiegetic observer and invisibility for the diegetic observer, this shifting presence-absence on the New York skyline emphasizes the significance of the Statue for the movie's meaning even as it renders that significance ambiguous, complex. In focus, the Statue's meaning seems certain, as fixed as its presence; out of focus, that meaning becomes uncertain, fluid. This brings us to the second image of a woman that I wish to discuss.

Linda Zerilli has persuasively argued that the Statue of Liberty is not the bearer of a single, uncontradictory, ahistorical, and universal meaning. Rather, it has always been caught up in the ideological wrangling "over the meaning of the American founding" (171) and American national identity. As a "political symbol" and "national monument," the Statue of Liberty is without parallel in the "creation stories that Americans tell themselves about the beginnings of their democracy" (171); but the certainty over the meaning of the Statue typical of much popular commentary serves to assuage "political anxieties" (169). My reading of *The Brother from Another Planet* above evokes immigration as the primary meaning of the Statue of Liberty. However, the Statue has not always symbolized this. Its "official meaning" at its unveiling did not include immigration, and as Zerilli notes, this meaning was deeply contested and opposed "through the late 1930s" (177). It was only after the passing of the draconian and racist 1924 Immigration Act,[10] which massively reduced the number of immigrants—especially those from anywhere other than northwestern Europe—entering the United States,[11] that the Statue "came to enshrine 'the immigrant experience as a transcendental national memory. Because few Americans were immigrants, all could think of themselves as having been immigrants'" (Zerilli 177, quoting Higham 81). It is unsurprising that the figure of the immigrant should become the totemic national symbol after so many "actual immigrants had been denied entry" because, Zerilli argues, the diversity of the American population is only partly a product of immigration, being equally derived from the terrorism of "conquest, invasion, and enslavement" (177).[12]

Although formally accepted by Congress in 1877, the component parts of the Statue of Liberty spent a number of years stored in crates until Joseph Pulitzer, a Hungarian immigrant, used his newspaper, the *World*, to raise funds from his "working-class and immigrant readers" (Zerilli 173) to construct a pedestal on which to erect the Statue. Zerilli argues that these largely impoverished sectors of society "were inspired by the revolutionary spirit" that was lost after the founding to transform "Bartholdi's folly" into "a site of intense mass-affect," known as "our Lady Liberty." The Statue's shift from symbolizing "transnational republicanism" to "immigration" was just the first of several; it later became symbolic of a United States "threatened by the wrong kind of immigrants," of "national heritage," of "democracy" (174). Moreover, from the moment of its unveiling, to which no women were invited, the meaning of the Statue of Liberty was contested; as a suffragette statement declared, "In erecting A Statue of Liberty embodied as a woman in a land where no woman has political liberty, men have shown a delightful lack of consistency which excites the wonder and admiration of the opposite sex" (171–72, quoting Shapiro 65). Zerilli's analysis critiques the notion, challenged by the suffragettes, that "sexual difference is the stable, prepolitical ground" on which "the far more volatile (because political) institutions of democratic equality" (183) could be constructed. However, she does also refer to two images of black women posing as the Statue of Liberty: Thomas Worth's 1884 "Liberty Frightenin' the World" and Jean Lagarrigue's 1972 picture of Angela Davis. Like the argument about sexual difference, these appropriations of the Statue can be seen to confront the way in which racial difference functioned as what Csicsery-Ronay Jr. calls a "nonnegotiable *essential* line of separation" (228; italics in original) capable of "authoriz[ing] in advance political arrangements" (Zerilli 185).

This overview of some of the meanings and the images of the Statue of Liberty is important because, as Zerilli notes, the Statue "was an image before she existed as an object." Stored as a collection of parts, some of which were put on public display, the Statue circulated as an image. It is unsurprising that such a potent symbol should have subsequently been used to advertise all manner of commodities, including "war bonds . . . Coca-Cola . . . Sure Deodorant . . . the Modern Language Association," because from the very outset the Statue of Liberty itself was a commodity. Zerilli refers not only to a variety of souvenirs (including photographic and ornamental reproductions) sold on both sides of the Atlantic to help fund its construction and a range of products that used the Statue's image but also to the world's fairs at which parts of the Statue were displayed "in all her fragmented, fetishistic glory." Such expositions were both a "testament to the imbrication of commodity culture and liberal nationalism" and the site at which, Anne McClintock argues, "a crucial political principle took shape: the idea of democracy as the voyeuristic consumption of commodity spectacle" (175, quoting McClintock 59).[13]

So even though the Brother never actually sees the Statue of Liberty, its presence in those opening scenes becomes relevant not only to the story of an illegal alien entering America but also to understanding the nature of the American society into which he assimilates himself. Although not overtly sexualized like the many other images of women the Brother notices adorning New York, the Statue of Liberty is merely the first spectacle offered for voyeuristic consumption.

As I suggested in my introduction, the final shot of *The Brother from Another Planet* has been prone to misdescription and misinterpretation, typically through emphasizing the movie's treatment of race in isolation from its more complex articulation of race, class, and gender within capitalism. For example, in his critical study of Sayles's movies, Jack Ryan writes:

> The shot that concludes the film is certainly hopeful: the Brother is happy, and smiling as he never has before in the film. He is, however, looking through a heavy-gauge wire-mesh fence at a Harlem high school. Like everything else in this wonderful film, there is a contradictory impulse at work here, an ambiguity that blunts a completely happy ending. It is a reminder that the Brother's struggle never ends. Sayles leaves his story looking ahead, to freedom, but also backward to the injustice of bondage. (114)

I would argue that, contrary to Ryan, there is no trace of hope in the closing image of the movie, just as there is no looking forward to a future freedom. The Brother has at best an ambivalent expression on his face as he heads up to Harlem—he looks like he is trapped on a train intent on dragging him away from his newfound community of illegal aliens—and it is difficult to see that his half-smile in the final shot signifies happiness. The double vision Ryan evokes, looking both ahead and backward, recalls the image that the Brother points out to Little Earl at the Harriet Tubman exhibition in which an escaped slave flees from a mounted pursuer and his slavering dogs; but Ryan is unduly affirmative, suggesting that bondage ended with slavery, and freedom can be achieved under capitalism once the racist aftermath of that bondage is overcome. As Malverne's experience as both an

African American and a woman suggests, replacing slavery with wage-slavery can offer only a very limited variety of freedom.

In *Framing Blackness*, Ed Guerrero writes:

> This last scene seems to suggest a tangle of unresolved ideological tensions and ironies as it reveals Brother, alone, smiling and looking through a chain-link fence across an empty schoolyard at a drab institutional building with a banner "Harlem Plays the Best Ball in the World" hung on its facade. This final shot frames Brother as an isolated individual seemingly released from slavery as well as the social unity necessitated by resistance, free to pursue the vicissitudes of the American Dream. Conversely, though, this final mise-en-scène also confronts and traps him. The barrier of the chain-link fence and the dreary school building with its ironic message (Harlem has always played the "best ball," but it is quality education that determines a people's future) all seem to signal Brother's absorption into a society where the opportunities and rights of blacks are uncertain and ambiguous at best. Despite a thematic emphasis on the social collectivity throughout the film, Brother standing alone, at the film's end, in a stark, spatial, and social emptiness, seems partially to recoup Hollywood's narrative strategy of ultimately resolving social and political problems in individual terms. (49–50)

Despite his emphasis on the movie's interest in collectivity, Guerrero fails to note that the depiction of communities, however compromised—such as Odell's bar; Randy Sue Carter's (Caroline Aaron) apartment; the welfare officers, Sam Prescott (Tom Wright) and Noreen (Maggie Renzi), who are dedicated to helping others despite the system for which they work; the Brother's liaison with Malverne; the illegal aliens who emerge to save the Brother from the Men in Black (John Sayles and David Strathairn) pursuing him—provide the few moments of unity amid the overwhelming isolation and alienation of capitalist social relations on which the movie insists.

The final shot of the Brother is not of a figure who has rejected community in favor of an isolated self now that he is free, but of continued unfreedom, entrapment, and alienation; as Guerrero initially acknowledges, this final shot is one of ideological irresolution. If the deaths of the Men in Black who were pursuing the Brother meant he was now free, he would not be constrained to return to Harlem. But presumably, as the ironic banner suggests, it is only participation in a capitalist endeavor that reduces the individual to an image, to a spectacle, to a commodity that can provide a way out of racialized impoverishment (a "quality education" certainly cannot guarantee it). The Brother's isolation is not a resolution, nor a cue to pursue the American Dream. Rather, it is an indictment of the illusion of freedom so central to the ideology of Western capitalism. As Slavoj Žižek notes, freedom is

> a universal notion comprising a number of species (freedom of speech and press, freedom of consciousness, freedom of commerce, political freedom, and so on) but also, by means of a structural necessity, a specific freedom (that of the worker to sell freely his own labour on the market) which subverts this universal notion. That is to say, this freedom is the very opposite of effective freedom: by selling his labour "freely," the worker loses his freedom—the real content of this free act of sale is the worker's enslavement to capital. (21–22)

The final shot of the Brother is, therefore, a condemnation of the prisons and slaveries constructed by the repressive violence of an economic system that, through the commodification of desire (drugs, prostitution, pornography, advertising, popular music, the sexualized thrills of computer games, sport) and the reduction of human subjects to commodities, replaces the "promised land" with what Virgil dubbed the "false salvation of the here and now."

NOTES

1. For a discussion of *Blade Runner* as being more concerned with passing for straight than passing for white, see Bould 2002.

2. Although Sayles's script-writing for hire and script-doctoring is often concerned with science-fiction subjects, his attitude toward the genre in *The Brother from Another Planet* is clearly one that considers it as part of a much wider popular cultural episteme. For example, alongside allusions to *The Andromeda Strain* (Wise 1971), *Invasion of the Body Snatchers* (Kaufman 1978) and *The Six Million Dollar Man* (1973–78), there are others to *Mogambo* (Ford 1953), *Being There* (Ashby 1979), *Splash* (Howard 1984), and *Dragnet* (1952–59).

3. See Bernardi 1998.

4. For an account of the sheer unlikeliness of this, particularly after 1994, see Nevins 2002. There are, of course, distinctions to be made between criminal law and treaty law, but the movie treats them as identical,

inasmuch as both exist to be administered/enforced by a hierarchy of state agencies, while tending to equate law enforcement with justice. Kay's apparently liberal treatment of terrestrial illegal aliens, which is actually little more than an assertion of his position within the hierarchy, functions to reinforce the otherwise unchallenged notion that extraterrestrial illegal aliens pose some kind of "genuine" threat. Notes 10 and 11 below suggest some of the ways in which this logic has permeated U.S. immigration policy. (Janus, of course, was two-faced.)

5. The casting of an African American star inevitably renders generalizations about a movie's racial politics more problematic. However, it is worth noting that Will Smith's star persona, from his early career as a pop hip-hop performer and his lead role in *The Fresh Prince of Bel-Air* (1990–96) through to starring roles in movies like *Bad Boys* (Bay 1995), *Enemy of the State* (Scott 1998), and the depoliticized biopic *Ali* (Mann 2002), has been predicated upon the desire to conform to the norms of a white bourgeois order. As Esther Leslie writes of Dumbo, once he "discovers that his quirk—those freakish oversized ears—is actually his winning and bankable asset, he becomes a highly paid star.... The circus... is turned into the sadistic arena where power parades its ability to buy off dissent, and injustice rules. There is no escape from the system, only conformity and the hope of triumphing within its terms" (201). For a critique of the supposed multiculturalism and ethnic egalitarianism of *Independence Day*, see Mair.

6. These tendencies of science-fiction cinema are exacerbated by the genre's post–*Star Wars* intersection with the blockbuster/event movie. *Men in Black*, with its presold source in Lowell Cunningham's comic and the casting of a transmedia star who also recorded the hit tie-in single, is clearly an example of the latter, regardless of its generic affiliations.

7. The voices that seem to reside or linger in the very stones of the Detention Center and that overwhelm the Brother are European. That this clamor registers disorientation, confusion, and pain, and that the Brother is swamped and devastated by them, are important pointers to the politics that develop throughout Sayles's movies, exploring multiple articulations of oppression around class, gender, and sexuality as well as race and ethnicity. Significantly, in a movie overtly about race, *The Brother from Another Planet* is careful to include, in this instance, a specific marker of the social class of immigrants.

8. It is worth comparing this treatment of alcohol consumption with that of Public Enemy's "1 Million Bottlebags" (1991), a track that criticizes the inordinate amount of alcohol advertising aimed at impoverished African American communities but that connects this to a genocidal conspiracy; at no point does it express any sympathy or understanding for those who find a haven in alcohol, and only in its closing sample does it connect alcohol to "other drugs."

9. On the way in which capital has already rendered us alien and posthuman, see Rikowski.

10. In 1921 the temporary Quota Act limited "the number of admis-

sions of any particular nationality to 3 percent of the group's population already in the United States as reflected by the 1910 census. This marked the first quantitative immigration restrictions in U.S. history" (Nevins 29). The 1924 Immigration Act, also known as the Johnson-Reed Act, "made the quotas permanent, but lowered the permitted percentage of immigrants to 2 percent and used the census of 1890 as its base" (Nevins 101), and "also required immigrants for the first time to obtain visas from U.S. consular officials abroad before traveling to the United States" (Nevins 29). The 1924 "legislation also included the Oriental Exclusion Act, which banned all Asian immigration except that from the Philippines. As opposed to the temporary Quota Act of 1921, economic arguments were secondary to ones of racial purity in 1924 ('alien indigestion' became 'racial indigestion')" (Nevins 101–2). In addition to creating "fixed concepts of 'race,' which the legislation effectively conflated with the concept of the 'nation,'" often regardless of the immigrants' self-identity or geographic origin, and valorizing both the classification of people by race and prejudices about which kinds of immigrants were capable of assimilation, the 1924 act "resulted in 85 percent of the new immigrant quota [being] allocated to North-Western Europe" (Nevins 102).

11. Immigration "came in three great tides, each stronger than the last. The first rose in the 1830s and 1840s to a high-water mark in 1854, when 427,833 new arrivals were recorded; the second, starting in the seventies, rose to a height of 788,992 in 1882; the third brought in an average of one million immigrants a year in the decade before the First World War" (Brogan 413–14). Brogan also notes that immigration "rose from 216,397 in 1897 to 1,218,480 in 1914" (456). The effect of the 1924 act was to end mass immigration:

> The annual average went down from 862,514 in the 1907–14 period to no more than 150,000—all that was allowed . . . and discrimination against suspect nationalities was built into the system. Immigration from the so-called Asiatic Barred Zone—China, Japan, Indochina, Afghanistan, Arabia, the East Indies—was stopped almost entirely; and immigration from everywhere else but Northern and Western Europe was made exceedingly difficult. (512)

Among the many tragic consequences of the implementation of this legislation was that of the 180,000 German Jews who might have entered the United States between 1933 and 1941, only 75,000 were given permission to do so (571).

12. Zerilli also notes that Bartholdi's original design for the Statue included "broken chains and Phyrigian cap" (326, n.27), traditional symbols of liberation from enslavement, but these were abandoned so as not to provoke offense among potential financial backers from the Southern states.

13. Sayles lampoons the voyeuristic consumption of democracy as spectacle in the mock interview conducted by Chip (Gordon Clapp) and Irene (Jean Passanante) in *Return of the Secaucus Seven* (1980).

WORKS CITED

Bernardi, Daniel. *Star Trek and History: Race-ing toward a White Future.* New Brunswick: Rutgers UP, 1998.

Bould, Mark. "Not in Kansas Any More: Some Notes on Camp and Queer Sf Movies." *Foundation: The International Review of Science Fiction* 86 (Autumn 2002): 40–50.

Brogan, Hugh. *The Penguin History of the United States of America.* London: Penguin, 1990.

Csicsery-Ronay Jr., Istvan. "Dis-Imagined Communities: Science Fiction and the Future of Nations." *Edging into the Future: Science Fiction and Contemporary Cultural Transformation.* Ed. Veronica Hollinger and Joan Gordon. Philadelphia: U of Pennsylvania P, 2002. 217–37.

Foucault, Michel. *This Is Not a Pipe.* Trans. James Harkness. Berkeley: U of California P, 1983.

Garnett, Rhys. "*Dracula* and *The Beetle:* Imperial and Sexual Guilt and Fear in Late Victorian Fantasy." *Science Fiction: Roots and Branches.* Ed. Rhys Garnett and R. J. Ellis. Basingstoke: Macmillan, 1990. 30–54.

Gordon, Andrew. "Science-Fiction Film Criticism: The Postmodern Always Rings Twice." *Science-Fiction Studies* 43.14.3 (1987): 386–91.

Guerrero, Ed. *Framing Blackness: The African American Image in Film.* Philadelphia: Temple UP, 1993.

Higham, John. *Send These to Me: Jews and Other Immigrants in Urban America.* Baltimore: Johns Hopkins UP, 1975.

Jameson, Fredric. "Postmodernism, or the Cultural Logic of Late Capitalism." *New Left Review* 146 (July–August 1984): 53–92.

Jones, Gwyneth. "Aliens in the Fourth Dimension." *Deconstructing the Starships: Science, Fiction and Reality.* Liverpool: Liverpool UP, 1999. 108–19.

Leslie, Esther. *Hollywood Flatlands: Animation, Critical Theory and the Avant-Garde.* London: Verso, 2002.

McClintock, Anne. *Imperial Leather: Race, Gender, and Sexuality in the Colonial Contest.* New York: Routledge, 1995.

Mair, Jan. "Rewriting the 'American Dream': Postmodernism and Otherness in *Independence Day*." *Aliens R Us: The Other in Science Fiction Cinema.* Ed. Ziauddin Sardar and Sean Cubitt. London: Pluto, 2002. 34–50.

Marx, Karl, and Frederick Engels. *Manifesto of the Communist Party in Collected Works, Volume 6: Marx and Engels 1845–1848.* London: Lawrence and Wishart, 1976. 477–519.

Moylan, Tom. *Demand the Impossible: Science Fiction and the Utopian Imagination.* London: Methuen, 1986.

Nevins, Joseph. *Operation Gatekeeper: The Rise of the "Illegal Alien" and the Making of the U.S.–Mexico Boundary.* New York: Routledge, 2002.

Public Enemy. "1 Million Bottlebags." *Apocalypse 91 . . . The Enemy Strikes Black.* Def Jam, 1991.

Rikowski, Glenn. "Alien Life: Marx and the Future of the Human." *Historical Materialism: Research in Critical Marxist Theory* 11.2 (2003): 121–64.

Roberts, Adam. *Science Fiction*. London: Routledge, 2000.

Ryan, Jack. *John Sayles, Filmmaker: A Critical Study of the Independent Writer-Director.* Jefferson, NC: McFarland, 1998.

Sardar, Ziauddin. Introduction. *Aliens R Us: The Other in Science Fiction Cinema.* Ed. Ziauddin Sardar and Sean Cubitt. London: Pluto, 2002. 1–17.

Shapiro, Mary J. *Gateway to Liberty: The Story of the Statue of Liberty and Ellis Island.* New York: Vintage, 1986.

Sobchack, Vivian. *Screening Space: The American Science Fiction Film.* New York: Ungar, 1991.

Zerilli, Linda. "Democracy and National Fantasy: Reflections on the Statue of Liberty." *Cultural Studies and Political Theory.* Ed. Jodi Dean. Ithaca: Cornell UP, 2000. 167–88.

Žižek, Slavoj. *The Sublime Object of Ideology.* London: Verso, 1989.

4

The Theo-Political Landscape of *Matewan*

Martin F. Norden

In 1987, John Sayles released a film based on one of West Virginia's most vivid historical events, the "Matewan Massacre" of 1920. This richly textured film, simply titled *Matewan*, reconstructs the unionization drive among coal miners in the movie's namesake community, an impoverished "company town" situated on the Tug Fork River across from eastern Kentucky. The film follows their conflicts with hired guns brought in by the coal-mine owners and concludes with the infamous shoot-out that left seven mercenaries, two miners, the mayor, and a bystander dead and led to the largest armed uprising in postbellum U.S. history.

The accolades for *Matewan* piled up quickly, with most mainstream critics reacting favorably to the film's construction of post–World War I Appalachian culture. They were particularly intrigued by the representation of the ethnic groups who worked the mines—native whites, African Americans brought up from the Deep South, and Italian immigrants—and the mine operators' strategies for keeping them divided.[1] In addition, *Matewan* won the Political Film Society's Human Rights Award and received multiple Independent Spirit Awards nominations, including a win for its cinematographer, Haskell Wexler. Perhaps more significantly, *Matewan* was showcased as part of the prestigious Directors' Fortnight at the Cannes Film Festival.[2]

For all of its appeal, *Matewan* left historians deeply divided over the accuracy of its depicted situations. Writing for *Radical History Review*, Stephen Brier objected to the film's lack of connection to historical events that preceded and followed the massacre and concluded his mostly negative review by opining that Sayles "flattened out, over-simplified and thus distorted a complex historical event" (127). Melvyn Dubofsky also dissented, stating in a *Labor History* review that the film turned the characters into horse-opera stereotypes and that Sayles "abuses history as much as he uses it" (489). Ronald Lewis was more charitable in his review for the *Journal of American History*, suggesting that the film's significance "lies less in its historical authenticity than in its power to draw viewers into the emotional lives of the strikers. . . . At that level, *Matewan* far surpasses most films about the American working class" (1048). Sympathetic, too, was Eric Foner, who in a *Past Imperfect* essay also underscored the film's lack of context but concluded that "the film's pleas for nonviolence, interracial harmony, and economic justice are hardly irrelevant today" (207).[3]

The debates over *Matewan*'s historical faithfulness have curiously neglected what I regard as an important area of concern: the film's representation of theological issues. Religious references abound in *Matewan*, but they are far more than simple background reflections of 1920s West Virginia culture; instead, I argue that Sayles took considerable dramatic license with them to further a not-so-hidden political agenda. As this essay will show, Sayles altered almost every religious reference in *Matewan* to support something far more secular than theological: the growth of unionization among the coal miners.

Sayles first learned about the West Virginia coalfield wars while a Williams College student during the late 1960s and early 1970s. Hitchhiking through the state several times during that period, he heard numerous stories about the coal-mining industry, United Mine Workers of America (UMWA) president Tony Boyle, and Boyle's political rival, Jock Yablonski. The region was then reeling from the news of the Yablonski family murder, but Sayles unearthed another compelling story, a half-century old, underneath the current turmoil. "Almost everybody would say, 'If you think this is wild and woolly, you should talk to my old man about the coal wars,'" he remembered. "I started to pick up a little oral history, even if I couldn't put it together" (cited in Vecsey 1). Intrigued by the area and its history, Sayles set part of his 1977 novel *Union Dues* in West Virginia coal country and discovered the details of the Matewan Massacre while researching the book.

Sayles started writing the *Matewan* script in 1978 but had to abandon the film temporarily in order to complete a number of other projects. Further delays threatened to derail the project altogether,[4] but Sayles persevered and eventually secured a distribution deal. With production funding in hand, Sayles began shooting *Matewan* in 1986 on location in the New River Gorge area of West Virginia. He and his cast and crew worked principally in the towns of Beckley and Thurmond, the latter of which—a nearly deserted community—was dressed to look like Matewan in the early 1920s.

Sayles had conducted considerable research for *Matewan* prior to filming and used the names of many organizations and people who played roles in the actual massacre. Among the institutions he "revived" for the film were the Stone Mountain Coal Company, the corporate owner and operator of the mines in the Matewan area; and the Baldwin-Felts Detective Agency, a company based in Bluefield, West Virginia, that contracted with Stone Mountain to quell dissent among the miners, by force if necessary. (Sayles represented the UMWA, too, of course, but strangely the union is never mentioned by name.) Sayles modeled the characters after people who actually lived in or around Matewan at the time, including such colorfully monikered folks as C. E. Lively (played in the film by Bob Gunton), "Few Clothes" Johnson (James Earl Jones), Cabell Testerman (Josh Mostel), and "Smilin' Sid" Hatfield (David Strathairn). His two main characters, however, were entirely fictional creations: Joe Kenehan (Chris Cooper), a union organizer dedicated to nonviolent means, and Danny Radnor (Will Oldham), a fourteen-year-old coal miner and lay Baptist preacher. Sayles's manipulation of religious issues to support the unionization movement is most apparent in these two latter characters.

Sayles described Joe as a composite of "a bunch of organizers, Wobblies, Socialists, and nonaffiliated guys who just got involved in things" (Sayles and Smith 121), but I submit that the union organizer is a much more complex character. Not only is he a presumed atheist ("I never was religious myself," he tells a dinner-table crowd at his boarding house), he is also—and with high irony—a Christ-like "good outsider" in the tradition of countless western and science-fiction movie heroes who intervene in the conflicts of the ordinary souls with whom they have come to live.[5] Indeed, when the film introduces him, Joe is on a train from Pittsburgh bound for Matewan and, while on board, witnesses a brawl between native white miners and black Alabamans hired as scabs.⁶ Blending a missionary's fervor with a homespun sincerity worthy of Abe Lincoln, Joe later convinces the two groups to work together alongside Italian immigrant miners to form a union local.

Joe defines himself as a radical, if in an understated way; when Few Clothes asks him if it is true he is a "red," he replies matter-of-factly, "Yeah, I suppose it is." His saintly dedication to pacifistic means of resolving disputes, however, is at odds with the more common tactics of the period's militant social activists. Joe even jokes about his refusal to carry weapons; when Few Clothes asks him why he does not pack a gun, Joe kids him by saying, "We carry little round bombs. Don't you read the papers?" In an attempt to add further credence to Joe's nonviolent convictions and diminish doubts that he might be a spy for the mine operators, Sayles had Joe talk about his experiences at Fort Leavenworth, a disciplinary camp where American conscientious objectors were incarcerated during World War I. As they sit by a bonfire, Few Clothes hanging on Joe's every word, the activist details his encounters with several members of the Mennonite Church of America, a religious denomination known for its refusal to espouse violence. As Joe reveals in the following passage, he sees the Mennonite war resistors as nothing short of heroic:

> When I was in Leavenworth there was a bunch of Mennonites, in 'cause they wouldn't fight in the war. It's 'gainst their religion. It's also 'gainst their religion to shave their beards or wear buttons on their clothes, and they was bein' forced to do both by the prison guards. So they refused to work. They went on a strike, right there in Hell's Half Acre. They were handcuffed to the bars of a cellhouse, eight hours a day for two full weeks. They were put with their arms up like this, so's they had to stand on their toes or those cuffs would cut into their wrists. Can't nobody stay on their toes eight hours, so pretty soon their fingers would start to swoll up, they'd turn blue and then they'd crack open. Blood would run down their arms—eight hours a day, day after day, but still they wouldn't work, still they tore the buttons off their uniforms every time they were sewed back on. They tore 'em with their teeth, 'cause their hands wouldn't close no more. Now I don't claim a thing for myself, but them fellas, they never lifted a gun in their lives, and you couldn't find any braver in my book.⁷

It would be difficult to imagine two groups more different in their beliefs and strategies than 1920s-style union agitators and members of an organized religion dedicated to resolving conflict through peaceful means, but Sayles succeeded in conflating qualities of both to create the character of Joe.

Despite Joe's prominence and unusual combination of traits, Danny Radnor ultimately becomes the pivotal figure of *Matewan*. "To personalize the backbone of the film, Joe's struggle for justice without violence, I created Danny Radnor," Sayles wrote. "Danny is an adolescent boy, a coal miner, preacher, and union man who has both the Old Testament values of righteousness and retribution and the New Testament dreams for peace and justice within him. Joe's fight becomes a struggle for Danny's soul, a fight to help him see beyond the cycle of blood feuds and meaningless revenge the company fosters among the miners. What is positive for me in *Matewan* is the sense of mission passed on from Joe to Danny, and so I try to concentrate on their points of view throughout the story" (Sayles 19). Indeed, Joe and Danny influence each other to such an extent that their lives become strongly intertwined and ultimately inverted; Joe, the miners' spiritual leader, dies while trying to better their lives, while Danny abandons some of his Christian beliefs while preaching a new gospel of unionization.

Danny's centrality is evident from the start of *Matewan*. Within seconds of the film's opening, we see the youth working in a coal mine while an old man offscreen begins to narrate the film; we eventually learn that the voice is Danny's many years later. In addition to his work as a miner and union supporter, Danny is also a lay Baptist minister known for his flexibility; he proudly tells Joe he preaches for both the "hardshell" and "softshell" Baptist congregations. Embodying an almost perfect balance of secular and theological concerns, Danny serves as Sayles's primary vehicle for expressing *Matewan*'s blend of religious and unionization issues.

An example occurs early in the film when Danny gives a sermon to the hardshell Baptists. He relates Jesus' parable of the vineyard found in Matthew 20: 1–16, in which a vineyard owner hires a number of men for the same daily wage even though they started work at different times of day. The men who began working earlier in the day believe they deserve more and complain to the owner, but, as Danny notes, he rebukes them by saying he may do with his money as he pleases and that they should be grateful that he hired them in the first place. Leaning forward, the boy preacher then takes his sermon in a decidedly different direction by connecting the vineyard tale to current events: "Now it's clear from this parable that Jesus hadn't heard nothin' about the union. If He was walking the earth today and seen the situation we got with these coal operators, He'd a'changed His tune." Danny startles the congregation further by speaking on Jesus's behalf: "'A man deserveth an hourly wage,' he'd say, 'for though the pit be gassy and the face fulla slate, a man still toileth by the sweat of his brow and wants a better deal here on earth, no matter what I got in store for him in the hereafter.' Praise Jesus!" Sayles added more force to Danny's words—powerful in and of themselves—by intercutting the boy's sermon with scenes showing the emergence of union activity among the disparate groups of miners.

Another example involving Danny's use of the pulpit concerns his efforts to preserve the fledgling unionization drive. Relatively late in the movie, Danny learns that C. E. Lively—a company spy on whom a miner has bestowed the heavily loaded biblical name, "Judas"—has encouraged Bridey Mae (Nancy Mette), a young woman whose love for Joe has gone unrequited, to spread lies about Joe's loyalties. The miners are so angered by what they believe is Joe's betrayal that they make plans to kill him, even as some of their number attend one of Danny's softshell Baptist prayer meetings. Danny knows that his friend's life and the unionization movement itself are at stake, but he cannot inform his parishioners directly because two Baldwin-Felts agents, Hickey and Griggs (Kevin Tighe and Gordon Clapp), have threatened to kill him and his mother if he leaks any word. Faced with an enormous dilemma, Danny uses the Old Testament narrative of Joseph and Potiphar's wife to communicate Joe's innocence to the townspeople. As Danny relates the tale, the congregation members quickly realize that, just as the Joseph of ancient times was victimized by rumors spread by a spurned woman, so too was his contemporary namesake. By the time Danny finishes his sermon with the line, "Draw your own conclusions," the only ones in the church oblivious to his analogy are Hickey and Griggs, cackling contemptuously in the back row. Danny's friend and fellow miner Hillard Elkins (Jace Alexander) slips out of the church unnoticed by the Baldwin-Felts agents to call off Joe's assassination, thus preventing the collapse of the fragile unionization movement.

If Sayles designed Danny and Joe as heroes of biblical dimensions, he constructed Hickey and Griggs, their main opponents, as utterly irreligious. Earlier in the film, Griggs needles Danny by suggesting the boy does not know any more scripture than he does, to which Hickey replies: "And that ain't a whole hell of a lot, is it, Griggsy?" When Griggs asks Hickey if he knows any scripture, Hickey says, "Never got no further than 'In the beginning was the Word'" and adds with relish, "Guess we both doomed to the hot place." Far from disagreeing with Hickey, Griggs chimes in with the following view of Danny: "The Lord relies on little shits like this one to spread His word, I don't want no truck with heaven." They frequently taunt the young minister, their mockery reaching its zenith when they drunkenly sing "There is power, power, wonder-workin' power in the precious blood of the lamb" to him. In the world that Sayles has created, atheism as embodied by Hickey and Griggs is tantamount to antiunionism at its worst. Moreover, Sayles implies that Hickey's and Griggs's irreligiousness is a fatal flaw; their inability to "read" Danny's sermon as a signal to the miners leads to their failure to stop the unionization movement and ultimately to their deaths.

A critical turning point in the film occurs when Griggs slashes Hillard's throat for refusing to name activist names and stealing a few pieces of coal, and this shocking death provides Sayles with another opportunity to appropriate religious issues for other purposes. Danny eulogizes his friend during the funeral, but his commentary contains a strikingly unchristian sentiment: "Sometimes people say how God willed it, how everything's His plan. Well, I don't think He planned on Hillard alayin' here amongst all these Elkinses, not this young in his life. I think all God plans is we get born, and we got to take it from there. So you rest in peace, Hillard. You rest easy, 'cause we gonna take up where you left off. [pause] Amen." This speech reflects a major change in the young preacher; Hillard's murder has shaken his faith to such an extent that now God is not much more for him than a Johnny Appleseed figure who places people on earth and then moves on—abandoning them, in effect. Danny's dramatic pledge to Hillard further demonstrates his changing perspectives. He offers it partly in a vengeful spirit driven by Old Testament

Danny's (Will Oldham) decisions epitomize the struggle between righteous vengeance and dreams of peace, reaching its ironic expression when he arms himself.

values and indeed later arms himself and participates in the Matewan shoot-out. (In a moment brimming with irony, one of Danny's would-be victims shouts, "Jesus, don't shoot me.") It is certainly arguable, though, that his pledge comes primarily from a desire to continue Hillard's work and keep alive the dream of unionization.

Danny's eulogy is immediately followed by a song performed a cappella by "mountain singer" Hazel Dickens, and it is well worth examining her contributions to the film at this juncture. Sayles employed Dickens's distinctive vocalizations at several points in the movie and saw her work as vital to the type of story he wanted to tell. "Hazel grew up in West Virginia coal country hearing the songs and sermons, and her voice carries all the mournfulness and strength of the hill tradition," he wrote. "We wanted to build a very spare, evocative sound from just a few elements, and Hazel's voice was central to that plan" (Sayles 113). Sayles's most pointed use of Dickens's singing occurs during the funeral scene noted above when she performs "Gathering Storm," a song written specifically for *Matewan* by Mason Daring and characterized by Sayles as "a mournful lament with overtones of Old Testament retribution" (Sayles 111). "Gathering Storm" is a religious tune on its surface and similar to "Amazing Grace" in its texture, but its powerfully rendered refrain—"deliver us from the gathering storm"—implicitly refers to the political violence to follow. "When [Dickens] sings at Hillard's funeral it is not only background sound but an important action in the story," Sayles observed. "There is a sense of tragic destiny in many hill ballads, and the expression of that resignation to doom [in "Gathering Storm"] is as palpable an antagonist to Joe as the Baldwin-Felts agents are" (Sayles 113). Although *Matewan* associates Dickens primarily with religious ballads such as the traditional tune "Hills of Galilee," the first song the audience hears her sing is "Fire in the Hole," a union marching anthem co-written by Sayles and Daring. By using the same singer and her unmistakable style to perform both union and religious songs (including the politically charged "Gathering Storm"), Sayles found yet another means of blurring religious and secular concerns.

The film's final example follows the legendary shoot-out between the Baldwin-Felts agents and the miners and their supporters. "The last shot in the movie is not the dead Baldwins on the street but Danny walking back into the mine, his voice as an old man telling us how he went on to work for the things Joe Kenehan stood for," wrote Sayles (27). During this concluding moment, the writer-director had Danny explicitly acknowledge the transformation of religion: "That were the start of the great coalfield war and us miners took the worst of it like Joe said we would. 'It's just one big union, the whole world over,' Joe Kenehan used to say, and from the day of the Matewan Massacre that's what I preached. That was my religion." The conversion of theological matters in *Matewan* has become complete.

An examination of the film's 1980s sociopolitical context may prove helpful in our attempt to understand Sayles's manipulation of religious issues. Sayles produced and released *Matewan* during what may safely be described as a most incongruous time for such a film: the Ronald Reagan presidency, one of the most conservative and antiunion periods in American twentieth-century history. With its class-warfare theme boldly on display,

Matewan stands in marked contrast to the reactionary movies and insipid entertainment characteristic of the Reagan years. As historian Carolyn Anderson has observed, these films may have acknowledged class differences but pointedly avoided the topic of class conflict almost completely (159).

Sayles was quite conscious of the fact that *Matewan* placed him in opposition to the prevalent Reagan-era antiunion mindset.[8] Indeed, he said that one of the reasons he wanted to make *Matewan* was to remind people why unions existed in the first place (Sayles and Smith 123–24). Sayles biographer Jack Ryan has astutely pointed out that the film operates on at least two levels: as a reconstruction of a 1920s historical event and as a commentary on its own time. As he puts it: "By examining the conservative 1920s, Sayles parallels the conservatism of the 1980s, a period dominated by the antilabor ideals of Ronald Reagan" (115).

If we extend Ryan's observation, we might argue that *Matewan* also has something to say about the fundamentalist religious thought that permeated the 1980s. The views of Pat Robertson, Jerry Falwell, Jim Bakker, and other charismatic leaders on the Religious Right (the "televangelists") held sway during the time, and *Matewan* taps into that zeitgeist with its many expressions of bedrock religious belief. It features a particularly potent blend of conservative politics and fundamentalist perspectives in the form of a character simply known in the film as the Hardshell Preacher. Onscreen for only a few minutes—and, tellingly, played by Sayles himself—the preacher explicitly equates the union organizer who has come to town with the devil himself. "The Prince of Darkness is upon the land," he intones. "In the Bible his name is Beelzebub. Lord of the Flies. Right now on earth today, his name is Bolshevist! Socialist! Communist! Union man! Lord of Untruth! Sower of the evil seed! Enemy of all that is good and pure, and this creature [pause] walks among us."

In a number of important respects, the Hardshell Preacher is an accurate embodiment of the fundamentalist antiunion beliefs of the 1920s. As Sayles pointed out, "The established Baptist churches in West Virginia really fought against the union, because very often the coal companies built the churches. On purpose." He further noted that the companies played a major role in the social life of the communities—a role defended by the local religious leadership: "[The coal companies] built the school, they built the church, they built the newspaper, and they controlled all the social organs. The hard-shell [sic] preacher I played really believes that his reading of the Scripture tells him that union people are in league with the anti-Christ—he's an absolute believer" (Sayles and Smith 129). The Hardshell Preacher's inflammatory rhetoric is similar to that employed by the renowned evangelist Billy Sunday, whom the coal-mine operators had recruited to defame the union organizers. Appearing at a rally in April 1922, Sunday removed his coat and tie, rolled up his sleeves in his trademark style, and proceeded to characterize the activists in no uncertain terms:

> I cannot believe God had anything to do with the creation of these human buzzards. I'd rather be in hell with Cleopatra, John Wilkes Booth, and Charles Guiteau than to live on earth with such human lice. The radicals would turn the milk of human kindness into limburger cheese and give a polecat convulsions. If I were the Lord for about 15 minutes I'd smack the bunch so hard that there would be nothing left for the devil to levy on but a bunch of whiskers and a bad smell. (cited in Jordan 115)

Yet, stunningly, the Hardshell Preacher provides *Matewan*'s only linkage of religion and antiunionism; as we have seen, Sayles used all other religious references in the film to support the unionization drive and thwart its opponents. *Matewan*'s powerful alignment of religion and pro-union politics emerges as the film's central paradox, one not easily explained away. As fitting as it might be to have the Matewan townspeople "see" the burgeoning unionization movement through the lens of their religious beliefs, it would be wholly inaccurate to suggest that they embraced it as a new kind of religion.

On one level, *Matewan*'s conflation of religious and political perspectives is related to Sayles's long-standing interest in making complex political issues accessible to ordinary people. In an oral introduction to a Sayles book reading, Bruce MacMillan noted that Sayles is one of the few authors and artists to explore not only the familiar sentiment, "The personal is the political," but also its reversal by translating abstract political concepts into situations that average people face daily (7 June 1991). As Sayles himself put it, "What interested me was how personal psychology can get into politics, and how politics can get into personal psychology" (cited in Aufderheide 27). A novelist and filmmaker known for creating socially aware material (one critic offered a backhanded compliment by referring to his "too-perfect liberal conscience" [Johnston 26]), Sayles noted that "politics are always at the mercy of human nature and custom, and the coal wars of the twenties were so personal that they make ideology accessible in a story, make it immediate and emotional" (Sayles 11). He doubtless concluded that religion, with its prominent role in so many people's lives, might work as an effective vehicle for facilitating that process.

On another level, Sayles quite possibly wanted to underscore the kinship between religion and politics as "belief-systems," particularly the fervor with which they can be espoused and their mutual susceptibility to subversion. As he argued, "There can be wonderful stuff in religion, but it can be used to chop people's heads off. And the same thing with any political belief; you can pervert it, just in the way you read it and interpret it" (Sayles and Smith 129). Although Sayles was referring here to the Hardshell Preacher's use of religion for political purposes, I might say in closing that the filmmaker's remarks resonate within a broader, and perhaps unintentional, context. After considering the fact that Sayles employed religious references throughout *Matewan* for a political agenda all his own, it might be reasonable to conclude that he and his onscreen persona, though on opposite sides of the political spectrum, are not so different after all. Such reflexivity, intended or not, only adds to the film's richness.

NOTES

1. As Thulani Davis has noted, however, some American critics "began to carp about his sentimentality for the downtrodden" as reflected in *Matewan* (49). Sayles observed the following on the relationship among the ethnic groups in the film:

> In *Matewan*, there is a very, very short alliance between these immigrant miners, the black miners and the mountain guys. It's basically there because there is a common enemy who is just as threatening to all of them, and they somehow realize that.... They really did put guards between the Italians and the Yugoslavs and the blacks and the hillbilly miners 'cause they didn't want them talking to each other. They said it was because they'd fight, but it was really because they'd talk. (cited in Davis 50)

2. A listing of the film's cast and crew credits, awards, and award nominations may be found online at the Internet Movie Database, www.imdb.com. Interestingly, Sayles's film was not the only fictionalized treatment of the Matewan Massacre to come out in 1987: see also Giardina's *Storming Heaven*.

3. See also Foner's lengthy interview with Sayles on pages 11–28 of the same volume.

4. More information on the *Matewan* delays may be found in McGhee 45.

5. Including, but certainly not limited to, the title character of *Shane* (1953), the Preacher of *Pale Rider* (1985), Carpenter of *The Day the Earth Stood Still* (1951), and Clark Kent of *Superman* (1979).

6. The African American miners had been riding the same train as Joe, which raises a question about the film's logistical consistency. It is not clear why Joe, coming down to West Virginia from Pittsburgh, would be on the same train as the blacks brought up from the Deep South.

7. For accounts of the mistreatment of Mennonites similar to the ones described here, see Hartzler 122–49.

8. When someone at the Cannes Film Festival asked him, "How [did] you make this movie in Reagan America?" Sayles responded in Kenehan-esque, low-key fashion: "I don't think he's worried about me" (cited in Vecsey 1).

WORKS CITED

Anderson, Carolyn. "Diminishing Degrees of Separation: Class Mobility in Movies of the Reagan-Bush Era." *Beyond the Stars 5: Themes and Ideologies in American Popular Film*. Ed. Paul Loukides and Linda Fuller. Bowling Green: Bowling Green State University Popular Press, 1996. 141–63.

Aufderheide, Patricia. "Coal Wars." *Mother Jones* 12 (1987): 24–29, 44–45.

Brier, Stephen. Review of *Matewan*. *Radical History Review* 41 (1988): 120–28.

Davis, Thulani. "Blue-Collar Auteur." *American Film* (June 1991): 16–23, 49–50.

Dubofsky, Melvyn. Review of *Matewan*. *Labor History* 31 (1990): 488–90.

Foner, Eric. "*Matewan*." *Past Imperfect: History According to the Movies*. Ed. M. Carnes et al. New York: Henry Holt, 1995. 204–7.

Giardina, Denise. *Storming Heaven: A Novel*. New York: Norton, 1987.

Hartzler, Jonas. *Mennonites in the World War, or Nonresistance under Test*. Scottsdale, AZ: Mennonite Publishing House, 1922.

Johnston, Trevor. "Sayles Talk." *Sight and Sound* (September 1993): 26–29.

Jordan, Daniel P. "The Mingo War: Labor Violence in the Southern West

Virginia Coal Fields, 1919–1922." *Essays in Southern Labor History: Selected Papers, Southern Labor History Conference, 1976.* Ed. Gary Fink and Merl Reed. Westport, CT: Greenwood, 1977. 102–43.

Lewis, Ronald. Review of *Matewan*. *Journal of American History* 75 (1988): 1047–48.

MacMillan, Bruce. Oral introduction to a book reading by John Sayles, Northampton, Massachusetts, 7 June 1991.

McGhee, Dorothy. "Solidarity Forever." *American Film* (September 1987): 42–46.

Ryan, Jack. *John Sayles, Filmmaker: A Critical Study of the Independent Writer-Director.* Jefferson, NC: McFarland, 1998.

Sayles, John. *Thinking in Pictures: The Making of the Movie* Matewan. Boston: Houghton Mifflin, 1987.

Sayles, John, and Gavin Smith. *Sayles on Sayles.* Boston: Faber and Faber, 1998.

Vecsey, George. "John Sayles Mines the Coal Wars." *New York Times,* 23 August 1987: B1.

5

Passersby and Politics:
City of Hope and the Multiple Protagonist Film
Greg M. Smith

More than any other contemporary American director (with the possible exception of Robert Altman), John Sayles consistently experiments with making films about groups. The maker of *Return of the Secaucus Seven, Matewan, Eight Men Out, Lone Star,* and *Sunshine State* explores how to tell stories where heroes and villains are deeply rooted in their communities, not isolated from them. For Sayles, community is not just a backdrop for action; it is the stuff of everyday drama and everyday politics.

Sayles also attempts an even more difficult juggling act: telling a story with multiple protagonists, each one crucial to the narrative's completion. In the commercial cinema (a medium whose structures are geared around telling stories about individuals), an auteur must necessarily rethink and reform basic narrative principles in order to deal with the intersecting desires of multiple protagonists. To do so may also require reinventing the visual strategies of storytelling, as Sayles does in perhaps his most narratively complicated film, *City of Hope*, a film with over fifty speaking parts and dozens of key players. *City of Hope* creates an urban environment in which people with only passing familiarity with each other may have profound effects on each other's lives. The fictional Hudson City is a network of apparently invisible but in fact strongly binding threads of causality, and Sayles creates this network through a beautiful linkage of Steadicam movement and staging. This essay in part examines the ways Sayles's *City of Hope* moves our attention from one character to another, and I compare Sayles's choices with similar aesthetic techniques chosen by previous filmmakers. I also tie these formal strategies to the larger thematic and political concerns of the film, arguing that the bravura transitions reveal the interconnectedness of urban life in a way that standard Hollywood practice cannot. Sayles's community politics are irretrievably bound up with his economic mode of filmmaking, but the visual style of each particular community portrait depends on a nexus of factors, including his collaborative approach and his understanding of a community's particularity.

City of Hope shows how graft, personal influence, and family obligation are the building materials used to construct an American city. It traces the way that a development deal is made to level a slum and build a high-rent condominium complex. The political machine seizes upon several seemingly chance events—a racially motivated mugging entangled with allegations of homosexuality, an inept burglary of an electronics store—and makes these the fulcrum for bringing about the development deal. Using the leverage provided by these events, the political operators exploit family and community ties for their own purposes. Fathers make deadly deals with the devil to protect their sons from prosecution, and politicians compound lie upon lie to gain a little ground. The bad guys and the good guys both play the same game: the local politics of expediency. Characters take advantage of a situation and try to exploit it for their own advancement or to further their cause. Mob furor over a mugging can become the spark that ignites positive political change if one plays it correctly, or a petty crime can create the opportunity for riches if one tweaks the players properly. What is doomed in this portrait is the politics of principle. Well-meaning citizens trying to hold onto their values become complicit with murder. A junior politician learns that he must compromise his high moral ground if he is ever to achieve any real effectiveness.

In order to transform these ordinary events into political forces, we must have a community so interrelated that even the most insignificant events can trigger a response from others in the network. Actions ripple across the surface of Hudson City, spreading from passerby to passerby, and Sayles conveys this connection by doing what he calls "trades."[1] Cinematographer Robert Richardson's Steadicam follows a set of characters until the camera "trades" its emphasis and begins to follow an entirely different conversation or action, often in the same shot. This carves individual scenes into dramatically separable miniscenes involving different casts of characters. *City of Hope*'s camera performs an intricate dance with the characters, trading partners over and over. Like a formal series of pas de deux, Sayles's staging is comprised of a set of simple maneuvers that, when used in different configurations, can provide an enormous number of expressive possibilities.

The dominant staging move involves two characters (or sets of characters) walking in opposite directions, passing each other. The camera takes advantage of this brief sharing of space and moves to follow the newly met characters. Often this "passing" move is staged in deep space with the characters moving toward and away from the camera. For instance, early on in the film we see Jeanette (Gloria Foster) walking down the street away from the camera, ignoring the obvious flirting from Levonne (Frank Faison) at the community center. As their interchange falters, Jeanette passes City Councilman Wynn (Joe Morton), who is moving toward the camera, preparing to speak to Levonne, and the camera now stays with Wynn for his next conversation scene.

On multiple occasions, Sayles does this passing maneuver several times in a single location, going back and forth trading conversation partners, showing how these characters' lives overlap unwittingly. For instance, one scene begins by following Asteroid (David Strathairn), a mentally ill man, as he shouts and walks down the street. As Wynn passes him (walking toward the camera), he glances at the pathetic figure, and then the camera begins to follow Wynn. Then as Wynn walks up the street, he glances at two women (Maggie Renzi and Marianne Leone) who are passing by, loudly haranguing two police officers (Jude Ciccolella and Jaime Tirelli), and the camera starts to trail the complaining women.

The passing maneuver duplicates and extends one of the basic experiences of being in a city: the sideways glance. It is acceptable to look briefly at the crazy homeless guy or the loudly arguing housewives, but one cannot stare without making contact with a stranger, which can be unsettling or even sometimes potentially dangerous. To walk down the street in a modern American city is to be constantly aware that there are odd or intriguing or frightening characters all around us. We intuit that some of these "characters" we pass on an urban street must have interesting stories, but we cannot allow ourselves to pursue these stories in the hurried rush of urban life. We know that there are a million stories in the naked city, but we cannot follow them. *City of Hope* takes this intuition and elaborates it, allowing us to follow these characters' lives instead of merely glancing at their faces. The passing maneuver in *City of Hope* gives us a sense of what it would be like to wander from story to story, a distracted spectator switching from one narrative to another. The shifts in perspective are naturalized by these movements, making Sayles's narrative orchestration seem like simply accidental crossings of passersby.

Another mode of city life (in addition to the exchanges of passersby) is exemplified by the traveler who flits from one thing to another in rapid succession. A jogger, for instance, moves quickly through the urban space, covering a great deal of ground without being able to linger in any one place. (In some ways, the jogger is Baudelaire's flaneur[2] passing by urban sights too quickly to be able to shop.) Not surprisingly, Sayles also uses versions of this figure to weave together his urban tableau. Les (Bill Raymond), the jogger who resumes running to overcome his fear after being mugged, roams the streets, providing a useful connective to help spectators move from one space to another. Les runs past a police car, and we linger on the car, noticing that Mike (Anthony John Denison) is spying on his ex-wife, Angela (Barbara Williams), from outside her window. We follow his gaze into the apartment where Angela is engaging in her first sexual encounter with Nick (Vincent Spano). Les's jogging also leads us past an arsonist disguised as a repairman, and we stay with the arsonist as he enters the soon-to-be-torched slum building.

The other traveler who structurally allows Sayles to flit from conversation to conversation is Asteroid, the lunatic who incessantly babbles as he lurches chaotically through city streets. When the poor people displaced by the slum fire gather in a makeshift emergency center, Asteroid is there, repetitively shouting, "We need help!" We follow him until we trip across a conversation between Levonne and Jeanette about the bureaucratic paperwork. Asteroid then crosses in front of them, and we follow him as he travels, shouting, "Why settle for less when you can have it all?" He confronts a startled social service worker, and we stay with her as Councilman Wynn approaches her and learns about the arson. At first, Asteroid seems to be no more than a narratively efficient excuse to move from one conversation to another without Sayles having to cut. However, as we encounter him again and again obsessively repeating dialogue and clichés from television commercials, he begins to function more like *City of Hope*'s wild-haired prophet or its schizophrenic Greek chorus. Phrases like "We need help" and "Why settle for less when you can have it all?" become commentary on the dire straits of the American dream and the shallowness of a consumerist society in which the power to purchase defines the citizenry, not an interest in the collective good. Like so much in this film that initially seems tangential, this traveler serves far more than his initial narrative function.

As the brief description of the scene in the makeshift emergency center indicates, Sayles does much of his trading between characters in public places. Restaurants, bars, police stations, and parties are places where a cross section of the community congregates, all with different purposes in mind. Such crowded spaces make it easier for Sayles to unite the characters with his camera, and these scenes truly showcase the stunning choreography of actors and camera that Sayles manages in *City of Hope*. In one example, the camera follows the young delinquent Ramirez into a bar. We walk with him until we trade to follow Zip (Todd Graff) and Bobby (Jace Alexander), who meet up with Nick, who is eyeing Angela lustfully. The camera moves with Zip as he goes to the bar, and we reencounter Ramirez. The two go back to the bathroom to do a drug deal, and we pick up construction foreman Riggs (Chris Cooper), who approaches Nick for a conversation about his brother who died in Vietnam. Nick leaves this conversation, and we see him go pay off his bookie, the arsonist/mechanic Carl (played by Sayles). Following Nick again, we then pick up the now coked-up Zip who reencounters Bobby, and the two move onstage to begin singing. Sayles uses these public places as ways to get an incredible amount of narrative business taken care of in a superbly efficient manner.

In so doing, Sayles also underlines the importance of public spaces to the community. They provide places for the urban "tribes," as the director refers to them, to congregate (Crowdus and Quart 145–46). Spaces such as police stations and bars provide opportunities for chance encounters to occur between tribes. An urban community depends on having such neutral spaces where the members' stories may intermingle, conflict, and resolve.

I have outlined a few of the most important ways that director Sayles and cinematographer Richardson "trade" perspectives among the multiple protagonists, but there are many more: using a single unmoving character as an anchor in space and bringing various characters into that space to interact; using sound to cue a switch in perspective; changing the visual dominant from foreground to background or vice versa; and so on. *City of Hope* is a veritable catalog of inventive ways to move our attention from one character to another. It is not, however, an infinite catalog; examining some of the choices Sayles does not make helps to clarify why he chooses the particular devices that he does.

The film is full of attention-getting transitions, but still Sayles avoids certain snazzy ways to change character perspective. The camera rarely floats away from characters (à la *Wings of Desire*) to show us other characters without some strong diegetic motivation (figure movement, sound, eyeline, and so on). The bar scene described above provides one such rare example in which the camera simply leaves Ramirez to anticipate and find Zip and Bobby. There are also few matches-on-action to take us to another time and space (the only significant one is when the film cuts from Angela and Nick having sex to Wynn and Reesha [Angela Bassett] in bed). Nor does the film generally give us an anticipatory cue of what is to come and then cut to a thematically resonant object. One example would be when Mrs. Ramirez (Miriam Colon) commiserates with Laurie (Gina Gershon) about her demanding relatives, ending the conversation by saying simply, "It's family." Sayles then cuts immediately to framed family pictures of a younger Nick and Laurie, revealing that we have begun another scene with Nick perusing old family photos. By and large, in *City of Hope* Sayles eschews cutting based on theme and action.

He avoids these transitions only partly because these devices emphasize the heavy hand of the director. Throughout the film Sayles emphasizes contiguity as the main principle underlying his transitions from one protagonist to another. When he cannot arrange to trade characters in relatively contiguous space, he tends to cut to the next set of characters using a rather unremarkable cut. The crossing passersby, the jogging traveler, and the crowded public space are favored people and places because these stagings require that the characters share space. Sayles wants to emphasize there's no avoiding bumping into other "tribes" in Hudson City. As much as one may want to isolate oneself from homeless madmen, dangerous muggers, or whiny housewives, there is no way to do it in an urban setting.

These collisions initially may appear to be inconsequential. We seem to trade perspectives for no other reason than having bumped into another character. When Councilman Wynn passes two African American boys, we leave his negotiation for computer access for low-income citizens to listen to the boys' inane conversation as they play video games. Only later do we realize that Sayles's naturalistically motivated but seemingly arbitrary decisions of whom to follow serve larger narrative purposes.

Such nonclassical changes of character perspective can provide surprisingly complex moral insights. For example, when Sayles follows two African American boys, Tito and Desmond, walking down the street at night, suddenly they are thrown against the wall and intimidated by two policemen. Our instinct is to side with the boys, who were doing nothing more suspicious than being two black boys walking down the street. We want to follow them to hear their reaction at being so roughly handled, but instead we trade to the policemen. After the confrontation ends, we hear the policemen discussing their doubts about whether they should have searched them at all. The public bluster of the aggressive cops suddenly shifts to reveal their private doubts. In a similar example, the policemen harass and threaten a mother and child living in a condemned building. We then follow the cops as they descend the slum stairs, only to learn that one of the policemen grew up in that same building and only left it due to the money his father earned by running numbers. Sayles's choices of character perspectives initially seem to be driven solely by the coincidences of contiguity, but as we learn more about the community, we discover that his stylistic choices also serve narrative, political, and moral goals.

City of Hope wants to give us the feeling that we could follow potentially any character we bump into, no matter how unimportant they might seem to the narrative at the moment. After the film builds up our expectation that characters will be traded, it then sometimes sidesteps an opportunity to trade perspectives, making us aware of the road not taken. As we eavesdrop on Nick and Angela's late-night conversation in an empty street, we follow their eyelines as they both notice a passing police car. Given the stylistic norms established thus far, we could easily have transferred our full attention to the police officers (perhaps even Angela's jealous ex-husband, Mike), but in this instance we stay with Nick and Angela. The expectation that the spectator will be asked to follow almost anyone who passes by radically changes the way we interpret the space. As such, passing cars and pedestrians are not ignored in the way that we ignore the extras in a mainstream film. We slowly learn that there is no such thing as a truly secondary character in this film.

Characters who seem unimportant when introduced to us soon return to play crucial narrative roles. The best example here is that of the two African American boys, Tito and Desmond. As mentioned earlier, we meet them in Mad Anthony's electronics store, where Anthony (Josh Mostel) and Councilman Wynn are discussing computer access for Wynn's constituents. As they walk they pass by Tito and Desmond playing video games, and Wynn and Anthony move out of the frame while we linger with Tito and Desmond for a bit of conversation that has little plot significance. Finally Wynn and Anthony return to the frame, stealing our attention away from the boys. We pass the boys again hanging out in a night street as we follow a conversation between Reesha and her brother Franklin (Daryl Edwards). Once again the camera's attention is directed toward these boys, who make suggestive comments to passing women. There seems to be no narrative reason to be interested in this pair, but they become the crux of one of the film's major plotlines when their mugging of Les, the white jogger, ignites a community uproar. This sordid event, covered with multiple lies, provides Councilman Wynn the opportunity to change from an idealistic, ineffective politician to a practical leader with real power. Thus, these minor characters become major players. Without them the plot of *City of Hope* could not move forward.

It is this leveling of the traditional character hierarchy of mainstream cinema that is most radical about *City of Hope*. The camera's tendency to be seduced into following passersby alters our expectations concerning who is a "lead" character. Because this radical equality is conveyed visually, this distinguishes *City of Hope* from other celebrated multiple protagonist films. For instance, Robert Altman's *Nashville*, which has been compared to *City of Hope* (Ryan 158), is similarly committed to giving a complex portrait of a society, but it does so without systematically connecting its characters through visual transitions. Without this tight connective tissue that binds the characters together, *Nashville* does not convey the sense that every character's slightest move could potentially have political ramifications upon others' lives. Sayles's Steadicam "trades" in *City of Hope* are not merely bravura flourishes; the style makes the political structure of the film possible.³

To see exactly how *City of Hope* uses its style, it is more useful to compare the film to its art-cinema precursors: Max Ophuls's *La Ronde* (1950) and Luis Buñuel's *The Phantom of Liberty* (1974). These films use related visual techniques, but they do so for significantly different purposes. Looking at how these films trade perspectives among characters will help us see better what Sayles accomplishes with his technique in *City of Hope*. The director humbly asserts that the style in *City of Hope* is "hardly original," pointing to the opening sequence shot in Orson Welles's *Touch of Evil* and to Ophuls's *La Ronde* (Baron 134). But *Touch of Evil*'s initial sequence shot follows a single nonhuman "character" (a bomb) without the elaborate passing back and forth of perspectives we see in *City of Hope*, and the long sequence shot operates as a showy, independent opening moment instead of structuring the visual style of the film as a whole. *La Ronde*, however, is a more complicated example of narrative structure wedded to visual transitions.

Ophuls's *La Ronde* is set up as a series of romantic entanglements in which, after spending a moment with a particular couple, we follow one character in the couple as he/she engages in an intimate moment with a different lover. Thus an interlude between a philandering husband and a young woman is followed by a rendezvous between the woman and a poet, whereupon that poet proceeds to a romantic scene with an actress, who then seduces a count, and so on. The baton is passed from one couple to the next, always having one character in common to anchor our understanding. To guide us along this narrative trajectory, *La Ronde* also has a superdiegetic master of ceremonies, a character (played by Anton Walbrook) who declares that he is neither author, announcer, nor passerby but rather the manager of the carousel of love. This master of ceremonies directly addresses the audience, announcing the next scene's participants ("The Maid and the Young Man"), but he also weaves in and out of various diegetic spaces, interacting with the characters, now serving as a maître d', at other times as a coach driver. The scenes are doubly glued together by the connecting lover and by our metaphysical narrator-host. In so doing, Ophuls makes explicit his metaphoric point: that love is like a merry-go-round. His lyrical camera moves passing from one character to another invite us to ask what is the connection between this couple and the previous one, and the master of ceremonies overtly gives us the answer: that romance is an amusement, a joyous ride that cannot last.

It would appear that using character "trades" encourages the audience to step outside the immediate plot concerns to find larger connections, either by pondering Ophuls's metaphoric carousel of love or by discerning the network of connection and coercion that runs a small city. Because Ophuls's film is constructed in circular, linear fashion (the soldier in the first couple salutes the count in the last couple, bringing the film's conclusion back to its beginning), it is more concerned with elaborating the overall metaphor of the carousel than it is with constructing a complex society. Characters interact, they pass the baton to the next character, and they disappear from the film.[4] In Hudson City, however, characters do not conveniently disappear from other people's lives. They keep bumping into each other, and these conflicts give much more particularity to the characters than the generic components of Ophuls's metaphoric wheel of love (characters who are often referred to as a type: "The Girl and the Soldier," "The Young Woman and Her Husband"). Sayles takes advantage of *La Ronde*'s metaphor-building technique to build a City that stands in for many real urban spaces. Visually intertwining the narrative threads creates more possibilities for conflict and gives his characters complexity that Ophuls's generic figures lack.

The other canonic art-cinema film that passes visual perspective from one character to another contiguous figure is Luis Buñuel's *The Phantom of Liberty*. Although Sayles does not cite Buñuel's film as an overt influence, the film demonstrates another instructive alternative for how the "trading" technique might be used. Like *City of Hope*, *The Phantom of Liberty* will leave one character in mid-storyline to follow another character who crosses his/her path. As Linda Williams notes, the physical trajectory of characters "has been translated into narrative trajectory, as if the restless generative force that propels the film's narrative cannot resist the impulse to follow a physical movement"

(162). We drift into a character's storyline and then abandon it for another passing character and his/her story. A man goes to a doctor for diagnosis, but a nurse interrupts the appointment, saying she must leave to visit her sick father, and we follow the nurse, never returning to the patient. After a Buñuellian trip to the country where the nurse encounters a military tank hunting foxes, a group of poker-playing monks, and a dominatrix couple, the nurse picks up a hitchhiker, and we follow him, never actually getting to the nurse's sick father. Susan Suleiman argues that *The Phantom of Liberty* operates based on a "principle of infinite suspension: every sequence is suspended by the intervention of yet another sequence" (287), with no closure for virtually all of the plotlines.

In this way, Buñuel uses the "trading characters" technique for two of his most characteristic purposes. By abandoning plotlines and never returning to them,[5] Buñuel once again violates the conventions of classical narration and uses this frustration to make the audience grasp the very conventionality of these narrational norms. In addition, the filmmaker wants to attack one of his favorite targets: the fatuousness of the bourgeoisie. As Joan Mellen notes, "Buñuel follows each character only to discard him when one more promising—that is, revelatory of bourgeois intransigence—happens along" (321). The film targets a running catalog of bourgeois foibles, including sexual perversions, irrational denials, and prohibited desires, specifically abandoning a storyline in order to poke fun at yet another class conceit.

Thus Buñuel takes advantage of the way that the "trading characters" technique encourages us to reach for broader associations between characters, as noted with *La Ronde* and *City of Hope*. But *The Phantom of Liberty* does not follow *La Ronde*'s example by presenting self-contained episodes with classical beginnings and endings. By leaving characters in the middle of plotlines and never reencountering them again, *The Phantom of Liberty* flaunts its violations of classical norms, frustrating our desires for closure. While *City of Hope* also leaves its characters at will, it continually returns to them, updating us on their stories. Sayles takes advantage of classical narrative closure to show the effects of characters' political choices. He does so without sacrificing the potential of the "trading characters" technique to make a broader political statement, as demonstrated by his art-cinema precursors. The result is a blend of the art cinema's ability to make more abstract statements with the classical cinema's narrative power.

Although beautifully handled, the Steadicam trading of characters in *City of Hope* does not feel as innovative today as it did in 1991. To find earlier points of comparison for *City of Hope*'s visual style, we had to look far outside of mainstream Hollywood to Ophuls and Buñuel; now we are used to seeing variations on this technique weekly on *The West Wing* and *ER*. The point is not that the "trading characters" technique necessarily carries a particular set of politics with it, but that a key aspect of Sayles's politics—the radical equality of characters—is made possible by this technique. *ER* and *The West Wing* may use similar visual transitions, but they do so within an economic and narrative structure that makes Sayles's vision of community impossible to convey. It is the combination of technique, narrative structure, and industrial film practice that makes Sayles's Hudson City a place where everyone, high and low, rich and poor, is deeply interrelated. In Hudson City, there are no stars.

On *ER* and *The West Wing* (and in mainstream Hollywood film), we are always aware who the stars are, and the camera follows them. We know that we are supposed to watch Tom Hanks and Meg Ryan, not the boys they pass on the street. Extras are literally part of the background, a living form of set decoration. We are meant to believe that the stars are simply more talented, more important, more interesting than ordinary people, instead of concentrating on the way the narrative rather arbitrarily confers this form of privilege upon them. *City of Hope* does not let us off so easily. Sayles's emphasis on contiguity as the guiding principle for following characters makes us realize that in this film anyone—any passing jogger or loiterer or madman—can become a major character. The technique levels the traditional foreground/background relations of mainstream cinema that keep stars privileged above all else.[6]

This distinction between stars and extras is deeply institutionalized in Hollywood practice, even to the point that actors and extras have different labor representation. To attempt a project such as *City of Hope* within the economic structure of the star system would be almost unthinkable. Imagine the cost of hiring a well-known actor for each of the dozens of crucial parts in *City of Hope* and then paying each of them to be present for all the elaborately choreographed scenes in public places. In order to portray this kind of community, Sayles must resort to his preferred strategy of relatively low-budget independent filmmaking. Hiring Joe Morton and Vincent Spano to participate in these massive group scenes is not quite the same as hiring Tom Hanks and Jim Carrey. The community portrayal here could only exist outside of Hollywood's dominant economic structure.

The aesthetics of classical Hollywood also make it difficult for the form to portray true community. Most Hollywood films center on a single individual and his/her struggles to achieve a goal. The musical and the romance are the primary exceptions, broadening Hollywood's focus from the individual to the couple. Antagonists are not faceless forces such as poverty, racism, and the government, but instead these forces are embodied in a single evil landlord, a particular racist, a specific politician. To defeat the lone antagonist is to overcome the entire social problem. When Hollywood does portray a stronger sense of community, it usually shows us one person's traversal through that community. It sometimes depicts a team, a group of people whose actions all move the plot forward. When it does show such a team, it usually gives them a common goal, giving the overall story a unifying singular thrust (for example, *The Dirty Dozen, Mission Impossible*). John Sayles recognizes the way this form validates American ideals of individualism, the romantic notion that one's own actions propel the universe, and he chafes at the restriction.[7]

An occasional Hollywood maverick may produce a rare exception to this trend in mainstream Hollywood filmmaking, and by comparing *City of Hope* to one such film—Lawrence Kasdan's *Grand Canyon*, which also uses elaborate visual devices to move among various plotlines—we can see how Sayles's deeply interrelated stylistic and economic structures make his distinctive political portrait of a city possible.

Just as Kasdan's *The Big Chill* (1983) provides an interesting study in contrast to Sayles's *Return of the Secaucus Seven* (1980), *Grand Canyon* seems to be examining concerns that are similar to Sayles's in *City of Hope*. Both films (each released in 1991) deal with the fragility of human connections, given the deteriorating state of race relations in American cities, and both follow a number of characters (*Grand Canyon* has six prominent ones) who accidentally bump into each other. But *Grand Canyon* is centered on Mack (Kevin Kline), the figure whose missteps provide an (assumedly) white, middle-class audience with an entrée into the darker urban environment. Mack is the figure whose well-intentioned interventions cause the other characters' lives to move forward. If Mack does not interfere with a character's life (as is the case with Davis [Steve Martin]), that character's life does not progress. *City of Hope*, lacking the economic star power of Kasdan's film, has no equivalent to this narrative privileging of one character.

In addition, *Grand Canyon* tends to move from one character to another with different stylistic devices from *City of Hope*. Instead of linking characters through contiguity, Kasdan emphasizes the disconnect between subcultures in this modern world. Kasdan frequently uses police helicopters and television sets as his transition devices, showing that impersonal forces bind the characters together. The only things these characters share are that they watch the same programs on television and that they in turn are watched by the passive eye of law enforcement. Bumping into someone from a vastly different part of Los Angeles is not an inevitable occurrence in *Grand Canyon*, as it is in the overlapping tribal culture of Hudson City. Such collisions are infrequent in *Grand Canyon*, and so when Mack strays into Simon's (Danny Glover) part of the city, the meeting is momentous, a rare moment of personal connection. By contrast, *City of Hope*'s structure makes it difficult to tell which of the multiple collisions will have important ramifications on the community. And so Kasdan's stylistic choices help him portray the grand canyon that exists between the communities; Sayles's aesthetic choices allow him to represent urban tribes that cannot avoid invading each other's turf. Kasdan's film blends Hollywood's individualistic politics with a style that emphasizes the disconnect between those characters to create a metropolis of rootless souls, not tribes.

To find comparable portraits of communities in American filmmaking, the obvious place to look is within Sayles's other group films. If Sayles is so concerned with showing the politics of groups, and if the character "trades" show interconnections so well, why does he use the technique only in *City of Hope*? Why don't *Lone Star, Matewan, Sunshine State, Eight Men Out, Men With Guns*, or *Return of the Secaucus Seven* switch characters similarly? The answer depends on some of the forces discussed earlier (Sayles's authorship and politics, his economic mode of filmmaking, the content of the film, Steadicam technology) and one other factor: key production personnel.

Although John Sayles's work is frequently considered to be visually unremarkable, this is clearly not the case (as *City of Hope* demonstrates). It is more accurate to say that the visual styles of his films vary widely, based partly on his funding and his choice of cinematographer. For instance, increased studio backing combined with the estimable talents of cinematographer Michael Ballhaus give the elegantly lit *Baby It's You* a sheen unlike any other Sayles film, and former documentarian Haskell Wexler lends *Limbo* a stark, sparse feel. Cinematographer Robert Richardson's suggestion to shoot *City of Hope* in a widescreen format allowed him to foreground his expertise with the Steadicam, thus elaborating on techniques he used in their previous collaboration (*Eight Men Out*).[8] Sayles's authorship and Richardson's execution were both fundamental components of *City of Hope*'s distinctive style.

But why didn't future Sayles films use the contiguous trading technique, once Sayles had mastered the Steadicam technology? Why show this particular community in this manner, and not other Sayles communities? Because *City of Hope* is Sayles's most urban film to date. *Sunshine State, Matewan, The Secret of Roan Inish*, and *Lone Star* take place in significantly smaller areas, communities where small-town ties (and frequently high school connections) still bind. To show that small towns are interconnected is a simple matter, given our American mythos of Mayberry and Grovers Corners. To depict the American city as equally tied (unlike the more typical portrait of city life as isolation, as shown in *Grand Canyon*) is more radical and requires a more radical technique.

Sayles's authorship does not impose a consistent visual style across his films. Instead, Sayles (true to his community-oriented politics) varies the look of his films depending on his collaboration with key personnel, particularly the cinematographer. For most of his directorial career, Sayles has chosen to avoid the economic structures that come with major studio backing, and this mode of production allows him to portray communities as interconnected. But his style can also vary based on the kind of community he wishes to portray. To understand why *City of Hope* looks the way it does and has the politics of equality that it does, we need to understand all these factors.

For Sayles, a community is not merely an aggregate of individuals; it is a network of bonds both small and large. Anyone can become a major player in the story of another person's life. In *City of Hope* Sayles gives us a glimpse of how this alternate view of community can be portrayed in an urban setting. In order to do so, he must liberate Hollywood's aesthetic and narrative strategies from their ties to the individual. As a result he depicts a city where people have unequal access to power but equal possibilities to change the course of human events. In Hudson City, Sayles shows us a world in which truly anyone can be a star, a scapegoat, or a savior.

NOTES

1. This is the term Sayles used (Smith 67) in the script for describing how the camera changes from following one character to following another.

2. See Baudelaire's "The Painter of Modern Life" (290–300) and also Benjamin's influential essay, "On Some Motifs in Baudelaire" (172–73).

3. Sayles describes the political structure of the film this way: "It's about people thinking that they are in these little enclaves, but they really are stuck together. What they do affects somebody else, even if it's like you send your kid to private school instead of public school—it may seem very personal to you, but it's a political act whether you like it or not. That was the point of *City of Hope*" (Smith 63).

4. At times they linger briefly in the subsequent scene. For instance, in the scene between the poet and the young woman, we hear the couple making plans for the woman to meet him outside the stage door after a theater performance. In the next scene, detailing the love between the poet and the actress, we get a glimpse of the young woman waiting by the stage door for a lover who will never come. Afterward, she disappears from the film as the carousel of love continues.

5. The only plotline he returns to involves a police investigation for a missing girl, and this is the only story that attains closure. Buñuel, of course, "solves" the puzzle in ways that poke fun at the narrative conventions of the detective story. First, the "missing" girl is actually there all the time, but no one seems to notice her. When she at last is "found," the inspector begins to read a report detailing what happened to her, but he instead leaves during the recitation of the solution for another meeting, and we follow him, never learning the facts of the detective story.

6. Sayles says that he told his actors, "Each of you, no matter what your piece in the puzzle is, we have to feel like that's a story worth following" (Smith 60).

7. One can envision a universe where Fred and Ethel are not merely Lucy's and Desi's sidekicks but are also the stars of a Fred and Ethel show, where Lucy and Desi play second fiddle. Spin-off television series such as *Rhoda*, *Phyllis*, *Frasier*, or *Angel* open up this possibility, but they rarely explore it. Key characters from the original series (such as Mary Richards, Sam Malone, or Buffy Summers) seldom appear on the spin-off show, and so these series often begin with the spin-off character moving away from the original community.

8. *City of Hope*'s trades have their origin in the sequence from *Eight Men Out* where the characters pop in and out of a hotel corridor. See Smith (67–68) for more details on the Richardson/Sayles collaboration.

WORKS CITED

Baron, David. "Sayles Talk." *John Sayles: Interviews*. Ed. Diane Carson. Jackson: UP of Mississippi, 1999. 133–35.

Baudelaire, Charles. "The Painter of Modern Life." *Baudelaire as a Literary Critic*. Ed. and trans. Lois Boe Hyslop and Francis E. Hyslop Jr. University Park: Pennsylvania State UP, 1964. 290–300.

Benjamin, Walter. "On Some Motifs in Baudelaire." *Illuminations*. Ed. Hannah Arendt, trans. Harry Zohn. New York: Schocken, 1968. 155–200.

Crowdus, Gary, and Leonard Quart. "Where the Hope Is: An Interview with John Sayles." *John Sayles: Interviews*. Ed. Diane Carson. Jackson: UP of Mississippi, 1999. 145–55.

Mellen, Joan. "*The Phantom of Liberty*: Further Investigations into the Discreet Charm of the Bourgeoisie." *The World of Luis Buñuel: Essays in Criticism*. New York: Oxford UP, 1978. 318–31.

Ryan, Jack. *John Sayles, Filmmaker: A Critical Study of the Independent Writer-Director*. Jefferson, NC: McFarland, 1998.

Smith, Gavin. "John Sayles: I Don't Want to Blow Anything by People." *Film Comment* 32.3 (1996): 57–68.

Suleiman, Susan. "Freedom and Necessity: Narrative Structure in *The Phantom of Liberty*." *Quarterly Review of Film Studies* 3.3 (1978): 277–95.

Williams, Linda. *Figures of Desire: A Theory and Analysis of Surrealist Film*. Urbana: U of Illinois P, 1981.

6

Of Spectral Mothers and Lost Children:
War, Folklore, and Psychoanalysis in *The Secret of Roan Inish*

Maureen Turim
and Mika Turim-Nygren

When she first saw John Sayles's *The Secret of Roan Inish* (1994), upon its initial U.S. theatrical release, my then seven-year-old daughter responded to the film so intensely that she chose as a new transitional object a stuffed seal that she named Selkie. The selkie spirits of Celtic legend that mark Sayles's film marked her childhood. As spirits capable of metamorphosis, selkies alternately take the body of a seal and of a woman. My daughter's Selkie became a necessity to cuddle while falling asleep, and subsequently went on all our travels. A selkie became a perfect transitional object, representing the mother in her absence, as well as a fantasy object connecting the mother with a sea animal of mysterious dreams. Her remembered reactions to the film from her earlier childhood and her present analysis (she is now fifteen) will serve to ground my own. In Mika's words:

> When I first saw this I must have been seven or so. It inspired me to name a stuffed seal Selkie, which I slept with instead of a teddy bear for several years. I cut off her whiskers because they were too scratchy, but other than that she's the perfect size to hug. In fact, there is now a Selkie II and baby Selkies (which happen to be slippers). The trouble with this is, when I told people my seal's name is "Selkie," they usually thought I was saying "Silky."
>
> I didn't remember a lot from that first viewing other than

the selkies; I just remembered my intense liking of this film. I had one picture in my memory of a little boy in a boat, and a girl running along the coast. I assumed these must be wrong, because they made absolutely no sense.

I saw it again a few days ago. I still liked it the second time; I had forgotten enough that it was like a new story, but with a strange sense of déjà vu.

Sayles's film, one of his most financially successful to date, is also the most anomalous in his oeuvre. A surprising foray into legend and fantasy from a director known for his intimate leftist social realism and his sharply focused eyes and attuned ears, this film does represent a departure in many ways. In others, however, it is quite consistent: it explores the patterns of communal life in which work and interpersonal negotiation are foregrounded.

Roan Inish is an adaptation of Rosalie K. Fry's *The Secret of the Ron Mor Skerry*, a children's book first published in Britain in 1957 as *Child of the Western Isles*, then in the United States in 1959 under the original title that highlights its secret. Fry illustrates her multichaptered tale with line drawings. The spare simplicity of these drawings matches her direct prose as she tells the story of a child's return to a skerry, the Scottish term for island. Sayles moves Fry's tale to 1946 Ireland, setting it on the coast in County Donegal, as the selkie legend is shared by the folklore of Ireland and Scotland. Despite the shift from Scotland to Ireland, Sayles strives for great fidelity to much of Fry's narrative, even returning to four of Fry's simple and elegant line drawings for the film's closing credits. He expresses his respect for storytelling by repeatedly embedding stories that are told, so that the film self-consciously navigates its filmic narration as the embodiment of oral legend.

The Irish setting gives Sayles the opportunity to journey through an intertextual landscape he associates with Robert Flaherty's *Man of Aran* (1934). Flaherty's landmark documentary explores a fishing community living on a similarly remote island off the coast of Ireland. Michael Powell's *The Edge of the World* (1937) becomes another intertextual touchstone, as a fiction film executed with the feel for setting reminiscent of documentary. It explores the lives of Shetland islanders who resist evacuating to the mainland. Powell rereleased the film in 1978 as *Return to the Edge of the World*, framed by documentary footage in which he discusses the making of the film; Sayles's voice-over track for the DVD version of *Roan Inish* provides his own parallel reflections on shooting in Ireland. The Flaherty and Powell precedents look specifically at the 1930s as a time in which the fishing economies of the islands collapsed, and residents moved to mainland cities in search of employment, precisely the history Fry explores from a childhood perspective in her book. That Sayles was attracted to this historical transformation of an economy as it affects a defined community should come as no surprise, nor that he finds fiction a useful means to explore a subject that documentarians have previously exposed. Another film worthy of noting in this context is John Ford's *The Quiet Man* (1952), which Sayles notes as affecting his decision on how to shoot the graveyard scenes in *The Secret of Roan Inish*; a tombstone also opens *The Edge of the World*. Ford wrested from two weeks' location shooting in Ireland indelible images of the landscape, and the film won Oscars for cinematography and direction. These films form an intriguing intertextual web; taken together they evoke the intersection of documentary and narrative film as descriptions of environments.

The cinematography by Haskell Wexler, which beautifully renders both village and fantasy seas, seeks to evoke the supernatural within a naturalistic painting of the island. Sayles avoids special effects except for the brief use of a seal animation, and then only in sea shots that are at great enough distance so that their bobbing in the waves is indistinguishable from footage of the actual seals used throughout the film. The near absence of technological means of producing the fantasy seems essential to Sayles's approach, which tries to create Fiona's point of view.[1]

> *What I realized was the most important part of the movie to me, the selkies, were in fact never actually in the story. Oh, they're implied, with the seals following everywhere and watching them. But the only time you actually see evidence that they are women and not ordinary seals is during the illustration of a story, a myth that is told to the little girl. Yet by the end of the movie the viewer believes firmly in the power of the selkies. I think it comes from the little girl's faith. She believes in Jamie when no one else will, and she turns out to be right. Therefore we can believe in the selkies with her, trailing on the edges of her vivid imagination.*

As Fiona (Jeni Courtney) arrives on a boat to live with her grandparents, the seal watches her arrival as they exchange looks.

Fiona's arrival by boat at the film's opening frames flashbacks to three significant scenes that explain the conditions of her journey to live with her grandparents. A funereal prayer begins on boat as voice-over, then the film dissolves from a tight shot of Fiona, her hair loose on the windswept deck, to a flashback image of Fiona, slightly younger, in a different coat, and wearing a knit cap. The scene from an as yet indeterminate past shows final moments of a funeral as the family gathers around the grave. We see this gathering from the subjective view of a child. The reverse shot that depicts Fiona in turn includes her full frame next to the grave marker but cuts off the head of the priest next to her, emphasizing how the scene is tailored to her height and perspective. Fiona's older brother holds a baby whose cries we hear continuously punctuating the prayer, itself worthy of being quoted in full, as its mystery colors the scene: "Lord of all spirit and all flesh, in whose ever embrace all creatures live, and whatsoever world or condition they be. I beseech thee to pull her hand to his name, and dwell into the every need thou knowest. Thou art life and rest, refreshment, joy and consolation, and paradise, and in companionship of the Saints, in the presence of Christ, and the hands that hold, all guide with love." Let me highlight here the mysterious way hands circulate in this prayer; the hand of the dead mother is extended to the Name, and we are promised hands that hold to guide us with love. Equally poetic and yet puzzling is the evocation of creatures who "live and whatsoever world or condition they be." Retrospectively, this phrase links the world of suffering humans to the familiar animals of Fiona's childhood that will circulate throughout the film, the gulls and seals. "Whatsoever world or condition they be" comes to stand for the strange metamorphoses of the selkies and the wild-child existence of Fiona's brother, Jamie.[2]

The final image of the funeral scene begins in close-up on the stone cross inscribed "Loving Mother/Brigid Coneelly/1910–1946," before the camera pans left across a sloping hill that descends to the sea. A dissolve links this to a shot of steam filling the frame in the interior of a factory, as the sound of steam bursting forth bridges the change of scene. Fiona enters the image, wending her way through an immense industrial laundry, where men load huge washing machines and fold linens. Care is taken to paint the arduousness of the labor, as the billowing steam creates a hellish image of this factory setting. Fiona stops at a large pressing machine to ask her brother where their father is. His answer, "The pub," links to a dissolve to beer tap levers, which in the context of the laundry just seen first seems to be just another machine part of that operation. Fiona once again fills the frame as she arrives at the bar, so that the men surrounding her are but headless, truncated presences on either side. Offscreen commentary over her image comes from the unseen barmaid and patrons who discuss her. Although sympathetic, their direct description of her appearance and circumstance names her status with disconcerting bluntness. The barmaid says, "Poor creature. She's only lost in the world, that's all. And what would you be in a strange land without a mother's touch? . . . This is no place for a child." The barmaid goes on to suggest that she go to live "with the old people" after having confirmed that her father's response to his own loneliness has been to become a "drunkard."

These three flashbacks are enigmatic scenes, presented without direct verbal explanation. Full exposition remains withheld, to be filled in retrospectively. Fiona's mother's death before they left the island seems to be linked to Fiona's exile to the city, a city that remains unidentified in the film, but as Sayles notes, historically the migration of Irish fishermen was often to factories in Glasgow.[3] Jamie, the baby who is being held at the funeral, seems to have disappeared, as Fiona wanders through the urban environment with only her drunkard father and older brother as family.

This opening offers an introduction to Fiona's subjectivity. Events happened that she apparently does not fully understand, and they haunt her. She stands courageously on the deck of the boat, holding onto the rigging, journeying into her future, yet the look on her face is one of pain and uncertainty.

Fiona's journey will be not only a search for the lost sibling but also a psychoanalytic journey into recognition of loss, and thus a journey through a symbolically imaged recovery. For what the film figures in its dreamlike landscape is reconciliation with the loss of the mother. The retrieval of her brother allows Fiona a purposeful contentment, as in the process she learns about herself in relationship to her mother; indeed, she learns self-sufficiency and how to become a nurturer.

The death of her mother stands as the precipitating event that forced the separation of young Fiona's immediate family from its ancestral island. Her abrupt remove to the subsequent alienation of an urban setting figures as a metonymic fragment. Loss haunts *The Secret of Roan Inish*'s characters, and the mystery of that loss is symbolized in a series of tales about Roan Inish told to the girl over the course of her stay with her grandparents.

First comes the tale by her grandfather of his "father's father's father," Sean Michael, from a time "when the English were still a force and you were punished for speaking Irish." The first part of this story tells of Sean Michael's punishment at school for insisting on his native tongue, being forced to wear a collar of thorns while his fellow students chant "Idiot! Idiot!" Indeed, Irish political contexts are brought home at the end of the story, as we are told Sean Michael was convicted of smuggling arms to the Fenians and died in prison.

However, Sean Michael's story is also a story of the founding of the Coneelly clan on the islands, a story steeped as well in a loss at sea, mitigated by the warming comfort of the hearth. When a storm hits, Sean Michael is the lone survivor washed to shore, while his fisherman father, uncle, and cousins all perish. He is rescued from the sea by a woman who wraps him between her cows to restore warmth to his frozen body at a time when cows still lived in a family's quarters. This narration, illustrated first with a long tracking shot of the woman running along the strand to rescue Sean Michael, subsequently takes on the amber firelit glow of a warm interior. Sean Michael tells of a seal that saved him, carrying him to shore. In a return to the storytelling frame setting, Grandfather sums up the animals' role in salvation, "saved by a seal and two cows," while Grandmother adds, "and the smart thinking of a woman." Linking the female and animals as saviors of a male ancestor anticipates Fiona's role in saving Jamie; this sequence of shots, strand and warm interior, find their echo in the final scenes of the film, and serve here as their foreshadowing.

Fiona seeks information about Jamie from her very first exchange with her grandfather. When he remarks on her light Coneelly coloring, Fiona says, "Jamie was the only dark one." This mention is clearly taken as a provocation, and her grandfather warns her, "Don't mention Jamie to your grandmother." It is significant that the first story her grandfather tells Fiona, in her grandmother's presence, while not being about the unmentionable Jamie, prefigures Jamie's rescue in both historical and narrative terms.

Tarring the curragh (the Irish term for fishing boat used in the film) provides Fiona time alone with her grandfather. Immediately she presses her second provocation: "You just want me to forget about Jamie."

"It was like a dream that day" are Grandfather's words of introduction as he responds with his story of evacuating the island Roan Inish, his acknowledgment that "none of us will ever forget wee Jamie." It is this evacuation that caused Fiona's younger brother, Jamie, to be swept to sea in his cradle. The visual narration is told with great economy, but also great violence, as we dissolve to the cradle on the beach, to see gulls attack those who try to rescue the baby. The cradle is swept out to sea, beyond the reach of those who give chase by boat. The baby loss to the sea becomes the second loss in Fiona's life, echoing the loss of her mother, and coinciding with the family's losing their ancestral home.

Looking back, I can appreciate the irony of naming my transitional object Selkie. My stuffed toy functioned as a mother-substitute. When I was very young I asked my mom to come in and rub my back every night; later on I shifted to needing Selkie to fall asleep. Indeed, the selkie myth often involves a nurturing female figure. In many stories, the selkie saves a fisherman's life or, alternately, becomes his wife and cares for his children. For Fiona, the selkies help to fill the void left by the death of her mother. By helping Fiona to reunite Jamie and her family, the selkies play an important protective role. Likewise, my Selkie helped comfort me in unfamiliar situations. Interestingly, it was my mom who convinced me to give Selkie up. Taking her advice, I left Selkie behind when we went on a long trip, and from then on Selkie ceased to be my constant companion.

Central to the series of tales is narration by Tadhg Coneelly (John Lynch), a family member Fiona meets while visiting the town with her grandmother as he works as part of a crew cleaning fish at a local market. The odd and unsettling Tadhg tells of an ancestor, Liam Coneelly, who took a selkie woman as his wife. Tadhg's violent anger as he stabs at a fellow worker who insults him serves as prelude to the tale's telling. It surrounds the entire tale with the unsettling atmosphere evoked by Tadhg's questionable sanity and exceeding strangeness as he relates the metamorphosis through which the seal becomes a human female by stripping off her skin, revealing a beautiful, wild woman. She will fall under the power of Liam once he seizes her seal skin. Tadhg's tale is infused with the evocative sensuality of both Liam and the selkie, Nuala. Tadhg tells us that Liam built a cradle to the specifications of his selkie wife. Having heard the grandfather's story earlier, we realize that this is the same odd cradle that one day will carry Jamie away. One of Nuala's children, also named Fiona, makes the mistake of asking Nuala about the leather coat her father keeps in the attic, a mistake because once a selkie finds her skin, she is bound to wear it once again to return to the sea. This selkie, then, figures as a lost mother, whom children like Jamie hope to rejoin.

The stories within the frame story add new layers for interpretation. Both Fiona's grandfather and her cousin Tadhg serve as narrators, feeding Fiona's natural curiosity and imagination. She believes wholeheartedly in all of these folktales, and her belief, at least in the legends surrounding Jamie, is eventually justified. This leads to speculation about the veracity of the connected stories, such as those about the selkies. Thus Sayles employs Fiona's faith to generate belief in the viewer as well. If one impossible tale could come true, why not the other? The legends surrounding the boy and the seals are undeniably linked, and it is hard to explain the presence of Jamie, alive and well after so long alone, without accepting the existence of the selkies. Yet Sayles never forces this critical decision: the second legend remains only a possibility, although it is supported by the events of the story. The final judgment is left to the viewer.

Madelon Sprengnether's *The Spectral Mother: Freud, Feminism, and Psychoanalysis* serves as a means of interpreting the implications of the embedded tales. Encapsulating much earlier feminist analysis that holds the psychoanalytical inability to fully theorize the preoedipal mother leads to a devaluation of feminist alternatives to male-centered scenarios, Sprengnether emphasizes the ghostlike function of the mother figure, as it creates "a presence out of absence." Although she uses the term preoedipal, Sprengnether actually is concerned with the multitude of associations one has with the mother, including the mother as desired and as ego-ideal. She is particularly attuned to how the mother's sexuality may become associated with dread and fears of loss. We can see that the selkie has elements of idealization and dread wedded within its image. Nuala's story suggests a dark lesson, that the price of ideal motherhood and domesticity entails forsaking a prior, more wild and free self. Further, the forsaking of freedom can only be enforced by an unnatural power over such a being; the selkie must return to the sea once she recovers that which was stolen and hidden from her, her very skin. One of the meanings of this myth within the story is to restore to motherhood its full sense of sacrifice, and with acknowledgment of sacrifice, a corollary ambiguity over the price mothers pay for what is lost. Even mothers who remain may attain a ghostlike presence within the mind of the child. So much more ghostlike is the mother who through circumstances or through death disappears. How could a loving mother ever leave? The myth of the selkies symbolically answers the question Fiona does not ask directly about her own mother's disappearance. The selkies provide a corollary mystery that Fiona sets out to solve.

Fiona's story remains that of a girl whose life will unfold in the absence of a mother. Returning to her ancestral island as a motherless child, Fiona is told not to discuss with her grandmother that which most troubles her, so that even this likely mother replacement exists at a remove from her. As we have shown, the initial flashback to her mother's funeral marks this absence. The absence is reiterated by the abandonment of her namesake, Fiona, by the selkie mother, Nuala, in the story Tadhg tells. Nuala, though adored by her husband and her numerous children, abandons them to return to the sea, where her other, more animalistic self, can reinhabit its longed for and stolen skin, to feel at home. Fiona will restore the family, bringing Jamie back so that her grandmother regains a happiness she seemed to have lost. There is a transgenerational restoration of nurturing, as the wild child is brought back to the hearth in a manner that attempts to find a balance between a wild and a cultural way of being. This is exemplified in the shot of Fiona cleaning up the graveyard on the island as her last act of restoration after the houses and garden had been made livable once more though her and her cousin's hard labor. She has a dream shown as a sequence in which her mother rocks Jamie's cradle with a foot, at the same time that she crochets and sings. This dream sequence appears to be from Fiona's point of view, a gaze on the mother as she would have appeared in everyday life. Fiona, upon waking, calls out to her mother. Through this dream, Fiona's mother's absence is now marked and named, instead of simply being ignored. Later, in order to weather the storm that greets their return to Roan Inish, Grandmother recreates the soup all the women of Roan Inish made from seaweed. Recall that Tadhg had told us that Nuala would "come back each day with her hands full of shellfish and seaweed which she'd simmer over a driftwood fire in a manner all her own." This matrilineal soup links Fiona through her grandmother to Nuala. Fiona's mother becomes restored symbolically as the bond between grandmother and granddaughter grows ever warmer and closer.

The sensuousness of the selkie as a shape-shifter who becomes a beautiful woman recalls the allure of the Greek Sirens as they migrate in folklore to become the mermaid and mermen of the legends of many coastal regions. In Ireland, the female merrow (*mulrruhgach*), also called a mermaid (*murœch*) or a seamaiden (*maighdean mhara*), is a beautiful creature whose mythic marriages with humans bear striking resemblance to many selkie tales:

> Mermaids are, of course, very well known in Scotland. Our northern shores seem to be a particularly favourite haunt of theirs; and sometimes, for hours, they may be seen, by those who have the eyes to see, sitting on a rock, or even lolling on the sands or the shingle, combing their long and luxuriant hair. The MaigAdean Chuain, like the sealwoman, and the ordinary land fairy-woman, is very fond of taking a handsome lad as a lover; and sometimes she will heap all sorts of riches on him: gold, and silver, and precious jewels, taken from the deep vaults of the sea. But, sometimes, too, she will lure her lover away beneath the waves, to keep him a prisoner bound by long, slender chains of gold. Out beyond Duncansby Head there is great storehouse of jewels, where the Mermaid in charge for the Sea-god, has a whole host of once-human lovers.
>
> There is danger in the love of a mermaid, for no matter how beautiful she may be, or how kindly, the affair always ends in disaster. That is why sensible fishermen, whenever they haul up a mermaid in their nets, always let her go. But, of course, there are fools among fishermen, as there are fools among other men,

War, Folklore, and Psychoanalysis in *Roan Inish*

The selkie (Susan Lynch) sheds her skin within the narrated rendition of the myth.

and sometimes silly and inexperienced lads will pull a mermaid aboard and keep her for their pleasure, only to rue it later—maybe even within an hour or two. (R. M. Douglas 112–13)

Compare this to the encapsulation of the selkie myth:

> The selkies are gentler creatures who are seals by day but men and women by night. In their mortal form the selkies are described as possessing an unearthly beauty with dark hair and eyes. Silently they emerge from the sea to shed their skins and frolic on the sand. Like the merrows they have webs between their fingers and toes (or at least wide palms that hint of their watery origin) and must obey anyone who secures their oily skins. Selkies, also, make excellent wives. But they are solitary and quiet by nature. They will frequently wander from their mortal homes to the sea cliffs to meditate and sing their melancholy songs. When their fishermen-husbands are lost upon the sea, they sing from the cliffs to guide them home. If they ever find their seal skins again, they, too, will return to the sea. But unlike the merrow, the selkie will not forget her husband and children and can be seen swimming close to the shore watching over them.[4]

We should also note that some versions of the selkie myth emphasize their protective and life-saving role in rescuing humans from the sea. Some versions present their transformation into human form less directly, preferring instead to personify the seals rather than magically have them shift shapes. The following excerpt (presented in an Irish dialect derived from Gaelic, and in its English translation) is an example of a version that does both; the protagonist is a seal hunter who thinks the better of killing two seal pups when he sees the soulful sorrow in the eyes of their mother. This excerpt picks up the tale at the end, when the former hunter turned fisherman almost drowns at sea:

> And then he gave up all hope of life, and saw nothing before him but dismal death. But just as the sea was coming round his neck, and coming now and then in little ripples into his mouth; just as he found the sea beginning to lift him from the rock something seized him by the collar of his jacket, and swung him off his feet. He had no idea what it was, or where he was, until he found his feet on the bottom, where he could wade in safety to the shore. And when the creature that had hold of him let him go, he waded to the dry land. He looked towards the place from whence he had come, and saw a large seal swimming to the rock, where she dived, took up his creel of fish, and swam with it to the land.
>
> He waded out and took the creel full of fish out of her mouth; and he said with all his heart, "God bless the seal that does not forget." And she looked at him as if she would have said, could she have spoken, "One good turn deserves another." She was the same seal that he had seen calving on Hacksness 40 years before. He said he would have known her motherly look among a thousand. But she had grown very large and old. So that was the seal that did not forget. I wish everyone would remember what is good, as well as that seal.[5]

This version of the selkie myth can be construed as an admonition against seal hunting, an aspect Sayles incorporates into his film by having Tadhg offer his narration of Liam's meeting with the selkie with the following introduction: "In them days seals was hunted, for their oil and their hides, clubbed to death and made into coats and pouches and pampooties for the feet. Liam never took a part in it, though. He believed, as many did then, that there was no worse luck than to harm a seal." As Tadhg closes his narration, he offers the final moral: "From that day on it was forbidden on the island to harm a seal, and man and beast lived at each other's side, sharin' the wealth of the sea. From

War, Folklore, and Psychoanalysis in *Roan Inish*

time to time the Coneellys would see her—in the waves, out basking in the sun on the Skellig rock, watching them. Watching her children." In his voice-over commentary offered as supplement to the DVD, Sayles notes that the selkie myth seems to stem from guilt a seal-hunting culture had about killing animals whose manner of looking at humans seems to display a human consciousness.

The Irish and Scottish selkie myths bear strong structural comparison to two Japanese tales: "The Serpent Wife" (related as she is to the kawakami) and "The Wife from the Sky World." Given that storytelling and folktales structure the film, comparative folklore sources will help us here, for there is much in common in these stories of brides from other worlds.

> "The Wife from the Sky World"
> Long ago a man who sold clay parching pans was walking in the mountains on the sixth day of the seventh month. He saw three maidens bathing and stole the robe of one of them. On his way home he found one of them crying. He took her home and married her. A child was born. While she was nursing her three-year-old child one day, she happened to notice a package wrapped in black paper and tucked into the rafters. She looked inside the package and found her lost robe. She realized for the first time that it had been stolen. She put it on hurriedly and held her child under one arm as she got ready to ride away on a cloud from behind the house. Her husband returned just then. She said she was Tanabata. She went to the sky after she gave him . . . instructions (on how to reach her again, which he proceeds to do, but ultimately fails). (Yanagita 25)

> "The Snake Wife"
> (The word snake is used, but it is a great Water Spirit, nearer to a Dragon Woman than a big snake).
> A beautiful woman appeared at the home of a man who was grieving over the death of his wife. They married and presently a child was to be born. When it came time, the wife asked her husband not to look under any circumstance. After making doubly sure, she went into the room to deliver her baby. The man could not endure his worry and looked in secretly. There he saw a great snake coiled around a baby. He was dumbfounded, but he withdrew and said nothing about it. The woman came out on the seventh day carrying a lovely little boy, but she was weeping bitterly. She said she could stay no longer because her true form had been seen. She scooped out her left eye and gave

it to her husband. She told him to let the baby suck it if it cried. He cared for the baby by letting it suck the eye, but the eye began to grow smaller after a while until it was completely gone. The father put his child onto his back and went to the pond in the hills to look for his wife. The great snake appeared and took out her remaining eye and gave it to him. She asked that a bell be hung near the lake and rung at the sixth hour of the morning and evening. She hid in the lake again. The father furnished the temple by the pond with a bell and arranged to have time marked. When the child grew up, he learned about his birth and went to the pond to meet his mother. She appeared in human form as a blind woman. He put her on his back and carried her home and lived with her as a dutiful son. (Yanagita 350)

Why consider Japanese folklore here? As island cultures with deep attachments to the sea, some of the common threads of their folktales speak to the ways folklore develops from the needs of an environment. Consider also the Japanese folktale "The Story of Urashima Taro, the Fisher Lad" who as a reward for saving a sea turtle's life is taken to be the groom of the daughter of the Dragon King of the Sea (Ozaki 26). He deserts her to return to his parents, at the cost of losing the immortality she granted him. This story allows us in its common fisherman protagonist to focus on the link between two cultures in which the hard life of fishermen often left men searching elsewhere for brides, even creating fantasies to describe their quest. This circumstance finds its echo in both myth and historical narrative: Liam finds Nuala, whose appearance Tadhg said is accepted because fishermen often searched elsewhere for wives, and similarly, Fiona's father brings her mother to the island from the mainland. Grandmother tells us later that Brigid grew to love the island: "She was the last to marry onto Roan Inish, and the last to die on it." Grandfather adds then that Fiona's father blamed himself for her early death, for "bringing her into the life of the sea," though he adds philosophically that "life is hard in the countryside too."

This comparative look at folklore helps us understand something of its structure and signification. These supernatural brides, the selkie, the water spirit, and the sky wife from different cultures show us how marital constancy or maternal nurturing may be somewhat at odds with the preexistent or wild nature of the bride and mother. The folktales split the mother's loyalties between her children and another calling; each version, for there are many variants on these tales within a culture, reaches its own balance between the wild and the civilized, the obligation of the mother to the form she first had and the love of the mother for her child. Sayles tells us that while shooting the film he heard a much harsher version of the selkie tale, one in which the selkie upon regaining her skin is followed into the sea by all her human children, who drown as a result. We should also note that the similar folklore cultures seem to have given the Sayles film a large audience in Japan. Fry's original story was translated as *Fiona no umi*, and published in Tokyo in 1996 to coincide with the film's release and the reissue of Fry's book as a 1995 Hyperion paperback, bearing this time the film's title, *The Secret of Roan Inish*.

The selkies are far from the only fantasy or mythic element of the story. The personification of the seagulls is nearly as important; indeed, the two species seem to work together throughout the story in protecting the children, sending messages, and such. Other components given a degree of consciousness include the ocean and the islands, although in these cases the sentience is more implied than explicit. Still, the waves play an uncanny role in some events, carrying boats away with seemingly meddlesome intent. Too, the islands, especially Roan Inish, are shown as intrinsically magical; with their seclusion and secrecy, they are natural sites of fantastical occurrences.

Throughout the film, Sayles emphasizes the importance of safety, especially within the home. One of the most important aspects of the selkies is their supposed power to protect. The selkies shadow Jamie during his time of need and abandonment, and likewise follow Fiona when she leaves her father and siblings to come to her grandparents. The selkies represent the comfort provided by family and friends; they take the place of a familiar community for Jamie and serve as surrogate parents for both children. In particular, the selkies replace Jamie's and Fiona's lost mother. Sayles repeatedly alludes to the connection between the selkies and the mother, most notably with the tale of the family's ancestral selkie mother. The theme of safety returns at the end of the film, with the efforts of the family to find Jamie and return him to the fold. However, in this instance the associations of security temporarily attached to the selkies shift back to the family. Jamie overcomes his fear and embraces his grandmother and grandfather; he, Fiona, and the rest are once again happy and secure in their home on Roan Inish. The selkies return to the ocean, to be left in the background, reminders of harder times and different lifestyles.

Let me also note the relevance for Sayles's film of the supernatural haunting as metaphor echoing a Marxist history that one finds discussed in Jacques Derrida's work in *The Specters of Marx*. Derrida's strategy reads *Hamlet* and the history of Marxism together as haunting discourses, linked by shades of the past. Sayles, too, proposes reading the history of a community in relationship to the mourning of a mother and a lost brother, and to haunting folk narratives that echo this mourning. Derrida connects the specter with the body as "that which remains," calling for the work of mourning. He emphasizes that it is language that names the meaning of death and the inheritance of generations to follow. He also makes the connection between this work of mourning, the work of the spirit, and work as such. So in asking "Whither Marxism?" Derrida asks us to know the specter of Marx that continues to haunt our thought, and speak of its remains through a recognition of the power of transformation, and through asking in the broadest possible sense, what is work?

The folktale gives its answer by telling us a story of working at the sea's edge as history has conspired to make that work unworkable. It is a fable that values the transformative power of useful communal work, but even if this involves restoring the graveyard, the future horizon is less predictable, given what we know to have happened in the past.

For if this folktale seemingly escapes the ideological social concerns of Sayles's other body of films to chart different territory, I hold that all is not as it might first seem. The film carries over social and historical concerns to this new territory. Many reviewers missed this haunting presence of the social throughout the film, perhaps due to their surprise that Sayles, the realist par excellence, would entertain myth, the supernatural, and the children's story. The film treats not only its folklore fantasy tradition but also the island fishing economy as a lost heritage that a young girl seeks to recover as she carves out her own identity as a survivor.

The film explores work in all its materiality, with attention to the visual details of work environments and processes.

For example, the early flashback scene in the industrial laundry steeps itself in the assembly-line process of mass cleaning and pressing. In contrast, but in equally discerning detail, the film depicts the artisanal process through which Grandfather restores the curragh with tar and canvas with Fiona's help. Often the dialogue underscores this attention to work, as when Grandfather reminisces, "The old people used cowhide for theirs, then it was calico, and now we make do with canvas. But the pitch is what it always was."

This attention to process carries over to the rehabilitation of the Roan Inish cottages that Fiona and her cousin Eamon undertake by themselves in secret. These work montage sequences edited to Irish music show the sweeping and cleaning, thatching, and weighting down with stones hung by ropes, whitewashing, the peat gathering, planting, and so on. While all children play house with siblings, cousins, or friends, Fiona and Eamon show an amazing capacity to make material their fantasy of returning to the island. While Eamon teased Fiona earlier about the danger of communicating with the seals as she was likely to be carried off to marry one, Grandfather teases Eamon that his ambition of one day returning to Roan Inish with a wife depended upon finding such a woman. Eamon proclaims he will not be, as Grandfather maintains, a "sorry sight, hauntin' the island all by yer lonesome" because "I'll have a wife." Grandfather responds, "But will she have you, Eamon? There's not many women these days attracted by the romance of work and solitude." The economy of the children's fantasy of restoring cottage life on the island then is dependent on an artisanal work ethic, in which solitary hard work has its own "romance."

This very notion then leads to another charge critics have made about the film: nostalgia. Implicit in this critique is a position similar to that taken by Fredric Jameson in *Postmodernism, or, The Cultural Logic of Late Capitalism*:

> Nostalgia films restructure the whole issue of pastiche and project it onto a collective and social level, where the desperate attempt to appropriate a missing past is now refracted through the iron law of fashion change and the emergent ideology of the generation. The inaugural film of this new aesthetic discourse, George Lucas's *American Graffiti* (1973), set out to recapture, as so many films have attempted since, the henceforth mesmerizing lost reality of the Eisenhower era; and one tends to feel,

that for Americans at least, the 1950s remain the privileged lost object of desire—not merely the stability and prosperity of a pax Americana but also the first naive innocence of the countercultural impulses of early rock and roll and youth gangs (Coppola's *Rumble Fish* will then be the contemporary dirge that laments their passing, itself, however, still contradictorily filmed in genuine nostalgia film style). With this initial breakthrough, other generational periods open up for aesthetic colonization: as witness the stylistic recuperation of the American and the Italian 1930s, in Polanski's *Chinatown* and Bertolucci's *Il Conformista*, respectively. More interesting, and more problematical, are the ultimate attempts, through this new discourse, to lay siege either to our own present and immediate past or to a more distant history that escapes individual existential memory. (19)

Reading Jameson's wording here is significant, as he does not mean this to apply to all historical films or novels. He speaks of a film that recuperates the past rather than presents it for critical scrutiny—in fact his term for a noncommercialized view of the past borrows from Theodor Adorno, valorizing what Jameson calls "individual existential memory" (19). He never analyzes in enough detail the films he cites as prototypes of the nostalgia films to indicate how their discourse differs either from other history films or other films that use history as a backdrop. A film such as *American Graffiti* only gives us a "mesmerizing lost reality" (19) rather than any critical insights. We might well grant him his argument if our own reading of that film sees its treatment of the 1950s as a superficial fantasy that only appropriates history as fashion, especially if we consider the best-selling soundtrack reissue that accompanied *American Graffiti* as indicative of what Jameson calls "aesthetic colonization" (19). However, others have tended to extend the critique of nostalgia by following Jameson's lead in citing Bertolucci's *Il Conformista* to any and all films that are set historically, no matter what their discourse is on history. *The Conformist* arguably presents a narrative view of the mass psychology of fascism, and one can argue that its high-fashion costuming is attempting to show that Italian fascist aesthetics played their role in glamorizing Mussolini.

Similarly, *The Secret of Roan Inish* asks to be seen as a self-conscious and critical discourse about the past, not merely a nostalgic marketing of it. The subject's relationship to the history of a family and a place are under scrutiny. Early on, Grandmother, while still in her state of emotional denial, takes a position that is so antinostalgic that it refuses to mine the past for any redeeming values: "The east is our future and the west is our past. The islands are to the west." The film then sets out to contrast a rural economy based in agriculture and fishing with an urbanization and a globalization that are quickly destroying it. It does examine the past for some positive traditions that it treats with respect, but never at the cost of ignoring the difficulties associated with earning a living at sea. Most importantly, it is a reflection on a period of economic transition for the seacoast dwellers of Ireland and, by extension, small fishing villages in all coastal communities.

Early on, Fiona asks Grandmother about Roan Inish, "Why did we have to leave?" Grandmother's answer, "It's the young people, dear. Like yer father and yer brothers. They were restless on the island, then comes the War, with jobs across the sea. And now as they've got the city in their blood—." Grandmother at the beginning of the film views the past with a combination of realism and emotional denial; she can articulate causes for historical change, but she cannot bear to talk about Jamie's loss. Her acceptance of a present that she seems powerless to change has her devoted to the rituals of everyday life, making tea and urging her charges to eat, while proclaiming, "What's done is done—there's no use moaning over it." She says, as she looks out the window at the islands, "I won't have nonsense and superstition under my roof," but we learn by the end of the tale that this insistence on realism is a defense mechanism that disappears once she regains hope of Jamie's return. It is the pain of loss linked to memories of the past that she tries to banish from her house; as she says directly, "There is nothing out there for us but sad memories."

In contrast, Grandfather's continuous working at sea makes him also far more emotionally tied to the islands, so that the past remains accessible and thoughts about it desirable for him. For him, Roan Inish remains beautiful and he relishes initiating his granddaughter and Eamon to his knowledge of the sea and his past experiences.

Sayles develops the historical and political nature of his attachment through Grandfather's narration of Sean Michael's story that we discussed earlier. We are told that Grandfather's great-grandfather was "born into the Famine," and that "the English was still a force in the country then, they had the schools and it was their language and their ways that you learnt there, or else." Grandfather initiates his granddaughter into the context of political struggle in telling of the punishment of Sean Michael for speaking Gaelic; he has to wear cingulum, a ring of thorns, around his neck as a punishment, which shamed him, causing him to rebel by shouting out in Gaelic, "I'm not your ox, you dirty foreigner, and you can shove this up your ass!" This phrase in Gaelic within Grandfather's story works to double purpose: it shields Fiona from the profanity, as she says she does not "have any Irish." Further, as Grandfather responds, "More's the pity for it." So Grandfather becomes the voice through which a history of political struggle enters the film. At the close of Sean Michael's story Grandfather answers Fiona's query about what happened to her ancestor that he was "jailed by the English and died in prison, a man of fifty. Smugglin' arms to the Fenians, he was."

This history of struggle continues into the present for Fiona's grandparents. Toward the film's end, it takes the form of impending eviction in favor of vacation dwellers, prefiguring the issue Sayles will take on in *Sunshine State* (2002) of the destruction of a community by land speculation for resort development. Grandmother tells Fiona, "You know we don't own this house? Well, the landlord says today he's an offer from wealthy people overseas that want a place to summer in. A goldmine, he calls it. . . . It was bad enough your grandfather had to come in off the island, but to take him away from the sea—I'm fearin' his spirit will fail him."

Grandmother links these problems with the landlord to her earlier assessment of the ongoing changes the community has suffered since the war: "It's the times darlin'. After a war people is always ready to cut off the past and go forward. We're just the ones that's left behind is all."

So even though the film celebrates folk culture and the sea, it does so in a very specific historical and political context. Too many critics saw the urban/rural dichotomy of the film as only nostalgic and apolitical, without considering how this is a film about the historical dimensions of a way of life. This past offers stories that haunt us as they offer us a way to mourn, and to learn from that process of mourning.

Perhaps the most magical, "secret" quality of the island, Roan Inish, is its ability to solve the family's problems. When

Grandmother and Grandfather are plagued with real-world troubles of rents and landlords, the abandoned island is suddenly put before them as the perfect solution. This solution is all the more fantastical for having been designed and implemented by children. It is Fiona's hope and determination that carries the family through from difficulties into a happy resolution. It is this childlike conviction, this wholehearted belief, that renders the island magical, as it is childish dreams that make the selkies seem real. The entire transformation of the island, along with its resettlement by Fiona's family, becomes a wondrous occurrence.

The most important differences between the film and the book can be found in the beginning and the ending. Both open with Fiona on the boat to her grandparents, but in the book the scene is cheerful and forward-looking. Fiona, excited and happy to be on the boat, encounters a friendly sailor who tells her a story of her destination. In contrast, the Fiona of the movie seems depressed by her journey. She clings forlornly to the side of the boat, rather than gleefully riding on the bow. Instead of a gripping tale of Roan Inish/the Ron Mor Skerry, Sayles presents a flashback to Fiona's mother's funeral. Not only does Sayles change the tone of the introduction, he also blurs the events leading to the boat trip. While in the book Fiona explains to herself that health reasons bring her to the isles, in the film her mother's death and the resulting sundering of her family seem to be the underlying cause. This sequence is a bit temporally misleading, but it does emphasize Fiona's confusion and grief over the separation from her family. Sayles equates Fiona's departure from the mainland with the death of her mother, thus successfully portraying her childishly muddled, but nevertheless intense, emotions.

An even more critical variation is found at the conclusion of the film. The book's end is quite definite, with the selkies satisfied over Jamie's return to the family. The last lines provide an answer to the mystery of the selkies, giving a sense of closure. Sayles slightly alters this ending, showing the selkies encouraging Jamie to return to his human family, then Jamie happy in Fiona's arms, followed by a final shot of a seal. This flow of scenes is certainly more abstract than the pointed conclusion of the book. The selkies, shown only as dark silhouettes in the waves, remain enigmatic. Sayles concludes the film with the secret of the selkies intact, reiterating his solidarity with folklore and children's fantasy as a form of knowledge.

NOTES

This essay is written in two voices. The paragraphs in italics were written by Mika Turim-Nygren; the rest belongs to Maureen Turim.

    1. Sayles speaks of this in his director's commentary to the DVD.
    2. For comparable theoretical and historical treatment of the feral tale, see Kidd.
    3. Sayles mentions this in his director's commentary to the DVD.
    4. http://members.tripod.com/~pg4anna/Mer_silkie.htm. 22 February 2005.
    5. "Orkneyjar—The Selkie that deud no forget—Translation from Orkney Dialect," http://www.orkneyjar.com/folklore/selkiefolk/selforget.htm. The site also offers the story in the original Orkney Dialect:

> He cried whill he wus trapple-hers', an' he could cry nee mair. An' dan he gae ap; a' hup' o' life, an' saw naething afore him bit dismal da-eth. An' dan, as de sea wus comin' roond his hass, an' comin' noos and dans i' peedie lippers tae his mooth, jeust as he f'and the sea beginnan' tae lift him fae the rock,—summin' grippid him bae the neck o' the co't an' whippid him aff o' his feet. He kent no' what hid wus, or whar he wus, till he f'and his feet at the boddam whar he could wad ashore i' safety. An' whin de craeter 'at hed haud o' him passed him, he wadded tae the dry land.
>
> He luckid whar he cam' fae, an' saw a muckle selkie swiman' tae the rock whar sheu dookid, teuk ap his cubbie o' fish, an' swam wi'd tae the land. He wadded oot an' teuk the cubbie fu' o' fish oot o' her mooth; an' he said wi' a' his he'rt, Geud bliss the selkie that deus no' forget." An' sheu luckid tae him, as gin, if sheu could hae spoken, sheu wad hae said, "Ae geud turn meets anither." Sheu wus the sam' selkie that he saw callowan' on Hacksness forty years afore. He said he wad hae kent her mitherly luck amang a thoosan'. Bit she wus groun a arkmae. Sae that wus the selkie that deud no' forget. I wiss' a'bothy may mind on what's geud, as weel as that selkie.

WORKS CITED

Brown, George Mackay. *The Island of the Women and Other Stories.* London: John Murray, 1998.

Carson, Diane, ed. *John Sayles: Interviews.* Conversations with Filmmakers Series. Jackson: UP of Mississippi, 1999.

Derrida, Jacques. *Specters of Marx: The State of the Debt, the Work of Mourning, and the New International.* New York: Routledge, 1994.

Douglas, George Brisbane. *Scottish Fairy and Folk Tales.* London: W. Scott, 1901.

Douglas, Ronald MacDonald. *The Scottish Lore and Folklore.* New York: Beekman House, 1982. 112–13.

Giolláin, Diarmuid Ó. *Locating Irish Folklore: Tradition, Modernity, Identity.* Sterling: Cork University Press, 2000.

Glassie, Henry H. *Irish Folktales.* 1st ed. New York: Pantheon, 1985.

Gose, Elliott B. *The World of the Irish Wonder Tale: An Introduction to the Study of Fairy Tales.* Toronto: U of Toronto P, 1985.

Jameson, Fredric. *Postmodernism, or, The Cultural Logic of Late Capitalism.* Post-Contemporary Interventions. Durham: Duke UP, 1991.

Kidd, Kenneth B. *Making American Boys: Boyology and the Feral Tale.* Minneapolis: U of Minnesota P, 2004.

Ozaki, Yei Theodora. "The Story of Urashima Taro, the Fisher Lad." *The Japanese Fairy Book.* Rutland: C. E. Tuttle, 1970. 26.

Ryan, Jack. *John Sayles, Filmmaker: A Critical Study of the Independent Writer-Director.* Jefferson, NC: McFarland, 1998.

Sayles, John, and Gavin Smith. *Sayles on Sayles.* Boston: Faber and Faber, 1998.

The Secret of Roan Inish. Directed by John Sayles. First Look/Columbia TriStar, 1994. DVD.

Sprengnether, Madelon. *The Spectral Mother: Freud, Feminism, and Psychoanalysis.* Ithaca: Cornell UP, 1990.

Yanagita, Kunio. *The Yanagita Kunio Guide to the Japanese Folk Tale.* Ed. and trans. Fanny Hagin Mayer. Bloomington: Indiana UP, 1986.

Yeats, W. B. *Fairy and Folk Tales of Ireland.* 2nd ed. London: Picador, 1979.

———. *Fairy and Folk Tales of the Irish Peasantry.* London: W. Scott and T. Whittaker, 1888.

———. *Irish Fairy and Folk Tales.* New York: Boni and Liveright, 1918.

Yeats, W. B., and Robert Welch. *Writings on Irish Folklore, Legend, and Myth.* Penguin Twentieth-Century Classics. London: Penguin, 1993.

7

Oedipus Edits (*Lone Star*)

Susan Felleman

> Minnie Bledsoe: Sheriff Deeds is dead, honey. You just Sheriff, Jr.
> Sam Deeds: Yeah, that's the story of my life.
> *Lone Star*

"I was a psych major," says John Sayles, "and I read Freud and all that stuff, and I always felt, 'well, Freud is just great literature. These are wonderful metaphors for things that don't have any scientific basis, that are nice ideas, but they don't necessarily live their way out.' I was much more of a believer in behaviorism, in B. F. Skinner and that crowd, than I was in Freud, even though Freud was more attractive because his theories were wonderful stories" (Sayles and Smith 74). But *Lone Star*, Sayles's version of the Oedipus myth, suggests that his attitude toward Freudian ideas might be more complex. Sayles, in a number of interviews, seems to oscillate about the oedipal aspect of the film and seems to express an ambivalence in which metaphor and Freudian theory are conflated. He may dismiss Freud's "wonderful stories" as "just" good metaphor, but he also characterizes the theme of "fathers and sons" as the "best" metaphor for history (West and West 214) and elsewhere maintains that the father/son theme is too close to life to be considered a trope; it is "beyond metaphor" (Sayles and Smith 220). If the whole "father/son" thing seems to lack clarity for Sayles, I argue that this is precisely a function of "Freud and all that stuff" that he has too casually put aside.

As this essay will demonstrate, *Lone Star*—one of Sayles's best and most complex films—is also one of the best instantiations of Freudian theory on film, in terms of film form and film history. Yet, although he does not dispute Gavin Smith's characterization of *Lone Star* as a "reworking of a classic myth, the myth of Oedipus" (Sayles and Smith 218), Sayles never explicitly mentions the subject of Freud and psychoanalytic theory in relation to this or any other of his films.[1] This despite *Lone Star*'s overt thematization of primal ambivalence, oedipal conflict, and the incest taboo, as well as its formal articulation of basic principles of psychoanalysis, including the return of the repressed and the essential timelessness of the unconscious. But, as Freud pointed out, denial itself—tacit or explicit—is often a symptom. And even with its striking originality, *Lone Star* is a film with its own considerable Oedipus complex. Beyond the influences of detective fiction (specifically Hammett and Chandler), to which Sayles admits,[2] its cinematic influences, anxious or otherwise, would seem to include such monuments as Jean Renoir's *Grand Illusion*, Orson Welles's *Citizen Kane* and *Touch of Evil*, Roman Polanski's *Chinatown*, and especially John Ford's *The Man Who Shot Liberty Valance*. Indeed, *Liberty Valance* seems to provide the basic narrative template, the meaning of which Sayles's film transforms in an intriguing instance of what Harold Bloom—who has best articulated the oedipal element of artistic influence—might call *Tessera*, whereby a poet "antithetically 'completes' his precursor, by so reading the parent-poem as to retain its terms but to mean them in another sense" (Bloom 14).

Beyond Metaphor

Briefly, I should like to identify within *Lone Star*'s narrative the thematic nexus of Freudian thought, starting with the obvious Oedipus complex. Sam Deeds, the foremost of the film's protagonists, struggles with and against the oversized image (or imago) of his dead and legendary father, Buddy Deeds. Sam, having returned to Frontera, a Texas border town, after years away working for his father-in-law, all too ambivalently now occupies Buddy's job as county sheriff. Buddy's own legend, moreover, which begins with him having faced down—some forty years before—the county's domineering, corrupt, and evil sheriff, Charlie Wade, at some level suggests the kind of primordial uprising that Freud imagined in "Totem and Taboo," in which a band of exiled sons unites to kill and devour the violent, feared, and envied father of the Darwinian primal horde. The catalyst of *Lone Star*'s narrative is the uncovering of a body that turns out to be that of Charlie Wade. In his investigations into this very old crime, Sam interviews a number of Buddy's buddies, including two town patriarchs, Mayor Hollis Pogue and Frontera's leading African American businessman, the so-called mayor of Dark Town, Otis Payne. In the complex denouement of the film, Sam, who has been convinced from the outset that his father must have been Charlie Wade's murderer, finally learns that Buddy, Otis, and Hollis together were complicit in covering up the circumstances of Wade's death long ago. This element of Sayles's story is particularly resonant in terms of Freud. The fable—or allegory—of the origins of the Law that Freud proposed in "Totem and Taboo" took Darwin's speculations as a point of departure and posited a historical and phylogenetic relationship between the father's legend and the son's conflict:

> We need only suppose that the tumultuous mob of brothers were filled with the same contradictory feelings which we can see at work in the ambivalent father-complexes of our children and of our neurotic patients. They hated their father, who presented such a formidable obstacle to their craving for power and their sexual desires; but they loved and admired him too. After they had got rid of him, had satisfied their hatred and had put into effect their wish to identify themselves with him, the affection which had all this time been pushed under was bound to make itself felt. It did so in the form of remorse. A sense of guilt made its appearance, which in this instance coincided with the remorse felt by the whole group. The dead father became stronger than the living one had been—for events took the course we so often see them follow in human affairs to this day. What had up to then been prevented by his actual existence was thenceforward prohibited by the sons themselves . . . they revoked their deed by forbidding the killing of the totem, the substitute for their father; and they renounced its fruits by resigning their claim to the women who had now been set free. They thus created out of their filial sense of guilt the two fundamental taboos of totemism, which for that very reason inevitably corresponded to the two repressed wishes of the Oedipus complex [patricide and incest]. (Freud 1913, 142–43)

The same "contradictory feelings which we can see at work in the ambivalent father-complexes of our children" can also be seen in Sam Deeds, who tells Pilar—the childhood sweetheart he lost to the interventions of his good ol' boy father and her Chicana mother—"I spent my first fifteen years trying to be just like Buddy and the next fifteen trying to give him a heart attack." And Sam's not the only one with contradictory feelings. The film's diverse storylines are fraught with oedipal conflict and filial love/hate relationships, as with the three generations of Paynes: Otis; his estranged son Delmore, an army colonel who has been assigned charge of the local military base; and Delmore's teenage son, Chet, an artistic youth clearly oppressed by his father's militaristic austerity and rigid expectations who longs for a history and an identity that speak to him. Pilar, too, stands in an oedipal shadow. Her widowed mother is another formidable figure—a successful businesswoman who spares no compassion for the ungrateful "wetbacks" who surround her, who has the phone number of the border control committed to memory, and who gives little away about her own past. And Pilar, like her mother, is now a widow, with troubled teenage children of her own. There is also a brief glimpse of Sam's ex-wife, Bunny, whose Dallas Cowboy obsession is part of a bigger Daddy-thing, whose very name seems calculated to remind Sam of his father, Buddy, and whom Sayles describes as like "a warning to Sam. In twenty years she's going to be in that room, bouncing off the walls, talking about how, 'I loved my daddy, I hated my daddy.' He'll be five years dead in the ground and she will still be living in his shadow and she's never going to get out from under it" (West and West 217).

One of *Lone Star*'s most effective currents has to do with the way history—societal, familial, and psychic—is figured as always still present, the way the then and there weighs down on the protagonists of the here and now. Inchoate, inarticulate—or unarticulated—knowledge, experiences, and pressures are palpable in the exchanges between characters, and in their solitary, often sad, silences. Thus, by the time the film delivers the shocking revelation, that the joyously reunited lovers Sam and Pilar are in fact siblings—Buddy is the father of both—the shock we feel is both a function of the greatness of the taboo that has been breached *and* the disturbing suspicion that we knew this already. The lovers confirm it. Pilar says, "From the first time I saw you at school . . . all those years we were married to other people, I always felt like we were connected." What she felt may have been the force that is literalized, or embodied, by the discovery of Charlie Wade's bones, the will to expression of suppressed knowledge or impulses (psychic or social) that Freud termed "the return of the repressed." It turns out that Sam's official investigation into Wade's fate, an investigation we knew to be tainted by oedipal hostility, was also all the time an investigation into his own private history and family romances, with all their bewildering implications. Nothing could be more Freudian than this discovery, that the supposedly objective apprehension of history is at best ultimately a subjective comprehension of the irrational and passionate currents that flow between the self and the world.

Sayles puts this best when he describes *Lone Star* as a story about borders, in all the manifold implications of that term: not only geographical or spatial, but also personal, temporal, and psychic. "In a personal sense," he says, "a border is where you draw a line and say 'this is where I end and somebody else begins.' In a metaphorical sense, it can be any of the symbols that we erect between one another—sex, class, race, age" (West and West 210). Sayles's insight relates to the film's most eloquent formal expression of Freudian ideas in its innovative, deceptively simple incorporation of scenes from the past. It seems wrong to call them flashbacks, since in most instances they are not separated temporally or spatially from scenes in the present. Of the seven scenes from the past in the film, six use and four begin and end with camera movements that shift fluidly from action in the present to action in the past and then back, without editing. These "seamless" transitions are generally motivated by direct narration—the stories that emerge as part of Sam's investigation, as for instance the first such scene, in which Sam asks Mayor Hollis Pogue to relate his version of Buddy's legendary standoff with Charlie Wade. By means of visual ellipsis, past and present are staged within the same mise-en-scène, collapsing historical time and geographical space into one narrative fold, locating Sam at forty in a continuum with his father, Buddy, at twenty-five or so.[3] The camera moves away from the elderly Hollis and across a basket of tortillas, the interlocking weave of which feels like the nexus between now and then, as the camera proceeds to reveal Charlie Wade, a dead man, now alive, now forty years ago.

Asked about these "fluid transitions," Sayles says, "The purpose of a cut or a dissolve is to say this is a border, and the things on opposite sides of the border are meant to be different in some way, and I wanted to erase that border and show that these people are still reacting to things in the past" (West and West

Oedipus Edits (Lone Star)

213–14). In this context, Sayles extends further the metaphorical meaning of the "border." The geographical border is radically questioned in *Lone Star*, in dialogue such as that between Sam, who has gone to Ciudad Léon in Mexico, and Chucho Montoya, a witness to Charlie Wade's murder of Eladio Cruz (Mercedes's husband and, supposedly, Pilar's father). When Sam asks him about Cruz, Chucho draws a line in the dirt with his heel and asks Sam to step over it. Sam obliges and Chucho says, "*Ay, ¡qué milagro!* You're not the sheriff of nothing anymore—just some Tejano with a lot of questions I don't have to answer. Bird flying south—you think he sees that line? Rattlesnake, javelina—whatever you got—halfway across that line they don't start thinking different. So why should a man?"

Beyond the geographical and the geopolitical, *Lone Star* reexamines the more metaphorical borders too, those boundaries between people, based on "sex, class, race, age," and along with these, the boundaries between past and present. The "seamless" or "fluid" transitions through which Sayles seeks to erase or belie the passage of time express one of Freud's most important assertions about the nature of the unconscious: "The processes of the system Ucs are *timeless:* i.e. they are not ordered temporally, are not altered by the passage of time; they have no reference to time at all" (Freud 1915, 187). This same insight is eloquently suggested by a quotation from William Faulkner meaningfully cited in an article about *Lone Star:* "The past isn't dead. It isn't even past" (Erickson). Sayles uses the magical properties of the cinematic medium to achieve a visual corollary to the rhetorical condensation of topographical space and historical time that he expressed in describing "edits" (e.g., dissolves, cuts) as "borders" and also achieves something that Freud attempted, unsuccessfully, to imagine in "Civilization and Its Discontents": "If we want to represent historical sequence in spatial terms," Freud wrote, "we can only do it by juxtaposition in space: the same space cannot have two different contents ... how far we are from mastering the characteristics of mental life by representing them in pictorial terms" (Freud 1930, 70–71).

But *Lone Star* does give the same space two different contents and thus succeeds in finding pictorial terms for mental phenomena. The film expresses the essential timelessness of the unconscious at every level: the social and historical as well as the personal ("How come it feels the same?" Pilar asks Sam when they've made love again after twenty-three years). The film ends with a resolution on the part of Sam and Pilar to defy the prohibition against incest. Although the ending is somewhat ambiguous, Sayles has claimed that the two lovers are about to make a profoundly antisocial decision: "they choose to cross that border," he says (West and West 215–16), extending even further the metaphorical properties of this term. "Forget the Alamo," Pilar says, perversely. She is, after all, a history teacher. Although Sayles adopts a rationalist, iconoclastic posture toward humankind's most universal and sacred taboo and inquires, although only after establishing that Pilar cannot have any more children, along with and on behalf of his screen lovers, "OK, what exactly is that rule?" the film must end where it does.[4] Who could tolerate the knowing exercise of incestuous passion? Its very exposure, however, is a testament to a world in which history is proved to be a timeless, always present, if always also forgotten, source of strangely obscure and irrational deeds and impulses that *do* "live their way out," as Sayles would put it—that shape the individual subject no less than the family, the community, and the society at large.

Just Great Literature?

"When the legend becomes fact, print the legend."
The Man Who Shot Liberty Valance

"Buddy's a goddamn legend. He can handle it."
Lone Star

Lone Star's oedipal concerns are not limited to those of its characters. The film works in the shadows of legends, much as its protagonist Sam Deeds does. As has been noted, *Lone Star*'s use of ellipsis is indebted to Orson Welles's in *Citizen Kane*, and so is its larger narrative strategy—the piecing together of a puzzle retrospectively through interviews that motivate the nonlinear sequence of scenes from the past.[5] In a deeply ideological sense, *Lone Star* owes much to Jean Renoir, again at the level of style and content. The essentially realist aesthetic of Sayles's work and his complex, interlocking narratives generally can be said to be descendants of Renoir. Sayles's films often employ long takes and a fluid, organic framing, similar to techniques Renoir used to attend to the strands of his sometimes-multitudinous stories. More specifically, *Lone Star*'s story seems to nod to *Grand Illusion*'s humanism and sense of absurdity. Chucho Montoya's discourse on national borders echoes the conclusion of Renoir's film, in which the French heroes are spared as they escape across an invisible national border in the snow. And *Lone Star* also echoes *Le crime de Monsieur Lange*, with its sympathetic murder of a loathsome tyrant and its Popular Front–inspired image of community.

If Renoir's influence—ideological and aesthetic—is evident in Sayles's oeuvre generally, *Lone Star* itself has other antecedents that signal its profound engagement with issues of genre. Sayles has directly acknowledged *Chinatown*'s script as influential on *Lone Star*'s for the kind of balance it achieves between the mechanics of a good detective story ("Hammett") and more complex, atmospheric, and psychological virtues ("Chandler"). Perhaps he does not need to note the striking "relationship" between the two films' revelatory denouements, but I shall: in *Chinatown* the imposing, corrupt Father is guilty of murder; in *Lone Star* he is absolved. But in both films, incest is the astonishing collateral revelation.

Two films stand out in *Lone Star*'s family tree, as its generic parents, so to speak: Welles's *Touch of Evil* (detective story) and John Ford's *The Man Who Shot Liberty Valance* (western).[6] One can almost see their ghostly traces playing on the empty, decaying drive-in theater screen that is the tabula rasa Sam and Pilar contemplate at the end of *Lone Star*—the same torn screen that Kim Magowan has described as "the objective correlative of their ambivalence" (27). It is certainly a testament to Sayles's strength and originality as a writer and director that he merges the profound narrative and thematic influences of these two masterpieces of his childhood (he would have been about eight and twelve, respectively, in 1958 and 1962, the years in which these were released) into a film that is very different in style and meaning from both.

Lone Star inherits from *Touch of Evil* (which was based on a Whit Masterson novel called *Badge of Evil*) the ugly and frightening figure of the Law corrupted, embodied by Welles himself, as physically repugnant police captain Hank Quinlan, and in Sayles's film by the morally grotesque county sheriff Charlie Wade, played by Kris Kristofferson. A striking common plot element has Quinlan and Wade finally stopped in their abuses and excesses, shot, by their own trusted deputies, Pete Menzies and Hollis Pogue, respectively. And, though not as viciously as Welles does with Vargas, Sayles also probes the righteousness of Sam Deeds, his essentially upright protagonist, who like Charlton Heston's character has a chip on his shoulder and a dangerous blind spot. But most striking is the way that both films mobilize the location of the U.S.-Mexican border as a metaphor that extends deeply into the cinematic project. As Terry Comito puts it:

> Welles's most fundamental theme, from the opening sequence on, is the crossing of boundaries; or rather, the impossibility of sustaining an effective boundary between a world we recognize as normal and a realm of violence at once uncanny and, as in a dream, disquietingly familiar.... The most precarious boundary is one overseen by no friendly customs man. It is the boundary between the apparent solidity of our rational daylight world and the dark labyrinth in which, if we yield to its solicitations, we will lose our way. Welles's "Mexico" is a place of the soul. (11–12)

Comito's characterization of Welles's undertaking makes it clear why, even as it shares *Touch of Evil*'s central problematization of law and borders, *Lone Star* opposes itself to Welles's nihilistic vision of a world in which the irrational threatens to subsume all. And the style of Sayles's film illuminates its opposition to Welles's. In *Lone Star* the boundaries between good and evil, self and other, between past and present, between racial and other social groups are blurred, or elided, but not obliterated. The boundaries that Welles explores, between good and evil, light and darkness, between material and psychic realities, are shattered in *Touch of Evil*. Welles's film achieves this shattering through the violent, "baroque" handling of spatial and visual relations.

Although it is entirely possible to imagine a character undertaking the kind of journey that Sam Deeds does in *Lone Star*—a journey that causes him to radically question his understanding of his own community, family, and sexual history—sucked into a vortex such as that into which *Touch of Evil* descends, that is not Sayles's objective. And the stylistic contrast between the two films underscores the essential realism of Sayles's vision in relation to the surrealism of Welles's. *Lone Star* is a version of the Oedipus myth, but it is also a film about race relations and police corruption, which are social and historical realities to Sayles. His story acknowledges but will not be overwhelmed by the irrational. Thus, while *Touch of Evil* is set in a disorienting and seemingly endless night and represents time as a tense and finite force—a ticking time bomb—*Lone Star*'s spatial and temporal fields are more balanced, measured, and contemplative.

Time has very different implications in Quinlan's world and Sam Deeds's. To Quinlan, the past *is* dead, to invert Faulkner's maxim. The events that embittered and corrupted him are inexorably past (his wife's murder, the shot he took for Menzies). The past is dead and there is no future, for as in so many noirs, there are no children. There's no Quinlan Jr. to reflect on his ambivalent legacy. As the gypsy Tanya (Dietrich) puts it when Quinlan asks her to read his fortune, "You haven't got any. Your future is all used up." This is a fundamental difference between *Lone Star*—which is so intent on mapping the relationships that take its story beyond the boundaries of the film—and the classic genre film whose themes it adopts. Genre films articulate larger cultural problems but cannot step out of their mythic frames into the world. Sam Deeds visits the border town of Welles's nightmare but need not spend eternity there. He returns to a dynamic, living society where history and the clash of cultures demand more than representation.

Perhaps no two masters of American cinema could be more different than Orson Welles and John Ford. But the past is dead, too, in *Lone Star*'s other mighty progenitor, Ford's elegy to the western, *The Man Who Shot Liberty Valance*. In fact, the past has just died, in the person of Tom Doniphon, whose funeral motivates the retrospective plot. *Lone Star* is, of course, a western as much as it is a detective story, and its theme has as much to do with the idea of legend as with that of borders. It is the retrospective examination of a legend in the making, as well as contemplation of the poignant fallacy of legends, that *Lone Star* inherits from *The Man Who Shot Liberty Valance*. Intriguingly, both films are characterized as "critiques" by one authoritative source. In his *International Dictionary of Films and Filmmakers* entry on *The Man Who Shot Liberty Valance*, Douglas Gomery describes the film as "a great filmmaker's own critique of the form in which he did his best work" (734). Philip Kemp's entry on *Lone Star* revises his *Sight and Sound* review of 1996, in which he was probably the first to note the narratological relationship between Sayles's and Ford's films. *Lone Star*'s "overall structure, and especially its final revelation, come so close to the crux of *The Man Who Shot Liberty Valance*," observes Kemp, "that it can only be intentional. The whole film, in fact, could be read as a covert critique of the earlier movie: where John Ford saw the passing of the old gun-law West as a matter for nostalgia and regret, Sayles celebrates the growth in tolerance and civic order it represents" (708).

If *The Man Who Shot Liberty Valance* is to be characterized by Gomery and many others as a critique, then *Lone Star* is a critique of a critique—a metacritique. The parallels that emerge from the source are twisted in *Lone Star*. The dreaded figure whose elimination is cause for such legendary remembrance, for instance, is portrayed in both films as evil incarnate: a sociopath. But while Liberty Valance is an outlaw—and stands archetypically for the wild, lawlessness of the Old West in the dialectical picture that the classic western draws—Charlie Wade is The Law. Sayles, by this inversion, gives the lie to the western myth. Righteousness is not always on the side of the law. *Lone Star* insists on the fuzziness of the border between right and wrong, law and crime. It shows honest "criminals" and dishonest law enforcers, and explores the motivations of those who transgress, as well as the rationale of the law. Buddy Deeds's old friend, Wesley Birdsong, tells Sam about Buddy's wild days after returning to Frontera from military service in Korea. "If he hadn't found a deputy's job, I believe Buddy might have gone down the other path," Birdsong muses, "gotten into serious trouble." This may be a common wisdom of our culture, but in some respects it is antithetical to the western myth. As Robert Warshow noted, the western hero embodies a kind of natural law:

> What does the Westerner fight for? We know he is on the side of justice and order, and of course it can be said he fights for these things. . . . If justice and order did not continually demand his protection, he would be without a calling. Indeed, we come upon him often in just that situation, as the reign of law settles over the West and he is forced to see that his day is over; those

are the pictures which end with his death or with his departure for some remote frontier. (Warshow 457)

But Ford's film seems to acknowledge the ambiguous territory between law and lawlessness, in fact to embody it in its most mythic character, Doniphon, who is, structurally speaking, exactly as close to the outlaw, Valance, as he is to the man of the law book, Stoddard. As Thomas Schatz points out, Doniphon's function within the process of mythmaking is to mediate between "Valance's primitive savagery and Stoddard's naïve idealism" (Schatz 78).

In a sense, Buddy Deeds serves the same function in *Lone Star*. He mediates structurally between the corrupt sheriff (Wade) and the righteous one (Sam). His son sees him as an abuser of power and as a cold-blooded murderer (which Doniphon termed himself)—as "The Man Who Shot Charlie Wade," so to speak. And indeed, Buddy's legend was built on having stood up to Wade, and he was credited with chasing him out of town (although not killing him). Here is another of Sayles's perhaps not so covert rereadings of Ford's myth. Like Ransom Stoddard's, Buddy Deeds's legend is built on a lie. "People liked the story we told better than anything the truth might have been," rues Hollis Pogue. But in Ford's legendary moment of the making of the West, a man's career as a lawmaker could be built on the lie that he had murdered a villain, whereas in the originary moment of Sayles's film, another man's career as law enforcer and leader could be destroyed by the truth that he had killed one. There are many twists in Sayles's remapping of Ford's terrain, then. Buddy, though parallel to Doniphon, is *not* really "The Man Who Shot Charlie Wade." The man who did—Hollis Pogue, the other, mild-mannered, less mythic, even rather cowering deputy—quietly went on to a successful political career.

Lone Star acknowledges the power of the legends to which society clings ("The day that man died," says Cody, the bartender, about Buddy Deeds, "they broke the goddamn mold") and the messiness of the realities that engender them. This is where it revolts against the bittersweet vision of Ford's late film. Again, as with *Touch of Evil*, the turning away from the source is effected foremost through stylistic choices. It is often remarked that *The Man Who Shot Liberty Valance* differs from many of Ford's westerns in its eschewal of location; it was shot almost wholly on a studio soundstage. As Gomery observes, the "narrative framework, the stark stylization of mise-en-scène, and the use of lighting render the flashback (and the flashback in the flashback) into nightmare. This is a stripped down western; the colorful legend and look of Monument Valley have become a barren world of broken dreams" (Gomery 734). In contrast, *Lone Star*'s narration and mise-en-scène are expansive, polyphonic, and diverse. To *Liberty Valance*'s one storyteller—Ranse Stoddard, who tells his tale in straightforward, unilinear progression, from beginning to end—*Lone Star* offers many tellers (Hollis Pogue, Minnie Bledsoe, Otis Payne, Chucho Montoya, Wesley Birdsong, and others) of nonlinear, often-overlapping fragments and versions of a tale that it is left for Sam and the audience to fit together. To the stagy, artificial, almost claustrophobic, black-and-white set of *Liberty Valance*, *Lone Star* offers, with relatively naturalistic color cinematography, an array of actual places—not mythic or spectacular locations like Monument Valley—in and around Del Rio, a typical Texas border town. The most dramatic contrast, though, is between the two films' framing of the narration. Ford's film graphically demarcates flashbacks in conventional ways, as recollection, while Sayles's film, through those seamless edits, visually folds the past into the present. There is no stylistic breach between past and present because the film refuses to give the past a different look, nostalgic or otherwise. To do so would thwart Sayles's desire to "erase that border and show that these people are still reacting to things in the past" (West and West 214).

So, as with *Touch of Evil*, *Lone Star* inherits thematically and structurally from *The Man Who Shot Liberty Valance*, but ultimately, as Bloom reminds us that strong art must, misreads or rewrites these themes and structures. As Laura Mulvey summarizes in her application of Proppian structuralism to the morphology of the western, in *The Man Who Shot Liberty Valance*, "the tension between two points of attraction, the symbolic (social integration and marriage) and nostalgic narcissism, generates a . . . splitting of the Western hero into two. . . . Here two functions emerge, one celebrating integration into society through marriage, the *other* celebrating resistance to social demands and responsibilities, above all those of marriage and the family." She demonstrates that with this splitting, in Ford's drama,

> The issue at stake is no longer how the villain will be defeated, but how the villain's defeat will be inscribed into history, whether the *upholder* of the law as symbolic system [Ranse/Jimmy Stewart] will be seen to be victorious or the *personification* of the law in a more primitive manifestation [Tom/John Wayne], closer to the good or the right. *Liberty Valance* as it uses a flashback structure, also brings out the poignancy of this tension. The "present-tense" story is precipitated by a funeral, so that the story is shot through with nostalgia and sense of loss. (Mulvey 34)

In *Lone Star* a villain is defeated, and the film is concerned with how this event becomes inscribed in history, but there is not so much clarity regarding the relative virtues of the villain's possible killer. Wade, Deeds, and Pogue are all supposed upholders of law, and to the extent that they manifest more primitive (narcissistic) qualities, the film presents them as abusers of the law, not its personification. Or, if Buddy Deeds does personify the law, then the law is an ambivalent abstraction, not a purely virtuous one. Thus the splitting in *Lone Star* is more oedipal. Instead of being doubled synchronically—as with the peer dyad, Ranse/Tom—*Lone Star*'s protagonists are doubled diachronically/generationally, with the father/son dyad, Buddy/Sam. This reinforces the essentially Freudian concept of the Father, who for his always ambivalent son both personifies the law and symbolizes it. If *Touch of Evil* and *The Man Who Shot Liberty Valance* are masterpieces of reflections upon genre, *Lone Star* is perhaps best seen as an oedipal engagement with genre itself. As Sam Deeds wears the hat and badge of his legendary father, but declines to carry his gun, the film around him also adopts the structuring and thematic trappings of its forebears, but strives to achieve a more tolerant, realist, and less mythic paradigm. The persistence of genre is the perpetuation of myths. The myths that it perpetuates are invisible parts of the status quo. It might be more precise, then, to say that Sayles wishes to go not beyond metaphor, but beyond genre: to demystify. But this demystification has an oedipal attitude. Cinematically and metacinematically, *Lone Star* is full of tensions, as well as insights, that can hardly be comprehended without the work that its author has called "nice ideas," "wonderful stories," "just great literature."

NOTES

1. For a study of the film's relationship to its classical source, see Bakewell.
2. "In my movies, very often there's a spine, which is the genre story, that's almost generic, but not quite. Here it's a detective story. But it's only a spine, it's not the most important thing. It's like the difference between Dashiell Hammett and Raymond Chandler. Hammett is very thin on the page, and it really is about who did what to whom, whereas with Chandler it's about the trip. When you can join the two of them—which is why *Chinatown* is such a good script—you're really doing something good" (Sayles, qtd. in Ryan 213).
3. On ellipsis as part of an "ethical" aesthetic, see Davis and Womack.
4. For a compelling reading of the way Sayles tries to create "a loophole which makes the taboo violable" and "incest, like miscegenation, gets recast . . . as a social prejudice, a 'rule' open to question," see Magowan.
5. The influence of *Citizen Kane* is mentioned by more than one critic, including Kemp's review in *Sight and Sound* (48) and Ryan (229, 240).
6. In an excellent, probing analysis of *Lone Star*, which I was unaware of when I originally wrote this essay despite its rather obvious parallels to my argument, Sam Girgus also connects the film to Freudian theory and makes a case for the influence of two other movies belonging to the period of Sayles's childhood, "two major films of 1956, John Ford's *The Searchers* and George Stevens's *Giant*, that also present Texas as a metaphor for America" (50).

WORKS CITED

Bakewell, Geoffrey W. "Oedipus Tex: *Lone Star*, Tragedy, and Postmodernism." *Classical and Modern Literature* 22.1 (2002): 35–48.

Bloom, Harold. *The Anxiety of Influence: A Theory of Poetry*. Oxford: Oxford UP, 1973.

Comito, Terry. "Welles's Labyrinths: An Introduction to *Touch of Evil*." Touch of Evil: *Orson Welles, Director*. Ed. Terry Comito. New Brunswick: Rutgers UP, 1985. 3–33.

Davis, Todd F., and Kenneth Womack. "Forget the Alamo: Reading the Ethics of Style in John Sayles's *Lone Star*." *Style* 32 (Fall 1998): 471–85.

Erickson, Ingrid M. "*Lone Star*: A Film by John Sayles," 1998. http://www.uwm.edu/People/ime/lonestarhomepage.htm. 15 February 2005.

Freud, Sigmund. "Civilization and Its Discontents." *The Standard Edition of the Complete Psychological Works of Sigmund Freud*. 1930. Trans. and ed. James Strachey. Vol. 21. London: Hogarth, 1961. 64–145.

———. "Totem and Taboo." 1913. *The Standard Edition of the Complete Psychological Works of Sigmund Freud.* Trans. and ed. James Strachey. Vol. 13. London: Hogarth, 1955. 1–162.

———. "The Unconscious." 1915. *The Standard Edition of the Complete Psychological Works of Sigmund Freud.* Trans. and ed. James Strachey. Vol. 14. London: Hogarth, 1957. 166–215.

Girgus, Sam B. "*Lone Star:* An Archeology of American Culture and the American Psyche." *America on Film: Modernism, Documentary, and a Changing America.* Cambridge: Cambridge UP, 2002. 40–64.

Gomery, Douglas. "The Man Who Shot Liberty Valance." *International Dictionary of Films and Filmmakers.* 4th ed. [Vol. 1, Films]. Detroit: St. James, 2000. 734.

Kemp, Philip. "*Lone Star.*" *International Dictionary of Films and Filmmakers.* 4th ed. [Vol. 1, Films]. Detroit: St. James, 2000. 708.

———. Review of *Lone Star. Sight and Sound* 6 (October 1996): 47–48.

Magowan, Kim. "'Blood Only Means What You Let It': Incest and Miscegenation in John Sayles's *Lone Star.*" *Film Quarterly* 57.1 (2003): 20–31.

Mulvey, Laura. "Afterthoughts on 'Visual Pleasure and Narrative Cinema' Inspired by *Duel in the Sun.*" *Visual and Other Pleasures.* Bloomington: Indiana UP, 1989 [originally published 1981]. 29–38.

Ryan, Jack. *John Sayles, Filmmaker: A Critical Study of the Independent Writer-Director.* Jefferson, NC: McFarland, 1998.

Sayles, John, and Gavin Smith. *Sayles on Sayles.* London: Faber and Faber, 1998.

Schatz, Thomas. *Hollywood Genres.* New York: Random House, 1981.

Warshow, Robert. "Movie Chronicle: The Westerner." *Film Theory and Criticism.* Ed. Leo Braudy and Marshall Cohen. 5th ed. Oxford: Oxford UP, 1999. 453–66.

West, Dennis, and Joan M. West. "Borders and Boundaries: An Interview with John Sayles." *John Sayles: Interviews.* Ed. Diane Carson. Conversations with Filmmakers Series. Jackson: UP of Mississippi, 1999. 210–18.

8

Men in Context: Gender in *Matewan* and *Men With Guns*

Klaus Rieser

John Sayles's oeuvre is often characterized as being progressive in terms of race, class, and ethnicity as well as for its portrayal of common people. Yet in terms of gender, his films are more inconclusive: While some of them feature female protagonists (for example, *Lianna*, *Passion Fish*, *Roan Inish*), others accommodate ambivalent or even conservative gender features. In this essay, I trace the gender scenarios in two of Sayles's films—*Matewan* and *Men With Guns*—in their heterogeneous and often contradictory implications. On the one hand, these films have distinct patriarchal aspects, such as the central position of white male heroes or the reliance upon oedipal trajectories. On the other hand, such conservative components are offset by more resistant elements that are intertwined with issues of gender: a contextualization of such features that undermines patriarchy, a vigilant attention to socioeconomic relations and power struggles, and a dedication to antihegemonic narratives. My intention, then, is to analyze the very specific configuration of hegemony's constituent elements (gender, race, and class), in particular the construction of gender in relation to ethnically and economically marginalized groups, in two representative Sayles films. I intend to unpack how, although in many ways his work is complicit with a hegemonic gender regime, Sayles is able to promote alternative masculinities through resistant characters and subversive story elements. In the criticism of patriarchal elements, I refer to well-established feminist and profeminist theories by Mulvey, Neale, and Willemen. Regarding the more subversive story elements, I rely mostly on a close reading of the two films and concepts of masculinities proposed by Robert Connell, an Australian-based sociologist who writes on masculinity.[1]

Patriarchal Structures

One of the most obvious patriarchal characteristics of both *Matewan* and *Men With Guns* is their problematic portrayal of women. Underrepresented and marginalized, female characters are given significantly less screen time than the male characters and are of less importance to the narrative. Furthermore, they are portrayed primarily in relation to the central male characters: Elma Radnor in *Matewan* is defined as Danny's mother and serves as a love interest for Joe Kenehan, as does the other female secondary character, Bridey Mae Tolliver. The women are in many ways the stock figures of patriarchy: Bridey is a sort of dim-witted town flirt, who turns to treason when rejected by the hero, while Elma Radnor, who "naturally" is also in love with Joe, is the retrograde stereotype of a good woman: the mother to a son. Consequently, *Matewan* recirculates the most pernicious dichotomy for female characters—as mother or whore. Similarly, Graciela in *Men With Guns* offers little challenge to such conservative representation. Out of the five major characters she is the only woman, and again is given the least screen time. She is resolutely depicted as a victim, traumatized and mute, and therefore—despite the sympathy the film creates for her—is also muted within the film, unable to speak for herself and to add her story to those of the other characters. In contrast, each film devotes much screen time to the two respective "male ensembles": In *Matewan*, Sheriff Sid Hatfield, Mayor Cabell Testermann, the miner Sephus Purcell, the Italian Fausto, the African American Few Clothes Johnson, plus the company spy C. E. Lively and the Baldwin-Felts agents who are the villains. In *Men With Guns*, the group comprises the orphaned boy, the AWOL soldier, and the fugitive priest, and most of the minor characters are male.

Most problematically, however, the protagonists of both films, Kenehan and Dr. Fuentes, operate as the primary figures for spectator identification because they are, like ourselves, only visitors to the worlds depicted in the film, serving as our guide to the respective social, historical, and geographic environments. This narrative strategy invites us to make a culturally preconstituted connection between the hero and a normative masculinity. As Connell has suggested, the figure of the hero—whether dominant or victimized—is central to the Western cultural imagery of the masculine (213). The resulting spontaneous association of heroism with masculinity, endlessly repeated in high as well as popular culture, endows male characters such as Kenehan or Fuentes with a naturalized authority, whereas in fact such power is a result of patriarchy. Although neither Kenehan nor Fuentes are immediately accepted as authority figures within the narrative, they quickly become focal figures in the diegesis, a consequence the films attribute to their ethical stance and moral stamina, but which is actually a patriarchal dividend.[2]

In addition to the unequal screen time devoted to male characters in comparison with the female and the positioning of the protagonists as key identificatory figures for the spectator, *Matewan*'s and *Men With Guns*'s oedipal narratives focus on a male succession achieved via the exclusion of women. In *Matewan*, the young miner/preacher Danny eventually succeeds Joe Kenehan within the narrative (as union organizer) as well as on the textual level (as locus of our point of view), for it is revealed at the end of the film that the offscreen narrator is actually Danny as an old man. In fact, the succession is classically oedipal, since Danny not only comes to take up Joe's position, but is also—like the mythical Oedipus—responsible for Kenehan's death in that he participates in the final shoot-out between the miners and the hired detective agents during which Kenehan, who has attempted to forestall this fight, is gunned down. Then, after Kenehan's death, Danny steps into his shoes, converting to pacifist union work. Dr. Fuentes in *Men With Guns* actually does have a daughter of his own, but is more concerned that his professional legacy be continued by his former students in the countryside. After starting his investigation into their whereabouts, his daughter is dropped from the narrative altogether. Instead, Dr. Fuentes picks up an orphaned boy and an AWOL soldier, to whom he eventually passes on his medical equipment.

Further, both films foreground another aspect that film theorists such as Laura Mulvey and Steve Neale have identified as patriarchal: male narcissism. In her article "Afterthoughts on 'Visual Pleasure and Narrative Cinema' Inspired by *Duel in the Sun*," Mulvey points out that unlike the Proppian Russian folk tale, the western hero has two options at the end of every narrative (33–34). He can either (as in the traditional plot analyzed by Propp) enter the symbolic through marriage, thereby gaining his "rightful" place in patriarchy, or he can reject the princess and remain aloof. The latter, most often embodied in the figure of the lonely hero riding out into the sunset in the film western, indicates, according to Mulvey, a nostalgic celebration of narcissistic omnipotence. While such a construction of the superactive male hero is a staple of various Hollywood genres, it is particularly evident in the western's glorification of the lonely white male hero. *Matewan*, which stylistically and narratively takes up the western formula, is no exception: Joe Kenehan rejects the flirtatious Bridey Mae and remains distant from the serious love interest Elma. His superior morals, which remain untainted by the triviality of common romantic bonds, further consolidate his narcissistic position. We cannot be sure whether Joe in the end would have succumbed to the lures of patriarchal family values and entered the symbolic by uniting with Edna, because he dies in the end. But throughout the film, he resists the obvious temptation. Thus, while on the surface he departs from the narcissistic western hero—pacifist rather than gunslinger, union organizer rather than pioneer, cowboy, or sheriff, herald of modernism rather than representative of the vanishing frontier—structurally he fits the mold of the narcissistic male hero described by Mulvey and others very well: restrained, silent, socially removed, guided by his own code of honor rather than law-abiding, brave, and so on. The same male narcissistic flight from women (first identified by Leslie Fiedler as a characteristic of American narratives) is also typical of the road movie/quest story, the structural basis of *Men With Guns*. In fact, here the hero had been integrated in society but gradually opts out. In fact, despite Dr. Fuentes's age, he follows the typical quest trajectory from innocence to knowledge usually reserved for adolescent characters. And he, too, conforms on a deeper level to what feminist criticism has revealed as narcissism.

Moreover, despite their compassion for other human beings, both heroes also prove to be tough guys who disregard their own physical safety: Kenehan continues to follow his quest although he is in danger of being killed by either side (the company or the coal miners), and Dr. Fuentes repeatedly makes light of the *hombres armados*. Being agents rather than victims, Kenehan and Dr. Fuentes exhibit the very heroic masochism that is a fundamental element of the most sacred occidental iconography: the bruised and battered male body as we know it from Jesus Christ via many of the Sebastian-style saints to the modern-day Rambos. The suffering inflicted on these characters is—again—not the suffering of victims (this position being reserved for the subordinated and marginalized) but instead is transformed into an attestation of virility, since it is presented as a willful choice, by which the hero, putting mind over matter, attains ultimate control over his (physically vulnerable) self. Both Joe Kenehan and Dr. Fuentes show such a power of will, such a subjugation of the body, for example by remaining steadfast in the face of armed opponents. The difference between the two lies mostly in that Joe suffers above all from a psychic torment: constant danger from thugs and the law, a distrustful sheriff, unreliable workers, inability to establish intimate connections because of the transitory and dangerous nature of his work. Dr. Fuentes is suffering bodily, much in the "saintly" manner described above: despite his failing health, despite the danger, and despite the continuing loss of his privileges, he pursues his goal.[3]

In sum, one can criticize Sayles's films for their tendency to conceal hegemony. Behind the apparent progressive veneer—the critique of the ruthless socioeconomic warfare in either West Virginia or Central America—the films foster a patriarchal gender politics. The superior morals attributed to the heroes of *Matewan* and *Men With Guns* are, one might argue, an implicit attempt to rehabilitate the "good white male." Both in *Matewan* and in *Men With Guns* the hero—despite his shortcomings (Dr. Fuentes's initial ignorance of the social strife in his country)—ultimately turns out to be an incarnation of the civil and humanitarian figure who always presents a genteel manner toward the natives. This is reminiscent of Connell's conclusion that advocacy of the patriarchal order does not necessarily require an explicit masculinity politics (212). Rather than joining an openly sexist or patriarchal vanguard, most men—and most representations of men—only implicitly foster ideas about superior masculinity. *Matewan* and *Men With Guns* do not, for instance, insist that men are more potent than women and therefore in charge of the latter's personal safety. Neither do the films claim that men are smarter than women and therefore legitimately in control of defining the terms of a common social and political utopia. Nonetheless, this is what these narratives suggest, whereas a more genuinely gender-democratic script would make room for women to speak about their own alternative social scenarios and political utopias.

Countering a Patriarchal Focus: Context, Ensemble Casting, and Social Relations

Despite the gender conservatism exhibited by *Matewan* and *Men With Guns* I have discussed above, these films in other ways mitigate the focus on the male hero, dismantling in particular the issue of male narcissism. Of particular importance in this regard is the focus on context, ensemble casting, diversity, and social relations—all Sayles trademarks.

The significance of context is first of all established by the location of the films. Sayles often uses unusual geographic settings—the Texan-Mexican border (*Lone Star*), Harlem (*Brother from Another Planet*), the bayous of Louisiana (*Passion Fish*), Alaska (*Limbo*), West Virginia (*Matewan*), or a Central American jungle (*Men With Guns*).[4] These disparate, neglected, or otherwise peripheral settings, however, never just serve as exotic backdrops but are paramount to the story in that their economic and social characteristics comprise the backbone of the narrative. For example, in *Men With Guns* we do not roam the jungle alongside Dr. Fuentes merely for picturesque sightseeing purposes as the American tourists in the film do, but rather are immersed in the lives of its inhabitants.[5] The characters we encounter (peasants, an orphan, a soldier, a priest, and so on) as well as the institutions and elements of the society they represent (the bourgeoisie, the church, the medical profession, the military, the guerrilla, the children, the indigenous farmers) have their own agendas that continue far beyond the encounter with Dr. Fuentes. Some may simply want to survive, or gain independence, while others want to fight oppression, run from their past or return to it, find work in the city, seek a hopeful future, maintain their precarious hold on power, revolutionize the peasants, reap a profit, or subdue a rebellion. Since their pursuits are deeply political, the films' attention to location also exposes power as it is distributed and fought over in these respective areas. And although both films present a struggle over gun power (be it wielded by the military, guerillas, company guards, detective agents, or the sheriff), ultimately the struggle (fought by means of speeches, preaching, argumentation, symbolic behavior, personal dedication, lies, spying, and so on) is over people's minds—over hegemony, that is—rather than over arms.

Context is further dramatized by a pronounced emphasis on music in these films. The soundtrack of *Matewan*, for example, ranges from a mournful Christian ballad to Italian workers' songs, from bluegrass music to the blues. Sayles carries this aspect to its logical conclusion in one scene, in which the camera moves from an African American playing a harmonica to an Italian strumming a mandolin to a mountain man fiddling a tune. They are all playing different melodies, and then suddenly, linked by editing, they comprise a harmonious trio playing the solidarity song. In *Men With Guns*, the soundtrack is perhaps even more important: paralleling the story's movement from city to backcountry and its emphasis on regional diversity, the soundtrack is a genuine amalgam of native and Latin styles, incorporating elements from urban and rural music, ranging from classical to popular, from Inca tones to Salsa tunes. Like locality, music is not just an emotional carpet for the narrative, but instead parallels and reinforces the stories' focus on diversity and context.

An emphasis on locality, a complex musical soundtrack, and other formal elements such as nonintrusive camerawork play an essential role in constructing a tight web of meaning around the central characters, but the single strongest element of contextualization is the sheer number and diversity of characters. This element in particular distinguishes Sayles's films from the standard Hollywood product, which favors the depiction of single individuals over a portrayal of a multitude of figures. In most of his films, secondary characters are well rounded and get a disproportionate amount of screen time. Sayles has gone to an extreme in this regard in the film *City of Hope*, where he interweaves various narratives with over twenty equally central characters (see Greg M. Smith's essay in this anthology). *Matewan*, while less extreme, nonetheless has the following otherwise "secondary" characters carry important story functions: the young miner-preacher Danny Radnor, his mother Elma Radnor, the leader of the black miners Few Clothes Johnson, the spokesperson for the Italians Fausto, the no-nonsense miner Sephus Purcell, the young widow Bridey Mae Tolliver, the sheriff Sid Hatfield, the town mayor Cabell Testerman, and last, but not least, the bad guys: the company spy C. E. Lively and the Baldwin-Felts agents Bill Hickey and Tom Griggs. Moreover, there is a small narrative strand with two other secondary characters — the local miner's widow Mrs. Elkins and the Italian immigrant Rosaria—which, although quite short, is very important on a symbolic level (their exchange is detailed below).

Similarly, in *Men With Guns*, Dr. Fuentes picks up an ersatz-family, made up of heterogeneous and complex characters. It is this group of characters—Conejo, the orphaned boy and scout to Dr. Fuentes; Domingo, the AWOL soldier and eventual successor; Padre Portillo, the runaway priest; Graciela, the mute woman; and Andrew and Harriet, the American tourists—that drives the storyline. Sayles has sometimes been criticized for his use of multiple characters, which supposedly are not well integrated in the narrative (see Kemp, Ryan, and Wilson), although other critics and reviewers (Ebert and Maltin) praise the films enthusiastically. Such criticism of the ensemble feature of Sayles's films posits as ideal a traditional storytelling model with a dominant central character and minor supporting players, and therefore misreads alternative character configurations as a shortcoming rather than an intentional challenge to the standard narrative formula. The intentional character of this narrative formation not only becomes clear from the films themselves, they are even stated explicitly by John Sayles in his book *Thinking in Pictures: The Making of the Movie* Matewan.

The many characters in *Matewan* and *Men With Guns* also represent a great diversity. Befitting *Matewan*'s story of interethnic conflict and cooperation, characters range from Italians just off the boat to blacks brought in as strikebreakers, from local backwater miners and hillbillies to union organizers and armed company agents. Cultural diversity is also manifest when Italian characters speak genuine Italian, which is subtitled, or, in some scenes, even left untranslated. As mentioned above, the film also incorporates original musical elements from each ethnic group to characterize them culturally. *Men With Guns*, too, features diversity beyond the main characters in background figures who are representative of a diversity of groups: "sugar cane people," "coffee people," "banana people," "gum people," as well as soldiers and guerillas. Sayles also makes a decision about dialogue that is highly unusual for a U.S. filmmaker: the film is in Spanish with English subtitles, while indigenous people speak in their own languages—Nahuatl, Tzotzil, Maya, and Kuna. Going far beyond a mere rendering of a local flavor, diversity in *Men With Guns* draws attention to the distance between the various groups and the resulting barriers to cooperation: "If everyone was speaking English, it wouldn't make as much sense," says Sayles. "Language is one of the main gaps between these people" (*Men With Guns* official homepage). Together with the soundtrack's amalgam of native and Latin music styles, this cultural diversity worked in counterpoint to the uniform violence exerted by the *hombres armados*, and—significant for our purpose—also subverts the straightforward progress of a typical oedipal or narcissistic story.

While in traditional narratives the (male) hero and his actions are foregrounded, our hero's decisions are of limited relevance to the other characters, just as they are of marginal importance in the wider picture. In a sense, the context may be defined as the true protagonist of both *Matewan* and *Men With Guns*, relativizing the male hero and the concurrent masculinism. For if traditional masculinity depends not only on the centrality of the hero but also on his exemplary status—he is both unique and representative—these films precisely break up this tie. Context, such as the local circumstances in *Matewan*, the jungle in *Men With Guns*, overwhelms the hero, and diversity—ethnic groups, local customs, individuals—is shown to be a life force of its own, which opposes uniformity both in the positive (one big union) and the negative (military rule). In his personal way (in difference to both the mainstream product and to the more formally radical techniques of avant-garde filmmakers), John Sayles therefore challenges the traditional narrative form of a central hero set off and ruling over a clearly identified background and its attendant ideological closure.

In Sayles's films, the context encapsulates the hero, embedding him in a rich set of social relations that run counter to bourgeois characteristics of separation and male narcissism. Social relations in Sayles's oeuvre are depicted as energizing and often decisive, running the gamut from conflict and strife to cooperation and community building. The most remarkable aspect of this rendering is the inherent dynamism of such social relations. Like other Sayles films, *Matewan* and *Men With Guns* depict social relations as procedural and dialectic; they admit and value conflict, arguing for an overcoming of such conflict where it is possible and advisable. They also argue strongly for resistance to power as well as against violence as a means to solve conflict. In *Matewan* the conflict between the company and the workers is not resolved, partly because of the company's unrelenting inhumanity to its workers, partly because the miners resort to violence. However, the conflict between the local miners and the strikebreaking Italians and African Americans, as well as conflicts between the various characters, is generally resolved in cooperative measures, depending on their views, status, or gender.

Further, while these conflicts are explicitly gendered only in *Men With Guns* (in a symbolic understanding of the title and in the issue of rape, for example), they are always conflicts between and within masculinities. For class and ethnic difference are, of course, major dividing lines between masculinities and therefore within patriarchy. By focusing on the conflict between such groups without resolving them immediately into individual attitudes, the films present a diverse and conflicted image of masculinity. And by focusing on social relations as defining marks of human subjectivity, and thus of masculinity, they implicitly present a codependent concept of masculinity that is at one remove from a conventional patriarchal heroic individualism.

A cardinal agenda of the films then is, as mentioned above, the building of community. In *Matewan*, the nonviolent coordination of diverse interests—symbolized in the building of a multiethnic union—is the single strongest element of the film. In *Men With Guns*, just as Dr. Fuentes is deprived of his individualist dream of a personal legacy, he gains in social relations, picking up a motley crew whose original dispersion is gradually being rectified. Initially, the doctor just wants to find his students and is not interested in anyone else, accepting the boy as a guide only reluctantly. The other characters are similarly self-centered: the boy at first has only the interest of self-preservation, the soldier robs the doctor and tries to force his will upon him, the priest just wanders aimlessly, and the traumatized woman lives in her social quarantine of muteness. The differences among these individuals—each with their own historical and social background—is never resolved tritely in the film, implying that mere goodwill is not enough to overcome their substantial differences. However, they do start to build a tentative community: Dr. Fuentes takes the priest and the mute woman on board without any self-interest; the boy starts to take care of the doctor; the priest saves the soldier from an army patrol, thereby endangering his own life; the soldier consoles Graciela by treating her psychosomatic illness; she in turn encourages him to take over Dr. Fuentes's medical legacy at the end of the film. The issue of community building, central to the narrative of both films, is reinforced by metaphors on the level of mise-en-scène and editing: *Matewan* features two montage sequences of the cooperative building of a tent city and of union organizing, and *Men With Guns* gives us the hopeful imagery of a poor but peaceful community being established in the jungle.

The importance of community over individuality, across cultural boundaries, which in my analysis counters the patriarchal principles of masculine independence and hierarchy, is most beautifully encapsulated in a small subplot in *Matewan*. In these scenes, interwoven within the main narrative, an Italian woman, Rosaria, and a local miner's widow, Mrs. Elkins, clash over cultural differences, mutual distrust, and individual interests. They initially meet at the building of a strikers' tent camp, in which the three groups—natives, Italians, blacks—experience close daily contact. Suddenly encountering the newcomers in such close proximity, Mrs. Elkins stares at Rosaria as she sets up a little Catholic shrine and, when challenged by her—"Cosa stai guardando?"—suspects Rosaria has "the evil eye." In a later scene, the two women engage in a material as well as cultural fight over a sack of cornmeal, which the American wants to turn into cornbread while the Italian wants to turn it into polenta. However, slowly, through cooperative work (tending the wounded young miners), cross-cultural values (Mrs. Elkins does not want the Italian children to starve), and emotional support (Rosaria sits vigil when Mrs. Elkins son is killed), the two women come to bond with each other. The film's superb cinematography provides a visual equivalent of this process by successively putting the two women closer and closer into one shot. At first, they are put at a distance via shot-reverse-shot imagery, later linked in a pan, and finally presented together in a close-up that succinctly conveys their newly established emotional intimacy. Although these sequences are not essential to the main narrative, they help maximize attention to the issue of community building. Just as the men's struggle to establish a union is not only anticapitalist but also antipatriarchal, female bonding also resists dividing practices, which, as Michel Foucault has extensively argued, are a central element of social rule.[6]

Problematizing Masculinity: Contestation of Power, Pacifism, Exit Politics

I have argued that detailed contexts, well-rounded and multiple secondary characters, and the emphasis on social relations redeem the conservative gender aspects, especially the heroic male individualism of *Matewan* and *Men With Guns*. Another progressive aspect of Sayles's films in terms of gender lies in their engagement with hegemony, problematizing masculinity through a pacifist contestation of power, establishing of alternative masculinities, and articulating an exit politics from hegemonic masculinity.

First, the films' narratives do not favor patriarchal succession into power, but on the contrary argue for a contestation of power in the form of opposition to capitalist exploitation and military repression. Such a contestation always takes us beyond a simple binary conceptualization of "norm" (patriarchal masculinity) versus "deviance." While in the main the films explicitly address class issues, this challenge also problematizes masculinity itself: Because of their antihegemonic stance, the main characters of these films are neither masculine role models representing the patriarchal norm, nor are they simply deviant (unmanly) characters. Their habitat is the always-precarious space of resistance that wavers between contestation and implicit reaffirmation of that power. This is made quite explicit in one scene in *Matewan* in which Joe Kenehan scolds the miners for their naïve pretensions to manhood:

> You want to be treated like men? You want to be treated fair? Well you ain't men to that coal company, you're equipment, like a shovel or a gondola car or a hunk of wood brace. They'll use you till you wear out or you break down or you're buried under a slate fall and then they'll get a new one, and they don't care what color it is or where it comes from. . . . It doesn't matter how much coal you can load or how long your family's lived on this land—if you stand alone you're just so much shit to those people! (Sayles 34)

In this rap-talk, the union organizer appeals to the miners' sense of masculinity trying to rouse their anger at the emasculating—even dehumanizing—working conditions (rather than their prevailing racism). But in terms of a contemporary text, this anticapitalist and antiracist stance (resistance) of course reaffirms a traditional, patriarchal concept of masculinity that the audience is requested to accept. This scene thus encapsulates the ambivalent construction between resistance and reaffirmation.

Further, in both films, the resistance to power does not occur with recourse to redemptive violence, but sans force. This pacifist agenda also runs counter to patriarchal masculinity. Joe's heroic pacifism is accompanied by a cool attitude when the Baldwin-Felts agents initially attempt to bring him down: "Joe raises his arms to his sides, turns to the crowd—*Joe:* 'Everybody see I don't have a gun on me?' *Hickey:* 'What do you think that'll do for you, Red?' *Joe* (shrugs): 'If you shoot me folks'll know it was murder.' *Hickey:* 'That's some cold comfort'" (Sayles 100). But at this very moment, the agents' gun power is also mocked when a group of hillbillies arrives. They ring out a shot and level their guns at the Baldwin-Felts agents. One of them points his gun at Griggs, whereupon the latter tries to talk down the situation: "*Griggs:* 'Where'd you get that thing, Pops, the Spanish War?' *Shep* [the hill person] gives a little smile and raises the muzzle to Griggs's head—*Shep:* 'Naawp. War between the States'" (Sayles 101–2).

In addition to its explicit criticism of power abuse by the military, *Men With Guns* also features an almost burlesque treatment of gun power: At a point early in the journey, Dr. Fuentes checks out the gun of the sleeping soldier and, finding it without bullets, sneaks it back to him. Thereafter he acts defiantly toward the soldier's commands, always assuming the latter's pretensions to power to be unfounded—while the audience knows that, in the meantime, the soldier was able to procure bullets. Although we smile about the doctor's mock bravery, knowing that he actually is in danger, the situation nonetheless does not escalate because the doctor's strategy really works: the pretension to power by means of the gun fails due to the doctor's defiance.

In both films, this resistance to and mockery of gun power carries meaning on the level of gender. It implies a refusal of violent masculinity in particular and of patriarchal power in general: the nonviolent agenda of the protagonists, which is already fairly atypical for traditional male heroes, has implications also on the symbolic level, where—in psychoanalytic terms—the gun may be seen as a symbol for the phallus that allows entrance into the patriarchal symbolic. In this sense, the pacifist stance portrayed in these films counters the patriarchal misrecognition of penis with power, against the cashing in on the dividend offered to men, particularly to violent men. *Matewan* and *Men With Guns* display an alternative—a more precarious, a more vulnerable—version of masculinity, one that is to be negotiated at the interface of resistance and cooperation, and that is to be achieved by bravery, and not by bravado. Both heroes represent castrated men, in other words "real" men, rather than adolescent fantasies of unlimited power. For they command neither mythical nor institutionalized power but are instead subjected to it: Joe is a pacifist union organizer in a time noted for its particularly violent suppression of all socialist or anarchist activities (such as the destruction of the IWW [Industrial Workers of the World], the Palmer raids, or the execution of Sacco and Vanzetti), and Dr. Fuentes is an old and dying man, whose distinguished social status becomes more and more tenuous out in the countryside. Within the films, their subjected status is taken even further, in that both Joe and Dr. Fuentes clearly fail in their personal endeavors. Joe Kenehan cannot prevent the miners from entering into armed conflict with the Baldwin-Felts detectives, and Dr. Fuentes finds out that his students either had to flee or else were assassinated. Finally, both protagonists die ingloriously at film's end. Thus, neither hero is a bona fide patriarch and, being tied to the real, neither manages to ascend to the level of a patriarch.

In fact, rather than representing patriarchal role models to their adopted sons, Kenehan and Fuentes signify an "exit politics" from hegemonic masculinity, away from patriarchal power, away from Othering and the consequential abuse of the Othered. Connell claims that such an exit politics usually consists in a backtracking through the oedipal as a precondition for antipatriarchal politics. And while the oedipal trajectory is about separation (the separation of the son from the maternal and the subject-object split inherent into entrance into language), as I have shown Sayles's heroes perform a reverse oedipal trajectory by trying to overcome separation in their many attempts of community building. Carol Siegel has warned against reading every film narrative in terms of a Freudian or Lacanian systematic, because this entails passing them through an oedipal grid (or the "family romance" as she calls it) regardless of whether this grid befits the text under question. This is especially true for films such as *Matewan* and *Men With Guns*, which feature narrative elements decidedly at a remove from the "family romance," such as class struggle and unionism. And even where these films seem to follow an oedipal trajectory, the depicted line of succession is not a move into power but into care and responsibility for our fellow beings, as when, right after Dr. Fuentes's death, the AWOL soldier takes over to treat the wounded indigene. What is being transmitted here is a genuine legacy rather than the passing on of an exclusive privilege.

Conclusion: Resistance to and Reproduction of Hegemony

In *Masculinities*, Connell distinguishes the following relations among masculinities: hegemony, complicity, subordination, and marginalization (76–81). Hegemony, here understood in the Gramscian tradition rather than the everyday use of the term, refers to a dominant group's power due to a successful claim to authority rather than due to explicit violence or simple domination. For example, bourgeois white men are the norm and privileged in most Western societies not by virtue of explicit laws or brute power, but above all, by hegemony—in this case, a pervasive acceptance of their superior position. Complicity refers to men who identify with hegemonic masculinity and support it without themselves necessarily embodying it—"masculinities constructed in ways that realize the patriarchal dividend [for example, better job opportunities, the subordination of women], without the tensions or risks of being in the frontline troops of patriarchy" (79). Marginalization stems from an interplay of gender with other demographic categories such as class and race. Connell sees marginalization as "always relative to the authorization of the hegemonic masculinity of the dominant group" (81). That is, the marginalized groups are not simply suppressed, but are linked to the dominant group because their resistance always has to be dealt with. In this way, dominant and marginalized groups are always linked in processes of negotiating for power. This also holds true to some extent for the relation between dominant and subordinated groups. Subordinated masculinity (for example, gay masculinity), according to Connell, tends to be "the repository of whatever is symbolically expelled from hegemonic masculinity, the items ranging from fastidious taste in home decoration to receptive anal pleasure" (78).

We should add a fifth relation, found most often in mass media representations, which Connell mentions at various points but does not recognize as distinct: exemplary masculinity. Rather than portraying the really powerful of this world (CEOs, tycoons, or other business barons), Hollywood provides embodiments of hegemonic masculinity that are incongruent with reality. What Connell claims for black sport stars—that they are merely "exemplars," because their success does not confer social and political authority to black men in general—can be applied to most Hollywood heroes. In this sense, overdrawn strong-men heroes à la Rocky or Rambo signify an exemplary masculinity, for muscular bodies have never been a trademark of the dominant group but rather of blue-collar work, and have become even less hegemonic in the shift from an industrial to postindustrial society. But they can serve to win over a significant number of men (or boys) who see themselves partly represented (working-class whites) or wish to identify with the strength portrayed. In other words, the construction of exemplars is itself resultant of a hegemonic struggle over signification between various social groups. Other, less starkly drawn characters (as, for example, those played by Harrison Ford or Tom Hanks) are more directly hegemonic (rather than exemplary), being accepted, as they are, to be "normal," perhaps even somewhat average, and unquestionably "believable." It is such figures with which and against which Sayles's characters are poised: meant to be accepted as heroic by the greatest possible audience (that is, claiming the hegemonic position), while also departing significantly from dominant models (union organizer, pacifist, socialist, and old man, who becomes enlightened)—who are disputing present hegemony. As Lawrence Grossberg puts it: "[p]ower in such a formation [a hegemonic struggle rather than one for domination] is always organized along many different, analytically equal axes: class, gender, ethnicity, race, age, and so on, each of which produces disturbances in the others" (208). Therefore, "if it is to win hegemonic leadership . . . the ruling bloc cannot ignore resistances to its specific struggle nor to its longer-term projects; it has to recognize and negotiate with at least some of the resistant fractions" (208). For a resistant fraction, therefore, it is important to engage with the dominant discourses, lest they might be excluded, relegated outside the hegemonic formation.

Neither *Matewan* nor *Men With Guns* simply reiterates a dominant model of masculinity. Granted, both the heroes are complicit, even hegemonic—for example, in regard to their status vis-à-vis women, their matter-of-course heterosexuality, their status as intellectual, analytical subjects who are, the films imply, vested with a natural and legitimate authority. This authorization of the protagonists—as masculine and (!) at the same time as degendered subjects, in other words, as generic subjects—is achieved via a narrative that surrounds them with a chorus of legitimizers: rural miners, Italian immigrants, African American workers, disempowered natives, and women. At the same time, this recreation of hegemonic masculinity is counterhegemonic, not only in terms of class and ethnicity but also in terms of gender. For example, as I have pointed out above, the political "innocence" of Dr. Fuentes in *Men With Guns* is revealed to be a sign of privilege and complicity: an implicit acceptance of the violence and oppression in his country for saving his own privileged status. As we have seen, both films also analyze relations and positions of marginality and subordination, particularly in the oppressed secondary characters: local workers, blacks, and recent immigrants in *Matewan* and various indigenous people in *Men With Guns*. Particularly in the latter film, the hegemonic position of Dr. Fuentes becomes subverted both by his dropping out of his elite societal position and by choosing fellowship rather than remaining aloof (the choice made by the western heroes described in Mulvey or the American tourists Andrew and Harriet). Concurrently, the young boy becomes essential as his guide (and as our guide) and a common soldier becomes the new doctor.

To summarize, the films *Matewan* and *Men With Guns* exhibit elements of both resistance and hegemony. The hero of *Matewan*, for example, while being a unionist, socialist, and pacifist, is nonetheless constructed as a traditional hero—a "naturally" strong and determined man. In many other ways too, antihegemonic features of the films (contextualization, ensemble casting, an older hero, portrayal of failure, and so on) are balanced by a gender-conservative representation. It seems that John Sayles wants to save the heroic quality of Kenehan and Fuentes so as to save the values they personify (such as political awareness and political activism), an attempt that only goes a certain distance. Yet I have argued too that the films' engagement with class and ethnic hegemony is always also an engagement with hegemonic masculinity and the gender regime because it opposes patriarchy's tendency to put men in relations of dominance to each other (higher vs. lower class, white vs. nonwhite, WASP vs. ethnic, and so on). Bending rather than outright breaking generic structures, Sayles constructs alternative masculinities as one attempt to exit from dominant masculinity.

NOTES

1. *Matewan* is a story of union foundation and union busting. It is set in West Virginia, in 1920. The local coal miners, brutally exploited by the Stone Mountain Coal Company, are outraged when the company recruits Southern blacks and immigrant Italians as strikebreakers. Joe Kenehan, a union organizer who comes to Matewan town, successfully unites the diverse groups—locals, Alabama blacks, Italians—to stand against the company. From that point on the main question is whether the workers will withstand the agents' provocateurs hired by the company and instead commit themselves to nonviolent union work. Disregarding Kenehan's pleas to avoid violence, the miners are finally lured into a shoot-out. Although Sayles centers the narrative on labor politics, he structures his story like an old-fashioned western: *Matewan* tells of a different American dream, that of the employed and exploited.

Men With Guns is a political odyssey into the most remote areas of a fictional Central American country, where indigenous people, already living in extreme poverty, are intimidated and violently oppressed by both the army and the guerillas. The protagonist, Dr. Fuentes, is an elderly physician living in an affluent neighborhood in the capital town. Due to a deteriorating heart condition, he decides to complete his legacy—a health program that he had set up in the past that trained medical students to work in the poor hinterlands—by setting out to check on the progress of his students. Thus begins a nightmarish adventure tour during which he loses his political "innocence" that characterizes his protected life, when he learns that his students were killed by either the army or, if they had helped soldiers, by the guerrillas. On his journey, he picks up a group of fellow travelers—an orphaned boy, a deserted soldier, a priest who had abandoned his village, and a young woman who has turned mute after a traumatic rape. Their journey becomes a quest for Cerca del Cielo, a mythical and peaceful plot of earth. In the end, the group finds a secluded hideout in an uncharted territory. Exhausted by the long journey, Dr. Fuentes dies at arrival. Yet there is a ray of hope in the closing sequence when the soldier picks up Fuentes's instruments to help a wounded indigene.

2. These patriarchal aspects of *Matewan* and *Men With Guns* in terms of characterization are reinforced by the visual structure. Cued by the findings of feminist film theory, we note that the gaze of the camera is most often aligned with either the male protagonist or with other male characters.

3. On the battered male body, compare Neale and Silverman.

4. This localism is responsible for some of the difficulty that Sayles's films encounter in European distribution and reception. On the one hand, his films are too far off the Hollywood mold in subject matter (unionism, antimilitary, third-world theme, lesbian love, antiracism, and so on) to be successful in broad popular distribution. On the other, they are too American for the European art-house circle, which can more easily incorporate the formally challenging but transnational abstractions of a Jim Jarmusch or a Hal Hartley.

5. Roger Ebert has pointed out that "*Men With Guns* is about the background. . . . If [Sayles] had taken this script to a studio executive, he no doubt would have been told to beef up the American tourist roles and cast the roles with stars. The film would have been an action sitcom, with Indians, doctors, priests and orphans in the background as local color."

6. Foucault sees rule in modern societies established on three related practices: dividing practices, scientific classification, and subjectification. As an introduction to these concepts, see Rabinow.

WORKS CITED

Connell, Robert. *Masculinities*. Berkeley: U of California P, 1995.
Ebert, Roger. Review of *Men With Guns*. *Chicago Sun-Times*. http://www.suntimes.com/ebert/ebert_reviews/1998/03/032704.html. 31 January 2002.
Fiedler, Leslie. *Love and Death in the American Novel*. New York: Stein and Day, 1996.
Grossberg, Lawrence. *Dancing in Spite of Myself: Essays on Popular Culture*. Durham: Duke UP, 1997.
Kemp, Philip. Review of *Men With Guns*. *Sight and Sound* 8.9 (1998): 48–49.
Maltin, Leonard. *Leonard Maltin's Movie Encyclopedia*. New York: Plume, 1995.
Men With Guns: Written, Directed, and Edited by John Sayles. Official homepage of the film. http://www.spe.sony.com/classics/menwithguns/index.html. 31 January 2002.
Mulvey, Laura. "Afterthoughts on 'Visual Pleasure and Narrative Cinema'

Inspired by *Duel in the Sun*." *Visual and Other Pleasures*. Bloomington: Indiana UP, 1989a [originally published 1981]. 29–38.

———. "Visual Pleasure and Narrative Cinema." *Visual and Other Pleasures*. Bloomington: Indiana UP, 1989b [originally published 1975]. 14–26.

Neale, Steve. "Masculinity as Spectacle: Reflections on Men and Mainstream Cinema." *Screening the Male: Exploring Masculinities in Hollywood Cinema*. Ed. Steven Cohan and Ina Rae Hark. London: Routledge, 1993 [originally published 1983].

Propp, Vladimir. *Morphology of the Folk Tale*. 2nd ed. Austin: U of Texas P, 1968.

Rabinow, Paul. "Introduction." *The Foucault Reader*. Ed. Paul Rabinow. New York: Pantheon, 1984.

Ryan, Susan. Review of *Men With Guns*. *Cineaste* 23.3 (1998): 43–44.

Sayles, John. *Thinking in Pictures: The Making of the Movie* Matewan. Boston: Houghton Mifflin, 1987.

Siegel, Carol. *Male Masochism: Modern Revisions of the Story of Love*. Bloomington: Indiana UP, 1995.

Silverman, Kaja. *Male Subjectivity at the Margins*. New York: Routledge, 1992.

Willemen, Paul. "Anthony Mann: Looking at the Male." *Framework* 15/17 (1981): 16–20.

Wilson, David. Review of *Matewan*. *Monthly Film Bulletin* 56.664 (1989): 141–42.

9

Tourism and Territory:
Constructing the Nation in *Men With Guns (Hombres Armados)*

Hamilton Carroll

In an era of globalization, transnational media conglomeration, and the increasing incoherence of national space, cinema stands as a fecund site for an examination of the legacies of nationalism and colonialism. Speaking of such a possibility, Rob Wilson and Wimal Dissanayake observe, "film, still the crucial genre of transnational production and global circulation for refigured narratives, offers speculative ground for the transnational imaginary and its contention within national and local communities" (Wilson and Dissanayake 11). John Sayles's *Men With Guns (Hombres Armados)* (1997) effects just such a contestation by refusing its own categorization within an American national cinema and through its meditation on the functions of narrative and historiography under national conditions. *Men With Guns* understands national hegemony to be maintained by multiple processes of narration and examines the constitutive power of narrative as a tool of national ordering. In this essay I interrogate the film's construction of a dialectical relationship between the national and the transnational by examining the film's meditation on the roles of narrative, cinematic form, and tourism in the formation of national imaginaries and hegemonic national practices.

Sayles's film examines how narrative functions constitutively for the nation-state. The examination of constitutive national narratives in *Men With Guns* functions on the twinned levels of narrative content and form. As such, *Men With Guns* casts local narratives of resistance against the metanarratives of nation and colonialism the nation's privileged subjects take for granted. The film's focus on the construction of national narratives illustrates how the process of hegemonic national identification functions to maintain uneven subject relations. This analysis is also affected through a related examination of the role U.S. tourism takes in the formation of (trans)national imaginaries. Tourism is shown to be both implicated in and constructed by the metanarratives of progressive modernization through which the nation is imagined. As such, the film's indigenous populations are silenced by national narratives and rendered invisible by transnational cultural imperialism in the form of U.S. tourism. The film not only illustrates the pernicious effect of national narratives on its indigenous characters but also opens up alternative representational spaces by disarticulating narrative from state practices. Moreover, the film's form distances the audience from the narrative through its use of subtitles, foreign languages, indigenous dialects, and a self-reflexive narrative structure.

"Like a Child": Willed Ignorance and National Narratives

A road movie of sorts, the film charts the growing disillusionment of its protagonist, Dr. Humberto Fuentes (Federico Luppi), as he travels from the capital city into the margins of a fictional South American country. As a society doctor in the city who ministers to rich women and corrupt Army generals, Fuentes can maintain an unquestioning innocence through which he is oblivious to the economic and social plight that surrounds him. This innocence is predicated on an absolute capitulation to the national narratives his status makes him a beneficiary of and entails a willed ignorance of the violence on which such narratives are grounded. Fuentes's position at the start of the film is one of assumed privilege in which he imagines himself part of a community of citizens with shared goals, assumptions, and aspirations. In one early scene, Fuentes is ministering to an Army general who is concerned that his illness be kept a secret in case his political enemies try to use it against him. Throughout this scene Fuentes's innocence/ignorance is foregrounded. In answer to Fuentes's naïve question, "Who'd want to give you trouble?" the general exclaims, "You're like a child, Humberto. The world is a savage place" (Sayles 5–6).[1] Slightly later one of Fuentes's ex-pupils, Bravo (Roberto Sosa), exclaims, "You don't know a thing about it, do you?" and tells Fuentes that he is "the most learned man [he has] ever met [and] the most ignorant" (12–13). Of course, Bravo and the general are each accusing Fuentes of a slightly different thing. The general's claim that the "world is a savage place" signals his own place within the same logic of citizenship as Fuentes, albeit at a different level. Bravo's lament underscores the ways in which Fuentes, because of his education, is able to avoid the harsh realities of his country's indigenous population—of the "savage place" the general bemoans. Fuentes's ignorance is linked to issues of privilege in which the doctor is able to maintain belief in the seamless interface between the nation and its citizen-subjects. As Sayles suggests in the introduction to the published script, "Fuentes is . . . ignorant of history—but . . . it's a careless, even willful ignorance, that of the man who subconsciously does not want to know" (Sayles vii). The doctor's perspective changes as he leaves the city and its socioeconomic hegemony and begins to see for himself the plight of peoples who are not only excluded from the benefits he takes for granted, but are actively marginalized in their constitution.

Fuentes's journey forces him to see how his own privilege has been made possible and at whose expense. His increasingly profound disillusionment is a result of the disruption of his belief in the logic of the nation in the face of alternative narratives that resist and destabilize the national narratives the doctor takes for granted. Donald E. Pease suggests that national narratives organized collective representations of the national people, transmitted the official scenarios wherein individuals were subjectivized as its citizen-subjects, and controlled the individual citizen's relation to the state. Overall, these narratives positioned a totalized community as the narratee of a story that structured the subject positions, actions, and events of that community within a master-plot that performed the quasi-metaphysical function of guaranteeing its perpetuity (5).

As such, national narratives guarantee a seamless interface between the nation and the state in which the citizen-subject, as beneficiary, is understood (and understands him/herself) to be part of a community of like people each enjoying the same benefits and beliefs. The ordering master-plot of the nation functions in such a way that its hegemonic operations appear natural and transparent. What *Men With Guns* does as it describes Fuentes's disillusionment is reveal the ways in which such national narratives are always predicated on the violent exclusion of a national Other, those who are marginalized in the inauguration of national affiliations.

Because Fuentes must leave the city, not journey toward it, in order to gain experience the film reverses the standard Western narrative of personal development in which the city figures as the apotheosis of the citizen-subject's transit from innocence to worldly experience.[2] This reversal illustrates one primary way in which the film rejects national narratives of citizen formation. Shown in the film to be a site of radical spatial delimitations, the city Fuentes leaves masks the reality of the interrelation between the metropolitan center of the nation and its rural margins. A place of mirrored skyscrapers and contained socioeconomic spaces, the city maps the unequal assimilation of the nation's people. As a white city-dweller, Fuentes can nonchalantly give an Indian beggar woman a few coins without either looking at her or really seeing her. As he is forced to encounter people like this woman on their own terms and in spaces in which he is denied the insularity of his own subject position, Fuentes (and, thus the viewer of the film) must confront the reality of the socioeconomic and spatial networks that allow for that insularity in the first place. By insisting on the relation, however unequal, between the city and its peripheries, Sayles's film complicates the very dichotomies of city/rural, center/margin Fuentes blithely disregards at the outset of the film. Removed from the ocular self-representation symbolized by the mirror-glassed skyscrapers he walks past, Fuentes is forced to see the interrelation between the city and the subordinate sites of rural production he travels to.

In *Men With Guns*, this reversed transit marks a shift in relationality in which, as Homi Bhabha suggests, "the postcolonial space is now 'supplementary' to the metropolitan center; it stands in a subaltern, adjunct relation that doesn't aggrandize the presence of the west but redraws its frontiers in the menacing, agonistic boundary of cultural difference that never quite adds up, always less than one nation and double" ("Introduction," 319). By redrawing the relationship between the metropolitan center of the nation and its subaltern periphery as one of unequal, inassimilable, and contested interaction, the film adumbrates a rent in the fabric of the nation in which the given position of the privileged national subject, personified in Fuentes, no longer obtains.

The typical journey into citizenship is mapped through the production of identification with the nation in which the individual conforms to idealized forms of subjectivity, thus performing and actualizing their citizenship. By reversing this trajectory (which is both geographical and ideological), *Men With Guns* rejects the paradigmatic telos of reconciliation with the nation. As he travels away from the putative center of the nation (the capital city) and encounters its margins, Fuentes does not so much gain experience as lose the innocence his capitulation to the national order has allowed him to maintain.

Despite the fact that he is searching for a number of doctors who have disappeared under mysterious circumstances, when he leaves the city Fuentes naïvely believes that his trip to the mountains will be commensurate with his more usual summer vacations at the beach. He is driving his son's brand-new Jeep sports utility vehicle, packed with cameras and other vacation paraphernalia. By the end of the film, all of these items appear to have been stolen, his car has been vandalized, and its wheels have been stolen. As the trappings of Fuentes's wealth and social standing drop away, the realities of his surroundings (and the conditions of possibility for his wealth and stature) become visible to him. As an old Indian man reminds Fuentes, "You can't see anything from a car" (Sayles 15). After his car's tires are stolen Fuentes's pace (and, as we shall see, that of the film itself) slows to a pedestrian speed and the luxury of ignorance/ignorance of luxury is taken away from him. Forced to walk, to encounter the country on its own terms, Fuentes is transformed from a naïve tourist into an experienced and disillusioned skeptic.

The loss of Fuentes's possessions signals a meditation on the act of consumption as a vital component of the hegemonic structure of the nation. In an early scene set in Fuentes's waiting room in which we encounter two of Fuentes's patients (rich society women), one woman complains to the other about the pain she gets in her kidneys from drinking red wine. She observes that "the more expensive the wine the sharper the pain" (Sayles 9). Conspicuous consumption is linked here to both socioeconomic issues and the maintenance of the hegemony of the nation-state. Quoting Arjun Appadurai, Canclini suggests that:

> consumption is not something "private, atomized and passive" ... but "eminently social, correlative and active," subordinated

to a certain political control by elites. The tastes of the hegemonic sectors have something like a "funneling" function, for they condition the selection of external offerings and provide politico-cultural models for the administration of the tension between what is one's own and what comes from afar. (43)

As such, consumption demarcates and authenticates socioeconomic distinctions between classes and groups. Sayles's ironic presentation of a rich woman afflicted as a result of her own consumption suggests that the cost of maintaining such distinctions is deleterious, albeit to a far lesser degree, for the assumed beneficiaries of national privilege as much as it is for the nation's subaltern subjects. What Sayles presents is the image of a nation destroying itself on multiple levels. Moreover, the desire of the guerillas Fuentes encounters late in his journey is as much for control of (or access to) the flow of commodities as it is to "free the people," a point made clear in a discussion between two young guerillas about what flavors of ice cream would be available to them in the capital city and who would control access to that ice cream and the rules governing its distribution. The most conspicuous consumption in the whole film, of course, is that of two American tourists, Andrew (Mandy Patinkin) and Harriet (Kathryn Grody), Fuentes encounters on his journey.

Fuentes's encounters with these tourists place the film's engagements with issues of willed blindness and socioeconomic national privilege in a transnational context. The doctor and the tourists are juxtaposed repeatedly in the film and, however ignorant Fuentes may be, the American tourists are shown to be doubly so. Andrew and Harriet travel in a world in which the plight of the country's indigenous populations is either rendered invisible or easily explained away within a logic of tourism that orders their interactions with their surroundings and the people who populate them. Andrew, for example, spends much of his time lecturing both his wife and Fuentes on the history of the local architecture and the rise and fall of earlier indigenous civilizations. On each occasion, the reasons he gives for historical events are equally applicable in the present, yet he is blind to the similarities. The tourists cannot see the realities of the situation they have placed themselves in precisely because they are tourists. An early encounter between the tourists and Dr. Fuentes takes place at a hotel called Pozo de los Caciques (translated as Well of the Chiefs). The scene begins with a shot of a pair of car headlights illuminating the sign for the hotel that depicts an Indian chief sacrificing a young virgin. This reference to the mythic history of the country's indigenous peoples as perpetrators of human sacrifice (transformed into a consumable tourist attraction) masks the country's history of imperial conquest. Andrew, thus, can relish telling Harriet of the thousands of virgins who have had their hearts torn out and thrown into the well without reading alongside this narrative his own implication—as a tourist—in the current socioeconomic realities of the nation's indigenous populations.

Fuentes, likewise, denies that the history being described to him is his own as he transposes the genocide Andrew describes to Mexico and blames it on the Aztecs. He tells the tourists in Spanish that it was "not our people. It was other tribes, attacking from the north" (Sayles 25). Harriet translates for Andrew (who speaks no Spanish), "Honey, he said it was foreigners from the north" (25). Of course, the only "foreigners from the north" are Andrew and Harriet and, as his claim that it was "not *our* people" shows, Fuentes is as much a "foreigner" to this precolonial history as the Americans are. The history Fuentes refutes is that of the nation before it was a nation in the context of his own, Spanish, colonial history. As a white city-dweller, Fuentes is as removed as the tourists from the realities hidden behind this mythic past. Indeed, following Andrew's insistent questioning about current political atrocities, Fuentes responds in exactly the same way, claiming that the stories Andrew has read in the New York newspapers about political murders "must be in another country. Not here" (Sayles 18). What the interactions between the American tourists and Dr. Fuentes limn is how the ideological figure of the nation is a collation of both internal and external sociopolitical forces.

What Fuentes has to give up in order to see the workings of this hegemonic violence is his belief in what Arif Dirlik calls the "metanarrative of modernization" as it is linked to the formation of the nation-state and is inherited from European Enlightenment traditions. As Dirlik has suggested, the "repudiation of the metanarrative of modernization" has had two consequences for the study of the nation. First, "it rescues from invisibility those who were earlier viewed as castaways from history, whose social and cultural forms of existence appear in the narrative of modernization at best as irrelevancies." Second, it "has allowed greater visibility to 'local narratives'" which call into question the myth of linear temporal progress that modernity inherited from the Enlightenment (Dirlik 25). As such, Men With Guns evidences what Walter D. Mignolo describes as the "decolonization . . . and transformations of the rigidity of epistemic and territorial frontiers established and controlled by the coloniality of power in the process of building the modern/colonial world system [by] absorbing and displacing hegemonic forms of knowledge into the perspective of the subaltern" (205). The stories Fuentes hears during his journey overturn the hegemonic national narratives he previously lived by and force him to account for his own position in the "coloniality of power." What Fuentes must relinquish at the close of the film is his desire for a legacy as he comes to realize that the progressive, benevolent liberalism of his privileged social position actively contributes to the maintenance of the oppressive socioeconomic structures his journey has forced him to confront. What Fuentes must give up, in short, is his stake in patriarchy.

This point is made most explicitly in the film in Fuentes's desire to preserve the Alliance for Progress program as his legacy.[3] This desire links Fuentes's personal quest to the patrilinear form and function of the nation. His belief in the Alliance for Progress program equally indicates Fuentes's capitulation to founding metanarratives as they are related to Enlightenment ideals of scientific progress. In a flashback to the training of his pupils for the program, Fuentes claims, "in a struggle against death, a small advantage in technology can win a battle. Cortes won an empire with a few men—but he had the horse and the gun and his adversary didn't. Where you're going your principal enemies will be bacteria and ignorance. Bacteria can be fought with drugs, but their ally, ignorance—" (Sayles 9–10). Medicine, the foremost science of the Enlightenment, and empire, its geopolitical result, are here linked in the person of Fuentes who is able to believe in one through his capitulation to the other. Unwittingly, Fuentes signals here the links between the colonial world system and the domination of subaltern peoples inherent in Enlightenment "narratives of transition, progress, development, and points of arrival" (Mignolo 205). His quest to discover the plight of his remaining pupils, then, starts out as a desire to ensure his legacy. In an argument with his son-in-law before he leaves for the mountains, Fuentes exclaims, "the [Alliance for Progress] program was a good idea! A good idea! It's my legacy" (Sayles 8). At the close of the film, however, he realizes that his legacy—and the legacy of the colonial world system he previously believed in—is Cerca del Cielo, the impoverished last bastion of refuge for the nation's indigenous peoples who have been decimated and have seen their land ravaged in the warfare between the nation's soldiers and the neonationalist guerillas. Sayles points out that Fuentes's trip is "a kind of Pilgrim's Progress, a journey where each turn brings new hardship and new knowledge. It is no odyssey, however, no way for him to bring back the news to his old home and live on as a wiser man" (Carson 225). Fuentes is forced during the course of the film to confront the myth of the nation and to examine his own culpability in its construction.

With his dying words, "every man should leave a legacy. . . . This is what I leave. . . . At least I don't have to climb any more" (Sayles 99), Fuentes acknowledges both his complicity in the nation's subordination of its indigenous populations and his failure to bring about any real social change through the Alliance for Progress program. Indeed, he comes to understand how complete that failure was as he realizes the extent to which the geopolitics behind the Alliance for Progress program functioned on an hemispheric level that, despite his own references to Cortes and the colonization of South America, he previously could not understand. Such is Fuentes's failure that the only recourse left to him at the end of the film is death. Ending with his death, the film rejects the myth of progress and national sovereignty that he embodies. As Fuentes is unable to save himself using modern medicine, he is unable, in the face of the local and contingent needs of the people at the nation's imagined peripheries, to preserve his belief in the Enlightenment myth of nation and progress. Domingo (Damian Delgado), the film's most complex character (soldier, Indian, thief, medic, coward, hero) stands at the close of the film in the place of the doctor and experience takes the place of willful ignorance. Clutching the doctor's medical bag after his death, Domingo states, "There is no doctor. The doctor is dead" (Sayles 100). Through this ironic inversion of the constitutive narrative of perpetual sovereignty—"the King is dead, long live the king"—the narrative logic of the nation-state is fractured and what is left to the viewer and the film's remaining characters

Rejecting bourgeois citizenship (Damian Delgado).

is the image of a moribund nation ravaged both from within and from outside its own borders.

Ruins Are U.S.: Mythic Pasts, Subaltern Subjects, and the Logic of Postmodern Tourism

Linking cold-war geopolitical practices to contemporary cultural imperialisms through the colonial history of the prenation, *Men With Guns* maps the conflicting—but often contiguous—relations between the nation-state, postcolonial neonationalisms, and a globalized economy. These relations are delineated most clearly in the juxtaposition of Fuentes with the American tourists. Sayles has suggested that, while Fuentes changes during the course of the film, the tourists remain essentially the same: "Fuentes has changed quite a bit. He's very sad. He listens to things in a much more philosophical way. He's not defensive anymore when they're talking about the massacres. He's started to hear his own stories about massacres and [to] see evidence of them. He's found skulls in a human body dump. So each time Fuentes sees [the tourists], they're the same—it doesn't affect them. But Fuentes is different" (Carson 225).

The encounters between Fuentes and the American couple become more and more disturbing as the film proceeds. Indeed, Andrew and Harriet stand as an index of Fuentes's own journey. This is in part because Andrew and Harriet *are* absolutely unchanged by their experiences. Fuentes, though, is forced to confront his beliefs about the unity of the nation. He witnesses events and hears stories that would previously have been invisible to him. Andrew and Harriet, whom Sayles calls "teflon tourists" (Carson 225), are unchanged because their experiences are mediated through a tourist gaze constructed equally by the logic of the nation in which they are vacationing and by their expectations as U.S. citizens in a foreign country. As Americans, the tourists expect to be protected from any harm by U.S. international state apparatuses such as embassies and consulates; as tourists they expect to have the harsh realities of the society they are visiting hidden from them through the careful orchestration of a national history that renders contemporary socioeconomic conflicts invisible. In this logic of tourism, national history is turned into spectacle for the benefit of the wealthy American tourists.

Andrew and Harriet evidence the worst form of multiculturalism, exoticizing indigenous cultural practices and histories as a means to their own sociocultural legitimacy. "The tourist," suggests John Urry, "is a kind of contemporary pilgrim, seeking authenticity in other 'times' and other 'places' away from that person's everyday life" (8). Andrew's fascination with local history is largely a fascination with the slaughter of indigenous peoples. By focusing on precolonial history, however, he is only able to understand events within this logic of tourism. In the transformation of local history into tourist spectacle, the realities of the present situation and their similarities to previous genocides are lost. As Urry suggests, such tourism, often connected to the burgeoning heritage industry, is "an essentially 'artefactual' history, in which a whole variety of social experiences are necessarily ignored or trivialized, such as war, exploitation, hunger, disease, the law, and so on" (112). All colonial, regional, or national particularities are lost in the museumizing of the nation's artifacts, and the tourists are able to incorporate the generalized monuments into a whole continuum of other possible vacation resorts available to them as the ruins undergo a process of reproducibility, typical of postmodernism. As a travel location, the ruins are emptied of any actual particularity, buttressing U.S. national identities rather than mobilizing any particular local, national identification. The trivialized history Andrew receives not only renders the events of the past as of no actual import, but also engenders a degree of blindness to current sociopolitical conditions that mirrors Fuentes's own position of willed ignorance. Andrew does, however, unwittingly reference the links between national historiography and current economic conditions when, after describing the ritual sacrifice of young, female virgins, he observes that the sacrificers "must have had a labor surplus" (Sayles 24). The ritual sacrifice of virgin maidens by the indigenous ruling classes of the colonial nation's prehistory is thematically related to the rape and economic exploitation of women in the present.

The effects of this postmodern tourism have an earlier corollary, as Benedict Anderson points out, in the construction of museums during a previous period of colonialism. Anderson suggests in *Imagined Communities* that "museums, and the museumizing imagination, are both profoundly political" (178). Further, "what was imagined [by the colonial preservers of ancient monuments] was a secular decadence, such that contemporary natives were no longer capable of their putative ancestors' achievements" (181). As historical monuments, these ruins position the indigenous populations of a colonized country in a relationship with the nascent nation-state in which they are rendered invisible or of no account. Anderson continues, "seen in this light, the reconstructed monuments, juxtaposed with the surrounding rural poverty, said to the natives: Our very presence shows that you have always been, or have long become, incapable of either greatness or self-rule." As such, "monumental archaeology, *increasingly linked to tourism* [italics mine], allowed the state to appear as the guardian of a generalized, but also local, Tradition. ... Museumized this way, [ruins] were repositioned as regalia for a *secular* [italics in original] colonial state" (Anderson 181–82). The ruins in *Men With Guns*, which Andrew and Harriet are visiting and which form the backdrop to Fuentes's travails, function just as Anderson suggests. A shift has taken place, however, in which the impetus of these mechanics of domination and subordination function in the new logic of postmodern tourism.

Ian Munt has suggested that a central facet of the appeal of such new tourism forms for tourists is related to "nostalgia for ancient traditions and environments [and] for the travel styles of yesteryear" (105). Such tourists, self-styled as "travelers" in distinction to the mass tourists of Disneyland and packaged tours, imagine themselves to be more learned, more sensitive to local conditions, and, as one travel brochure suggests, "custodian[s] of the ancient relationship between traveler and native which throughout the world has been the historic basis of peaceful contact" (Munt 115). Such evocations of the "ancient relationship between traveler and native" unwittingly highlight the extant links between travel and imperialism. In one particularly illuminating scene, Fuentes overhears a different pair of American tourists discussing Bali as a possible alternative vacation spot. In this conversation, one reads from a travel brochure: "There is a place where the air is like a caress, where gentle waters flow, a place where your burdens are lifted from your shoulders on wings of peace.... A place to forget, a place to grow, a place where each day is a gift and each person is reborn.... Where is this paradise on earth, this haven, this safe harbor?" (Sayles 26). Such narratives, which clearly place the tourist in a privileged position in relation to the "native" akin to the colonial domination Anderson describes, serve to shore up the tourist's own identity through a dual process of relationality. More advanced than the native populations and their mythic monuments, the tourist also differentiates him/herself from his/her own fellow citizens in a process that Munt calls tourification that produces a "socio-spatial process of economic, cultural and class distinction" (116). Such tourism, Munt suggests, "signals a cultural and social *reaction* of the new middle-classes to the crassness which they perceive as tourism, and their craving for social and spatial distinction from the 'golden hordes'" of mass tourists (199). Postmodern tourism of the type Andrew and Harriet are engaged in, then, shores up domestic class distinctions. Harriet and Andrew are able to construct a reading of the nation in which the "history" they see, emptied of any but the most reductive particularity, obfuscates the actual conditions surrounding them. Because of this, despite the fact that she and Andrew have recently been carjacked at gunpoint, Harriet can remark to Fuentes, "it is so peaceful here. *Como tranquilo?*" (Sayles 89).

The nation Andrew imagines, Harriet ignores, and Fuentes long refuses to see exists within the Enlightenment logic of progress Anderson points to in *Imagined Communities* when he states that "the idea of a sociological organism moving calendrically through homogeneous, empty time is a precise analogue of the idea of the nation, which also is conceived as a solid community moving steadily down (or up) history" (26). Within this logic, the nation *must* have progressed through the course of history and thus the genocide that is contemporaneous to Fuentes's quest and Andrew and Harriet's sightseeing cannot actually exist. By mythologizing genocide in the prehistory of the (colonial) nation, both Fuentes and the American tourists can ignore how these myths belie the material, present-day conditions of the nation's poorest and most disenfranchised subjects. Both the nation's privileged subjects such as Fuentes and extranational subjects such as the American tourists are able to participate in the construction of the nation-state through its continual renarrativization. State hegemony is maintained through a constant narrative process in which sense is made of otherwise unequal and inassimilable subject relations. While Fuentes, Andrew and Harriet, and the other tourists can mobilize the mythic past of the nation to their advantage, the actual inhabitants of the region are denied the same privilege and have correspondingly different relations to the state.

In *Men With Guns* the nation's marginalized characters are shown to understand themselves as existing primarily as functions of the economic interests of the state, even while they acknowledge their exclusion from its benefits. The indigenous populations of the film are each demarcated by their function within the economy of the nation. Each group of people Fuentes encounters describes themselves according to the crops they grow or harvest: salt people, sugar people, gum people, coffee people, and so on. By self-reflexively writing themselves into the nation's economic structure in this way, the people Fuentes encounters effectively refuse their categorization as of "no account" and insist he come to understand how his privilege is founded on their subalternity. By rejecting and pragmatically understanding their own relations to the state, the subjects at the periphery of the nation recast national narrative as what Bhabha calls the "site of an ambivalent identification; a margin of the uncertainty of cultural meaning that may become the space for an agonistic minority position" ("Introduction," 317). Such counternarratives not only refuse national narratives in the here and now but also insist on the already unequal value of their production. Caught in the midst of the conflict between the crumbling power of the colonial nation-state, the neonationalist struggle of the guerrillas, and a shifting, increasingly transnational, economy, the film's indigenous populations construct their own, postnational, myth of resistance.

"What's the Word for Fajitas?" Language, Narrative Structure, and Postnational Critique

Situated at the interstices of U.S. national cinema, *Men With Guns* complicates its own position as producer of hegemonic national allegiances and rejects an easy didacticism that would undoubtedly slip over into exoticism and the romanticizing of the film's indigenous characters. Orchestrating a doubled formal disruption—on the level of language and of narrative structure—that complements and reinforces the critique it engages on a thematic level, *Men With Guns* prompts the audience to examine their own positions, as consumers, in the very structures of dominance its content critiques. Narrative cinema continues and transforms the function of the realist novel in the nineteenth century as a producer of national affiliations and imagined relations. Ella Shohat and Robert Stam claim that, in the twentieth century, "national self-consciousness, generally seen as a precondition for nationhood, that is, the shared belief of disparate individuals that they share common origins, status, location, and aspirations, became broadly linked to cinematic fictions" (153). In this way, cinema was uniquely positioned to join, even replace, the novel as a principal form of hegemonic production, shoring up and evoking identification with the nation for its citizens. Indeed, as Mike Featherstone contends, "the development of the film industry facilitates [the] process [of imagining communities] even better [than newspapers and the novel], as film provides an instantiation and immediacy which are relatively independent of the long learning process and institutional and other supports necessary to be able to assimilate knowledge through books" (54).

Yoking the culture of empire to an easily disseminated ethnographic gaze, cinema recontextualized the imagined communities of the nation in a transnational, colonial context, offering a specular relation with colonial others against which national subjectivities could be grounded.[4] Cinema, as much as tourism, then, allows for an imperial gaze as it "has offered the spectator a mediated relationship with imaged others from diverse cultures." Further, "if the culture of empire authorized the pleasure of seizing ephemeral glimpses of its 'margins' through travel and tourism, the nineteenth-century invention of the photographic and later the cinematographic camera made it possible to record such glimpses" (Shohat and Stam 104). Like tourism, the "mediated relationship" with other cultures that cinema affords places the viewed subject in a subaltern position vis-à-vis national affiliation. Cinema, however, can equally occupy an antagonistic position in relation to national culture; *Men With Guns* holds just such a position. Through an intricate articulation of narrative, plot, and linguistic form, *Men With Guns* insistently critiques a Western European historiography that assumes a temporal, progressive history as constitutive of national identity. Refusing to allow any one of these components to stand unexamined, the film lays bare the constitutive structures of national narrative.

The dialogue in *Men With Guns* is a mix of Spanish, six Indian dialects, brief snippets of English, and (in the United States) the film is subtitled in English. Extending the trenchant critique of the hegemonic processes its narrative content delineates, the film's use of language disrupts the (English-speaking) audience's relationship to the events that unfold on the screen. Subtitles estrange English-speaking viewers from the spoken dialogue and place them in an equivalent position to Fuentes and the American tourists. In this way, *Men With Guns* examines the links between language, narrative, nation, and the legacies of colonialism and U.S. imperialism. Understanding language to be a potent hegemonic tool, the film charts the structures of power embedded—nationally and transnationally—in a monolingual, (neo)colonial worldview.[5] Not content with mere illustration, Sayles places the viewer of the film within these power structures by linking the tourist gaze to cinematic spectatorship. The audience is forced to acknowledge their own potential positions, as possible "armchair conquistadors" (Shohat and Stam 156), in the structures of dominance such spectatorship allows. Faced with what is essentially a foreign-language film, the audience "come[s] to share an experience common to dislocated Third World and minoritarian audiences; the feeling that 'this film was not made for us'" (Shohat and Stam 165). *Men With Guns*, however, is not simply a "foreign-language film," but an American one in which the decision to marginalize spoken English was a conscious and important one. It is, in short, a film that "*was* made for us," but which demands a reappraisal of exactly who that "us" is and how any such community of viewers is constituted.[6] *Men With Guns* is, in many ways, a film that is "foreign" to every viewer. As Sayles himself has suggested, "There is no such thing on this one as domestic and foreign. It's all foreign" (Carson 233). Denied the transparency English-language films allow, the viewer is made to identify with the insularity of Fuentes and the American tourists.

The insularity of both Fuentes and the tourists is foregrounded early in the film in Fuentes's first encounter with Harriet and Andrew and in his subsequent encounter with a blind woman in the first village he visits. In this first scene, Harriet complains to Fuentes, "when we speak to the Indians they don't understand Spanish" (Sayles 16). Moments later, Andrew asks "why they don't have fajitas here. . . . Que no—what's the word for fajitas?" (Sayles 18). This foreignness, grounded as it is at the most mundane level, contrasts markedly to Andrew's self-professed expertise about the local history. This knowledge is shown to be marginal and of little relevance to the current sociopolitical conditions of the local populations. In the scene immediately following this conversation with the tourists, Fuentes's equivalent ignorance is foregrounded as his status as a Spanish-speaking city-dweller marks him as foreign in the eyes of the villagers he attempts to communicate with. The tourists' communication difficulties are juxtaposed with Fuentes's ability to speak *only* Spanish and none of the country's indigenous dialects. Equally foreign, the privileged citizen-subject is here linked to the tourist and the subordination of the nation's indigenous populations is shown to take place at the intersection of foreign and domestic cultural practices. Through the film's use of subtitles, the viewer is placed in an equivalent position of insularity to Fuentes and the tourists, thus prompting an examination of the structures of knowledge embedded in the dominance of colonial language practices. Refused a transparent relation to the film on the level of dialogue, the viewer is equally denied—with Fuentes—the comforts of a strictly linear narrative progression and resolution.

The narrative of *Men With Guns* is bookended by a frame story in which an Indian woman tells her daughter of Fuentes's quest and his arrival at Cerca del Cielo. Yoking an indigenous, oral tradition of storytelling to the cycle of stories that makes up the film's principal narrative, the frame story places Fuentes's quest within the realm of myth and outside the bounds of national narrative. Like the use of foreign languages and subtitles, the subtle disruption of the frame story, coupled with the episodic nature of the plot's narrative progression, disarticulates the audience's relationship to the events that unfold before them. The national historiography Andrew espouses and Fuentes believes in is replaced by a more complex, nonprogressive narrative that is attendant to the conditions of the subjects Andrew's history (for example) refuses to acknowledge. Edward Soja claims that "we can no longer depend on a story-line unfolding sequentially, an ever-accumulating history marching straight forward in plot and denouement, for too much is happening against the grain of time, too much is continually traversing the story-line laterally" (23). The framing device used in *Men With Guns* unseats such forward motion and illuminates the hegemonic function of narrative.

In response to the query "What do you think they'll find?" the author of the frame story tells her daughter, "it doesn't matter so much. When people start into a story they have to see the end or they aren't happy" (Sayles 96). As this exchange shows, the frame story both disrupts the narrative logic of the film on a formal level, but also foregrounds the audience's need for that structure. Indeed, through the oft-repeated phrase "the common people love drama," the film reminds us that drama—in the form of national narrative—performs hegemonically as it interpellates the citizen-subject, making sense of discrete and often inarticulate events. Emanuel Levy has criticized the film, claiming that, "plodding along with pedestrian tempo, *Men With Guns* does not benefit from its inherently dramatic format of a murder mystery" (93). While the claim that *Men With Guns* is primarily a murder mystery is itself debatable, this statement also misses the importance this tempo holds in the film's critique. As Fuentes's plight worsens with the loss of his possessions and the theft and vandalism of his car, as he is forced to walk, the narrative pace of the film itself slows down and linear progress toward the resolution of the "murder mystery" (which is never "solved" as such) is derailed.

The film's tempo slows down as Fuentes movers deeper into the mountains, farther away from the city, and the narrative becomes an episodic series of encounters with the characters he meets on his journey. Developing the film's meditations on narrative and hegemony, each of these encounters is built around the telling of a story that complicates and develops those that have come before. What these interrelated stories make clear is that the mystery of Fuentes's missing students cannot be "solved" in

Seeing from ground level (Federico Luppi).

any recognizable way. The events within which the mystery is embedded form a labyrinthine structure of power relations, ranging from contemporary neonationalisms to the U.S. "good neighbor" policy toward South America in the 1930s and the Alliance for Progress of the 1970s, for which the narrative structure of a murder mystery would be inadequate. The macrological view Fuentes begins the film with is not adequate to make sense of these complexities. Thus, the "pedestrian tempo" Levy bemoans must be understood as an essential facet of the film's broader critique.

The easy answers Fuentes desires do not exist because the complex interrelations between the components of the problem—tourism, economics, religion, colonialism, language, nationalism, and such—refuse the reductive reading he wishes to give them. Assuming the form of an odyssean quest, the film contextualizes Fuentes's story within a Western European, epic tradition of storytelling, which it then cites as inadequate. If "films arrange events and actions in a temporal narrative that moves toward fulfillment, and thus shape thinking about historical time and national history" (Shohat and Stam 154), such narrative resolution is ultimately refused in *Men With Guns*. Fuentes is denied the opportunity to make good on the knowledge he has gained, Andrew and Harriet remain blind to the reality surrounding them, and the viewer is finally left in no better position. Forced to walk with Fuentes, the audience is ultimately refused the linear progress and narrative resolution—signified in

Domingo's refutation of the narrative of perpetual sovereignty—they expect and is asked to reflect on why such narratives consistently fail the majority of the film's characters.

NOTES

1. All dialogue from the film is taken from the published shooting script.

2. I would like to thank my colleagues Tyrone Simpson and Laura Shackelford for pointing out the importance of this reversal.

3. While the film is ostensibly set in a fictional country, the Alliance for Progress was an actual program, instigated by John F. Kennedy in 1961 with the intent of curbing revolutionary politics (i.e., communism) in South America. The program lasted until 1973, when the standing committee created to oversee the allocation of funds (the U.S. had pledged $10 billion) and the administration of the program was disbanded. See http://www.bartleby.com/65/al/AlliancPro.html (19 February 2005) for a brief history of the program, and http://www.Fordham.edu/halsall/mod/1961Kennedy-afp1.html (7 March 2005) for a copy of Kennedy's address.

4. See Shohat and Stam 147–51.

5. Mignolo suggests, for example, that "one of the strong weapons in building homogeneous imagined communities was the belief in a national language, which was tied up with national literature and contributed, in the domain of language, to the national culture" (218).

6. One should not be surprised, perhaps, that *Men With Guns* is often classified as a "foreign film" in video rental stores, and is cataloged accordingly—a point that would seem to highlight the troubling ease with which the requirements the film places on a domestic audience can be refused precisely by placing the film "outside" an American national cinema.

WORKS CITED

Anderson, Benedict. *Imagined Communities: Reflections on the Origin and Spread of Nationalism*. London: Verso, 1991.

Bhabha, Homi K. "Dissemination: Time, Narrative and the Margins of the Modern Nation." *Nation and Narration*. Ed. Homi Bhabha. London: Routledge, 1990a.

———. "Introduction: Narrating the Nation." *Nation and Narration*. Ed. Homi Bhabha. London: Routledge, 1990b.

Canclini, Nestor Garcia. *Consumers and Citizens: Globalization and Multicultural Conflicts*. Trans. George Yúdice. Minneapolis: U of Minnesota P, 2001.

Carson, Diane. "John Sayles: Filmmaker." *John Sayles: Interviews*. Ed. Diane Carson. Jackson: UP of Mississippi, 1999.

Dirlik, Arif. "The Global in the Local." *Global/Local: Cultural Production and the Transnational Imaginary*. Ed. Rob Wilson and Wimal Dissanayake. Durham: Duke UP, 1996.

Featherstone, Mike. "Localism, Globalism, and Cultural Identity." *Global/Local: Cultural Production and the Transnational Imaginary*. Ed. Rob Wilson and Wimal Dissanayake. Durham: Duke UP, 1996.

Levy, Emanuel. *Cinema of Outsiders: The Rise of American Independent Film*. New York: New York UP, 1999.

Mignolo, Walter D. *Local Histories/Global Designs: Coloniality, Subaltern Knowledges, and Border Thinking*. Princeton: Princeton UP, 2000.

Munt, Ian. "The 'Other' Postmodern Tourism: Culture, Travel and the New Middle Classes." *Theory, Culture and Society* 11 (1994): 101–23.

Pease, Donald E. "National Narratives, Postnational Narration." *Modern Fiction Studies* 43.1 (1997): 1–23.

Sayles, John. *Men With Guns & Lone Star*. London: Faber and Faber, 1998.

Shohat, Ella, and Robert Stam. *Unthinking Eurocentrism: Multiculturalism and the Media*. London: Routledge, 1994.

Soja, Edward. *Postmodern Geographies: The Reassertion of Space in Critical Social Theory*. London: Verso, 1989.

Urry, John. *The Tourist Gaze: Leisure and Travel in Contemporary Societies*. London: Sage, 1990.

Wilson, Rob, and Wimal Dissanayake. "Tracking the Global/Local." *Global/Local: Cultural Production and the Transnational Imaginary*. Ed. Rob Wilson and Wimal Dissanayake. Durham: Duke UP, 1996.

10

Psychic Borders and Legacies Left Hanging in *Lone Star* and *Men With Guns*

Rebecca M. Gordon

Postcolonial theories of nation, narration, and sexuality; recently created political associations like NAFTA and the EU; the emergence of transnational capitalism; immigration, birth rates, and other demographic shifts all call the notion of a nation's singular identity into question. Implicitly and explicitly, these developments also recast the normative masculinity that sustains it. For if the concept of "nation" is exposed as a fiction, then the association of masculinity to nationhood as similarly coherent, whole, and impenetrable is weakened. Furthermore, if a nation is conscious of other national stories—of other paternal legacies within its borders—then those who are traditionally entrusted to carry on the national story, namely men, have more than one legacy to choose from. Kaja Silverman and other gender theorists have attempted to show that the development of normative masculinity is not invariable but susceptible to identifications and fantasies that the Oedipus complex cannot always contain. If the "son" (the citizen, the subject) chooses a story of nation that differs from that offered by the "father," not only does he choose a different explanation of the nation's coming into being but also a different set of psychic identifications not available to him under the dominant story. Likewise, should a paternal legacy be exposed as a mistake, not only is the legacy rendered null but so too the psychic identifications it might have engendered. In either situation dominant masculinity may endure, but it cannot sustain itself as exclusive.

Two recent films by John Sayles explore these themes along parallel but as it were opposite sides of a psychic and geographical border. *Lone Star* (1996) and *Men With Guns* (1997) show what happens when a son refuses to take up the paternal legacy and also what happens when the father can find no one to carry it out or, worse yet, when the legacy turns out to be wrong. *Lone Star* takes place in a border town whose population reflects America's racial mix in microcosm. Frontera, Texas, struggles consciously with the fact that the overwhelmingly Mexican population will soon hold the reins of local power and of local history. Sam Deeds, a sheriff following reluctantly in his father's footsteps, is called upon to solve a forty-year-old murder. He could walk away and accept the story offered by his father's old cronies—and with it that story's erroneous conclusions—but instead decides to negotiate the many "unofficial" stories told by Frontera's residents. The patrician protagonist of *Men With Guns* decides to visit the medical students he trained years ago to treat the indigenous peoples in their villages. Innocent and naïve, the doctor does not know that rumors of civil war in the mountains are true, nor that his students have been murdered by men with guns—whether guerrillas or soldiers no one knows—in their villages. Set in an unnamed Latin American country, a sense of generic horror permeates *Men With Guns*. In neither film do the characters have a single culture or language to cling to or rely on as true, let alone a unifying story of the past. Furthermore, in each film, memory and the stories on which memories are based—the local paternal legacies—turn out to be the constructions of fathers, constructions that inevitably wound their sons.

Sayles's choice of subject matter invites the question of whether, perhaps, these films qualify as hybrid cinema on the same terms as hybrid literature, for the films' narratives are both "artificially organized system[s] for bringing different languages in contact with one another . . . system[s] having as [their] goal the illumination of one language by means of another, the carving out of a living image of another language" (Staiger 15). In *Lone Star*, characters speak border Spanglish and English, sometimes interchangeably, and who speaks what is often as much a sign of political affiliation as ethnic group or generation. *Men With Guns* was shot and directed in Spanish and given English subtitles, but many of the actors speak indigenous languages (Nahuatl, Kuna, Tzotzil), not Spanish. Taken together, the films provide a wide—and politicized—view of history, masculinity, and responsibility for knowledge of the Western Hemisphere. Especially in the age of NAFTA, in which the limping official story of progress for all simply has not happened, Sayles's films may be an example of third-world cinema coming from a first-world nation.

To the extent that Sayles's films incorporate experimental visual techniques in order to express images and memories not otherwise expressed in a given dominant culture, and to the extent that Sayles puts marginalized voices in conversation with dominant voices in order to "ironize and unmask the other within the same utterance" (Young 20), I submit that these films are hybrid works that participate in the aesthetics and politics of Third Cinema. Chiefly, however, I contend that Sayles's films demonstrate that the singular nature of history, story, and culture that keeps the paternal legacy afloat (and defines "the nation") will be challenged in a hybrid society. Furthermore, once a society recognizes itself as hybrid, the psychic identifications that subtend the singular view—in particular, normative masculinity—may be altered. Taken together, *Lone Star* and *Men With Guns* interrogate the function of the paternal legacy not only to comment on the exhaustion of the motif but also to suggest that the paternal legacy as a source of cultural formation is bankrupt.

Lone Star

The central plot of *Lone Star*, though not its locus of meaning, is a murder mystery. The remains of Sheriff Charlie Wade, missing since 1957, are discovered on a local rifle range. His disappearance allowed the rise of deputy Buddy Deeds, who took over as sheriff for the next several years, building himself a legend as a peacemaker and peacekeeper after decades of rule by the crooked, trigger-happy Wade. Sam Deeds, the new sheriff of Frontera, Texas, reluctantly investigates the murder and his father's possible role in it.

When Sam goes to see longtime Fronteran Minnie Bledsoe about her late husband's relationship with Sheriff Wade, he introduces himself as Sheriff Deeds. "Sheriff Deeds is dead, honey. You just Sheriff Jr.," she says. Sam replies, "Yeah, that's the story of my life." Although he has taken up his father's legacy, Sam clearly cannot fill his father's shoes. He has donned the sheriff's uniform not out of a desire to enforce the law in Rio County but to confront other "issues." In particular Sam bears a grudge against his father for separating him from his first and only true love, Pilar Cruz. Having experienced "an intense love . . . opposed by an almost equally powerful hatred inseparably bound up with it," Sam resembles Freud's Rat Man, whose obsessive, and impotent, hatred for his father derived from being thwarted from marrying his love object (*Three Case Histories* 24). Like the Rat Man, Sam's life is stuck in a similar sort of "paralysis." Although he would like to know the truth about his father's involvement in Charlie Wade's disappearance, he would much rather find weakness in the man who terrorized him as a teenager, and perhaps find out why his father, hero to everyone else, was so unheroic to him.

Sam is driven to investigate his father's past, which he expects to find inextricably linked to local justice and also to Wade and to graft. More important to the film than Sam's quest, however, is Frontera's history and psychogeography. The incidental characters in *Lone Star* are much like tour guides, sharing distilled versions of Frontera's history as they know it, which explains less about whether Sheriff Buddy Deeds was a good man or a bad man than telling Sam and the audience about their social space, their particular ethnic or generational enclaves, and how they connect to where they live.

Formally, *Lone Star* revisits *Citizen Kane:* other people tell a story about what a man was like, from their own perspectives. However, in *Lone Star,* more often than not, one story that begins with one teller and from one perspective—a medium shot pushed into a medium close-up by tracking, a pan, or a flashback—will end with another person finishing the story. Or a pan rather than a cut will merge the "present" into the "past," proof that Buddy's story is still very much alive for some people. As the pan shots suggest, however, that story is circumscribed within tight circles or areas of knowledge that one teller cannot escape, or will not, because there are things Sam does not and should not know.

Hollis's story is the first, recounting in tall-tale fashion the time Buddy Deeds challenged Charlie Wade. He begins his story at the Santa Barbara Café, a joint owned by Mercedes Cruz that used to belong to someone else. The camera tilts down to a plate of tortillas, the light changes from goldish day to dark red night, and Charlie Wade's hand picks up the bread, shifting us to the past. Hollis's story ends in the past with Buddy Deeds facing down Wade. In search of other stories, Sam visits Minnie Bledsoe, who tells Sam about the way Charlie Wade used to treat her late husband, Roderick, and indeed all the blacks in town who used to go to the club they managed. Her story begins in full day on her front porch; her flashback ends in Big O's—the club Otis bought for himself, years after Wade's disappearance—and in the middle of another family's story.

Minnie's tale chronicles the differences between the terror Wade wrought on the town's minorities and the much fairer rules set down by Buddy Deeds, but also indicates Sam's "unfearsomeness" as sheriff. Part of it is his lack of charisma, perhaps, but part of it could be the weakening, over time, of the "sheriff" legacy. There is also a generational factor. On his way to a celebration unveiling a statue of his father in the town square, in front of Buddy Deeds City Hall, Sam is flanked by Danny, a Kickapoo city councilman; Ray, an activist Chicano high school teacher; and Cliff, a city deputy and old friend of Buddy's. Sam is surrounded by three generations (and ethnicities) of Frontera men. Ray walks slightly behind the group, declaring that renaming the city hall is a desecration; he recounts that among Buddy's sins was the eviction of one hundred Kickapoo from a little village on the edge of Lake Perdido, done so Buddy could invest in a housing development. Realizing he may have insulted Sam, Ray says, "I just think people should know the truth about Buddy." "That makes two of us," Sam replies. He's hardly a one-story sheriff.

Wesley Birdsong, the Kickapoo Indian who sells bric-a-brac on a lonely back road, gives Sam more information than anyone else, perhaps because he's further at the fringes than anyone else—literally more marginal. He mentions that Buddy "had that woman on the side," but "can't remember her name" after so many years. Shaking a rattler skin, he tells Sam, "Be careful 'bout where you go looking. Don't know what you'll find." The repeated line "Your father was a legend; your mother was a saint" should be warning enough to Sam that he might uncover an oedipal nightmare. And in fact it turns out that Sam's first love and newly reclaimed lover, Pilar, is the daughter of Mercedes Cruz and Buddy Deeds. Thus Sam's lover is his half sister; his father's infidelity makes Sam's only love taboo. Even now, Buddy has the power to mess up Sam's life.

At least one review of *Lone Star* posits the incest subtheme as the central point of the film. This, however, is a red herring.

Sam and Pilar's decision to be an incestuous couple is certainly dramatic, but it does not involve the rest of the community of Frontera. Theirs is an antisocial decision, as romantic love often is. They will have to leave Frontera, where "people will know," but on the whole their decision is an individual way of wresting from social rules and the shadow of the Father—who is, for them, their father—some independence and peace.

For Freud, the incest taboo and the Law of the Father are enmeshed: the incest taboo is necessary to keep the paternal legacy afloat. Silverman comments,

> Rather than isolating it as the site at which human culture emerges, he subordinates it to a more primordial event, of which it is merely a consequence or extension. Its inception becomes one of the concluding moments in a phylogenetic narrative, a narrative in which a horde of sons murder and incorporate the father, and then elevate the paternal principle to a Law. Freud consequently makes it impossible to conceptualize the incest taboo outside the context of a phallocentric symbolic order. (40)

Silverman pulls the two concepts apart to emphasize instead the way "the ideology of the family functions to arouse in the subject conventional Oedipal desires and identifications. The positive Oedipus complex is consequently the normative psychic response not to kinship, but to the dominant fiction" (40).

Whether the law of the father and the kinship structure overlap or not, however, Sam and Pilar are already mixed: White and Hispanic, already proof that there is more than one originary story for them. They commit incest before and after the fact of knowing, and they are able to drop Buddy's paternal legacy—of being sheriff, of being "in control" of Frontera's history—because it can have nothing to do with them as both mixed people and incestuous lovers. Their story has more to do with desire than continuance of "the" story.

Men With Guns

Lone Star tells a local story in extensive detail, detail that links that story to a larger image of America. *Men With Guns* is a simpler story both in form and content, though it suggests a grander

Searching for his former students, Dr. Fuentes (Federico Luppi) must eventually confront the truth of their murders. *Shane Young, courtesy of Vulcan Productions.*

political scope. The film is a road movie whose "quest" literally takes its characters up the side of a mountain. Although prosaically structured, *Men With Guns* is psychically much more unnerving than *Lone Star*, which still falls within the purview of Freud's Oedipus complex. The end of *Lone Star* reveals that the father's shadow also hid the father's sins, which put the son at risk in ways he was never warned about. In *Men With Guns*, the father does not know what has happened to his "children," and his own blindness would have made it impossible for him to warn them.

Dr. Humberto Fuentes, physician to generals and upper-middle-class ladies in his fictitious country's capital city, trained several medical students years ago to be doctors in the Indian villages in the *campos*. His wife dead and his own children no particular comfort, Fuentes decides to track down his former students to see how they have fared. Impossibly naïve about the atrocities carried out by his nation's government against the indigenous people, Fuentes is unprepared for the discovery that every single one of his students has been murdered, either by the army or by guerrillas—whichever group of "men with guns" has come through the village and decided to destroy rather than evacuate it.

One of the first images in *Men With Guns* is of Dr. Fuentes in his office giving a rectal exam to a uniformed general. Dr. Fuentes literally has his finger in the ass of official knowledge, yet knows nothing about the state of his nation. *Men With Guns* offers the antiromance of the man on intimate terms with state power. If the typical (or stereotypical) notion of masculinity in Latin American dictatorships includes a machismo fed by proximity to power, then certainly Fuentes is not typical. Although so close, he has decided not to see any more or learn any more, willing to remain in bourgeois comfort in the capital city until, narcissism taking over, he begins to worry about his legacy. His character is out of line with his counterparts, though Dr. Fuentes perhaps has precedents in Spanish hidalgo culture, and in an older idea of the Latin American nation.

As a member of the metropolitan upper middle class, Dr. Fuentes inherits the tradition of the European creole elite who, in the early nineteenth century, sparked the independence movements against Spain that led to the creation of Latin American nations. Mary Louise Pratt, focusing on the politics of the contact zone, and Doris Sommer, reviewing Latin America's literary history, have explained the central importance of fictional founding narratives to the work of nation building in Latin America. Pratt recounts how the revolutions for independence were led by intellectuals and writers, who sought to exert imaginary control over the nation through fictions that encouraged racial mixing—a fait accompli that reinforced the fiction of European beneficence (175–81, passim). According to Sommer, Latin American literature of the independence period consisted largely of "stories of star-crossed lovers who represent particular regions, races, parties, or economic interests which should naturally come together" (75). The novels from various regions across South America illustrate particular national contexts, but "the novels . . . read together, . . . reveal remarkable points of contact in both plot and language. . . . [Their] coherence comes

... from their common need to reconcile and amalgamate national constituencies, and from the strategy to cast the previously unreconciled parties, races, classes, or regions, as lovers who are 'naturally' attracted to and right for one another" (Sommer 81). The Latin American nation needed to be deliberately mixed, for it was necessary and desirable to know everyone in the land in order to consolidate it.

Dr. Fuentes's failure in *Men With Guns*, then, may in part be his alliance with this older, more romantic nationhood of "natural families" and of his nation's leaders as "civilizing fathers." He has perhaps believed the foundational narratives too much—that is, believed that the mixes took place and all is now well, for such a view would fit the narrow bourgeois "cultural box" he knows in the capital city. What has intervened in this national romance is revolution. Perversely, Dr. Fuentes is alive but his "children," the students, have been murdered. His situation is the inversion of Freud's "horde of sons" come to kill the father, for rather than being an established professional on his way to replacement by former students who might envy his comfortable position, Dr. Fuentes has sent these students, unwittingly, to their deaths. In contrast to the father whose secrecy creates suffering in the son, this father created suffering through sheer ignorance and vanity, a mistaken belief in the power of his paternal function. Dr. Fuentes's *méconnaissance* in regard to his own nation and his own culpability render him not the Father, but a father manqué.

While searching for his students Fuentes attracts a ragged troupe of fellow travelers: a starving boy, an army deserter who has himself committed vicious crimes, and a hunted priest. Fuentes's new "family" is an unnatural amalgam—it consists entirely of men until the army takes Padre Portillo away. They are then joined by Graciela, a mute Indian girl who has been raped by a soldier (perhaps the deserter, or certainly a man much like him). As this ragged family scours the countryside, they encounter, in turn, the "sugar people," "cane people," and "coffee people." Each community "tells" Dr. Fuentes what has happened to the local doctor he sent. He does not understand them, however—they speak mostly in silence, answering his questions about his former students by ignoring him. Conejo, the boy, tries to make Dr. Fuentes understand that the students have been murdered. "Why?" he asks. "Because they were doctors," replies Conejo.

Marginalized voices enter into conversations with dominant voices in *Men With Guns*. Here Dr. Fuentes (Federico Luppi) and the boy Conejo (Dan Rivera González) sit at a campfire. *Shane Young, courtesy of Vulcan Productions.*

Still confused, Conejo explains to the doctor that soldiers and guerrillas are like dogs. "Dogs can't be blamed for what they do; they're just dogs." Yet Dr. Fuentes fails to comprehend—indeed, he resists comprehension—until the last possible moment, when he dies under a tree after finding out that hearsay of a last surviving student, a woman, was a lie.

Eerily, though the country is never given a name, *Men With Guns* is redolent with the markers of "nationhood." In an uncanny manner produced to some extent by Sayles's "magical realist" cinematic effects, the apparatus of the state makes itself felt offscreen while the countryside is terrorized. Indeed, the film's ability to invoke an invisible torture-machine recalls Michael Taussig's work on the imagery of colonial terror. The unnamed nation in this film attempts to control men through recourse to the standard lures of dominant masculinity—machismo, the attainment of rank, a gun, local power—but the pleasures of these lures have ceased to be attractive. Dr. Fuentes leaves the capital, Domingo deserts the army, and Padre Portillo abandons his flock (at their insistence). However, the men's resistance to the official story broadcast from the metropole cannot stem the unofficial violence they find in the countryside. As long as someone pays soldiers to kill the Indians (whether it be the United States in the mid-1980s or the Mexican government in the 1990s), the men with guns will show up.

Men With Guns is an allegory of the extreme case of a figure who has grown old and not paid attention to the fact that his country is no longer under the sway of "civilizing fathers" who are "feminized and sentimental" but of brutish sons in civil war. His legacy, in which he has so much proud faith, is a good idea but wrong for the times. In life, he can find no one to take it over.

Paternal Legacies Left Hanging

Obsessively returning to the paternal theme, these films remind us of the Rat Man's confession to Freud: "Thoughts about my father's death occupied my mind from a very early age and for a long period of time, and greatly depressed me" (*Three Case Histories* 9). The fathers fail to protect the sons in either case, though Sam and Dr. Fuentes hold opposite positions in that relation. Neither man doubts he deserves a measure of power in his respective society, nor does either decline opportunities to wield it; but neither Deeds nor Fuentes is able to control the narrative in which he is placed as the ostensible hero. Sam Deeds allows himself to take up the sheriff's badge, which in turn allows him access to privileged information, but his investigation is the engine for a story that has more facets than he can perceive, and he will learn more than he wanted to know. Dr. Fuentes, the patriarch, is certainly not ambivalent to his phallic inheritance, yet he cannot palm off his legacy on anyone because his (substitute) children, those who should be "killing him" for his legacy, are already dead. Both men have some power; but Sam chooses to abandon his while Fuentes, who discovers that his legacy is not of the quality or quantity he thought, mournfully lets it drop from his hands. Through different devices, Sam Deeds and Dr. Fuentes are made to see the wounds on which their masculinity rests, and to know the pain that mistaken memories—by extension, mistaken histories and national stories—can cause.

It is possible, however, for the suffering son to suffer no more *and* to break the legacy of the father. In *Lone Star,* Sam suffers no consequences for breaking the Law of the Father—namely, for committing incest (leaving aside Silverman's separation of the two concepts for the moment). This suggests a masculinity that has freed itself somewhat from alliance with the dominant fiction. In *Men With Guns,* Domingo, the army deserter, proves that there are soldiers who no longer want to be men with guns. He takes the medicine bag from Dr. Fuentes to help a woman wounded by a land mine, metaphorically embarking on a career of healing rather than violence. Domingo becomes the unintended heir of Fuentes's paternal legacy. Because he takes over the legacy with no prior preparation, he offers hope of bringing a different story to this paternal legacy, one that is cognizant of the terror in the mountains and the government's lies. The will to perversion at work in these films discloses an antipaternal, antimasculine spirit. To dispute Silverman's opinion on the subject, a change in the dominant fiction may not necessarily rely on the "collective acknowledgment" of the abyss on which male subjectivity is erected. But the will to pervert the dominant fiction does depend on having a better story, a more varied story, than the one suggested by the paternal legacy. Granted that the nation is a fiction, the story of the nation is still important for social and psychological stability, for a nation in want of or in the process of telling itself its story is likely to be a nation at arms.

As I mentioned earlier, Silverman divides Kinship structure from the Law of Language in order to demonstrate, as Gayle Rubin and others have done, that Freud conflated the two, and to show where the Law of the Name of the Father is invariable, and where it is not. According to Silverman, "[t]he positive Oedipal complex represents the primary vehicle through which the subject affirms the 'reality' of the family and the phallus, as well as the other ideological elements with which they are intertwined" (40). The dominant fiction, for Silverman, is about fantasy first. So too is the nation a fiction, a fantasy. It makes sense, then, that if a man does not respond to the paternal legacy, he has not responded to a crucial component of the dominant fiction, and may have already recognized his masculinity as resting on an "abyss."

What I am contending is that the nation is the most widely visible manifestation of and metaphor for the outcome of the positive Oedipus complex. If the positive Oedipus complex, though, is, as Silverman says, "the psychic consequence of a conventional interpellation into [the dominant fiction]," and the dominant fiction "not only offers the representational system by means of which the subject typically assumes a sexual identity. . . . but forms *the stable core around which a nation's and a period's 'reality' coheres* [my emphasis]," then a choice of national stories makes it possible for a nation's citizens to be interpellated into a quite different dominant fiction (40). When a nation knows itself as hybrid, the nation's story of itself changes; the details of its foundational narrative are transformed: who fought where, when, and against whom; which languages are spoken where, by whom, and why; how many people live where, under what conditions, since when. When being a mixture of what was once "other" or "different" is the norm, not the exception, a hybrid nation's foundational narrative will have imbricated within it an assortment of ways to tell its story.

The love/hate relationships of sons to fathers and, perhaps, of men to national stories that do not include the whole range of possibilities, remind us of Freud's judgment of reality in "Totem and Taboo," a judgment clearly related to his Rat Man findings: "The asocial nature of neuroses has its genetic origin in their most fundamental purpose, which is to take flight from an unsatisfying reality into a more pleasurable world of fantasy. The real world, which is avoided in this way by neurotics, is under the sway of human society and of the institutions collectively created by it. To turn away from reality is at the same time to withdraw from the community of man" (74). But what would Freud do with a hybrid nation? A nation formed of multiple and contentious communities? A nation with multiple foundational stories and paternal legacies, not one?

A fairly standard reading of nationalism understands it to have "typically sprung from masculinized memory, masculinized humiliation and masculinized hope" (Nagel 242). But the responsibility to be Masculine on so many fronts carries a high price:

> Patriarchal masculinity cripples men. Manhood as we know it in our society requires such a self-destructive identity, a deeply masochistic self-denial, a shrinkage of the self, a turning away from whole areas of life, [that] the man who obeys the demands of masculinity has become only half-human. . . . To become the

man I was supposed to be, I had to destroy my most vulnerable side, my sensitivity, my femininity, my creativity, and I had to pretend to be both more powerful and less powerful than I feel.
(Roger Horrocks, qtd. in Nagel 246)

It is hardly news that being a man in a man's world is difficult. But if a society begins to know itself as hybrid, then the single paternal legacy can be allowed to relax its hold. When represented in cinema, refusal of the paternal legacy in favor of mixtures and profligate others may well be a sign of the desire for a different story in the wider culture. The dominant fiction does not exist in the abstract; it is in part determined precisely by images in culture. As history, fiction, culture, politics, and the vicissitudes of capital have shown us, reality itself can be altered.

For some time it has been argued, especially in postcolonial studies, that the hybrid form allows the subaltern to speak—usually meaning an ethnic or gendered minority. Perhaps it is also possible for a nondominant masculinity, or the desire for a nondominant masculinity, to "speak" through hybrid forms. According to Laura Marks, "[h]ybrid cinema doubts the assumptions that structure conventional films about minority history, fiction and documentary alike: namely that there is an intact oral history out there waiting to be tapped, recorded, and proffered to a community" (247). Furthermore, "[f]ilms that are hybrid . . . are forced to use hegemonic languages to speak from positions of diaspora," and "take advantage of this disjunction between the visual and the verbal" (244). Considering how, theoretically, the language of a nation is associated with those who dominate it, the fact that *Lone Star* and *Men With Guns* use more than one language within their narratives suggests a conscious effort to avoid that association with dominance.

John Sayles, an American director, shot and directed *Men With Guns* in Spanish. By taking his scripts to Spanish-speaking script doctors he also avoided any particular Spanish-speaking country's cadence by effecting a Spanish devoid of national and local resonances. Sayles is rather self-congratulatory on this point, feeling he has found a desirable "genericness." This discomfited a Spanish-speaking *New York Times* reviewer, for the lack of linguistic integrity meant the story had no historical integrity, which made it seem—rightly so, perhaps—that Sayles was colonizing a region and blurring its linguistic and historical differences into an allegory for the Yanquis. At the same time, "for Spanish speakers, the comic potential for this idiomatic hodgepodge is staggering" (Rodriguez 4).

Before we draw a neocolonial authorial phantasmatic from Sayles's films, it may be helpful to remember that "[t]he minority artist dances along the border. He/she must undo a double colonization, since the community is colonized both by the master's stories and by its own, that have been translated and annexed by the colonizer" (Marks 262). It certainly would be possible to interrogate Sayles's cachet as an independent filmmaker with outspoken leftist politics; his long-standing interest in Hispanic American life and culture; his own authority as an inhabitant of several American towns, cities, and boroughs. However, as Homi Bhabha points out, textual hybrids have effects on colonizers. The recognition of hybridity calls into question the transparency of colonial authority; further, to recognize a hybrid forces the dominant culture to look back at itself and see its presumption of universality. As Janet Staiger argues, "Hybridity always opens up the discriminatory presumptions of purity, authenticity, and originality from which the textual hybrid is declared to be a deviation, a bastard, a corruption" (15–17). Despite the didacticism in some of his films, it seems much more fruitful to take Sayles's political commitments at their word, for his work produces just such a recognition even among annoyed critics.

Touring the Psychic Borderlands

In a 1996 *Cineaste* interview on *Lone Star*, Sayles explains, "When you cross the border and go into some kind of new territory, you don't necessarily have the power that you had on your side of it" (West and West 14). The action the main characters take in these films is precisely border crossing (physical and psychical), which demands a concomitant giving-up of power, whether it be Sam Deeds's delving into the past discovering nuggets of knowledge forbidden him before, or Dr. Fuentes's accidental discoveries of villages, peoples, and languages he did not even know his country contained. In addition to individual masculine psyches, Sayles presents sociopsychic images of the U.S.-Mexico border, and of the territory between public and state knowledge in South America.

Lone Star takes up the concept of "the border," including

its psychic meanings, in a bluntly conscious and self-conscious way. One might even argue that the border is so clearly in view of Frontera's inhabitants, that they live with the past and remember it so well, that the concept "border" almost functions as an ego formation. It is anything but repressed, and it is the concept that keeps the town moving, even giving the town a name. In *Men With Guns*, the borders are not so neatly drawn. The Latin American country in which the film takes place is left unnamed, though it looks like Mexico and could stand in for Guatemala, given the recent civil war and Sayles's research for the film. As Dr. Fuentes's naïveté suggests, the Official Government has control of the mouthpieces of the nation and, by extension, control over public memory. Unlike Texas where every ethnic group has its own recollection of what happened and has the right to speak that memory, the Indians in *Men With Guns* are at the mercy of two fighting forces who treat whoever's in their path the same way. In the words of a 1998 *Esquire* magazine review, this film "might seem so very 1985" if it were not for the recent murder of Mexican Indians in Chiapas ("*Arriba* Sayles!" 42).

Structurally, the border crossings that take place in these films invoke a perverse form of tourism. Tourists most often cross borders as outsiders to a place or to a time, seeking to know more about the past of a place or the present life of its people. Most tourists follow well-laid paths to museums, monuments, and other sites, accepting as they do so the paradigm of commercial tourism in which, as Keith Hollinshead explains, "most interpreted sites are national 'sacred' sites or are enunciations of some well-resourced set of stakeholders or of a traditionally minded elite" (135). At such sites, Hollinshead continues, "it is commonplace for the value-coding of the exhibitry to be seized and restrictively controlled, so that only storylines with a discursively closed circle of interpreted traditions are allowed to be revealed" (135). Thus tourism in modern societies often functions as a support for a nation's narrative of itself. Toward a similar end, tourism may also be used as a force to control populations who might otherwise live independently from the national entity. As anthropologist Jean Michaud has found in his studies of Northern Thailand and India, central governments use international tourism to influence the balance of power between local communities and the centralized state, even though distant communities may themselves be ambiguous in their feeling toward and support for the state. Hence, "tourism is used as a form of governmentality which helps dominate outlier communities, which lose their own freedom to be ambiguous as they are inscribed as 'national' by the central government through tourism and through related social and political forces" (Michaud, qtd. in Hollinshead 139).

Ironically, Dr. Fuentes is on vacation when he learns that his former students have all been killed. His encounters with his nation's outlier communities—the salt people, the cane people, the sugar people, the coffee people—are the stuff of travelogues, except that Fuentes meets them on the run. Hunted by the soldiers and guerrillas, they are attempting to escape to Cerca del Cielo, a refugee village in the mountains. The government soldiers scoff that Cerca del Cielo is a myth, a superstition, but are nonetheless exasperated by the people's attempts to find it, understanding that the village, mythic or not, stands for the possibility of slipping through the cracks of state surveillance—and of living as testaments to the lie of the "official story." Fuentes, Conejo, Domingo, and Graciela—themselves more refugees than tourists—decide to follow suit. Fuentes hopes to contact the last of his students who might be alive; Graciela hopes to hide from the army and other men who might brutalize her; Conejo and Domingo tag along because they have nowhere else to go, having been abandoned by or deserted from the army. Midway through the trip, Fuentes discovers Graciela on the point of committing suicide. To convince her to continue with them rather than kill herself, Dr. Fuentes describes Cerca del Cielo for her as a mountain paradise of clear water, fresh air, peace, and plenty. He wants her to believe she is close to safety, but he could just as well be describing a health spa or a resort, so unreally perfect and distant does it sound. That Fuentes's description echoes the stilted language of travel brochures also indicates his own skepticism about ever finding Cerca del Cielo.

After the first two days the travelers must abandon their jeep and hike the mountains. While lunching at a hidden temple in the jungle, two Americans Fuentes had long presumed dead suddenly reappear, fully outfitted in backpacking gear. They are not worried: "My husband's got an excellent sense of direction!" The situation is absurd. Ultraindustrious and ultraperky, the Americans make a mockery of Fuentes et al.'s trip with their ease of travel and absolute confidence in their right to be there.

Graciela (Tania Cruz) makes a mute appeal. *Shane Young, courtesy of Vulcan Productions.*

These tourists are particularly hilarious because they reject "preferred commodity forms" in exchange for "traveling"—rather than being satisfied with the deluxe hotels and other pleasures provided specifically for them in the tourist zones, they are "extreme tourists" in search of the "real" nation—which does not, in fact, exist. At the same time, however, the tourists underscore how much more Fuentes has in common with first worlders than with the indigenous peoples of his own country, among whom he sent his students. He first came across the couple, in fact, at a tourist-class hotel a day's drive outside the capital city, early in his own travels. The Americans also remind the viewer that they knew more than Fuentes did about what was happening in the mountains, having read books and heard in the American press about "atrocidades aqui."

At the end of "Totem and Taboo," Freud cautions his readers against "being influenced too far in our judgment of primitive men by analogy of neurotics" (161). We must "avoid transplanting a contempt for what is merely thought or wished from our commonplace world, with its wealth of material values, into the world of primitive men and neurotics, of which the wealth lies only within themselves" (160). It would seem that Freud's warning, spiked with the red-flag words "material" and "wealth," suggests a perfect tourist destination, where an escapee from the materially wealthy West can inspect the indigenous folk or watch the compulsive behaviors and hear the muddled stories of an obsessional neurotic from the safe haven of a normative psychic tour bus—replete with normative notions of nation, self, and other. And if the wealth of the primitive men "lies only within himself," for the tourist that is precisely where the primitive man's wealth should be, for that is what he has to offer the tourist who has everything else. And once the primitive man learns he can be safe from guerrillas by being a tourist attraction—for helping the tourist industry enrich the coffers of whatever government is in power—then he or she can be an attraction simply by being "him-" or "herself."

Tourism near Frontera is likely to be limited to the nearby Alamo, which, in painfully self-conscious Frontera, most people would like to forget (both for the local meaning of that site, and for the embarrassing Disneyfication of that meaning for an international audience). Other attractions include Lake Perdido, a man-made reservoir and housing development owned primarily by Mercedes Cruz and Hollis, who have Buddy Deeds to thank for the money to invest in it; and the nearest town across the border, Ciudad León, famous for its radio commercials: "Chucho, Rey de las Llantas!" (Chucho, King of the Tires!). Fronterans may be too aware of themselves and their hybridity to attempt toying with "authenticity," crucial to any successful tourist mission. Pilar invites her mother, Mercedes Cruz, to come down to Mexico with her and her kids, Amado and Paloma. "Amado's into this big Tejano thing," Pilar explains, and wants to know the "real culture." "What does he want to go to Mexico for?" her mother asks. "There are Mexicans all over the place. Look around you!"

At work in both *Men With Guns* and *Lone Star*, on a metaphoric if not diegetic level, is the tension between universal civilization and national culture—between the involuntary mutual awareness and dependency of every people and region made possible (and inevitable) by "civilization," as well as, to quote Tim Brennan, "the dogged persistence of defensive movements helping subject peoples carve out a bit of space on the earth's turf" (46), for "[i]n order to take part in modern civilization, it is necessary at the same time to take part in scientific, technical, and political rationality, something which very often requires the pure and simple abandonment of a whole cultural past" (Ricoeur, in Brennan, 46). For Bhabha, the idea of a "whole" cultural past that could be abandoned "purely and simply" is ridiculous. As he argues in *The Location of Culture*, the categorization of peoples, places, and pasts is not a matter of unswerving fact about a universally accepted character or property of that population, region, or inheritance. Instead, it is more usefully seen as something contained within discourse itself—as an ongoing matter of debate, negotiation, and ideological struggle. In this process, "everyone actively and continually competes to advance their own vision of nationhood or group heritage" (Hollinshead 133). But these two films suggest that the struggle over discourse is bound to be difficult. The communities of Frontera might debate the state of their heritage, partly because the sheriff's legacy is fading and because the military base in town is about to close: that means fewer jobs but also fewer visual indications of a troublesome national story. The situation in Dr. Fuentes's unnamed country is far different— not a matter of negotiations at all but of brute force. The state of masculinity thus also differs in each film. Whereas Fronterans have an opportunity to redefine masculinity for themselves as the markers of dominant masculinity slowly disappear, or reveal their power as outdated, the markers of dominant masculinity in *Men With Guns* seem to be in dangerous flux: rather than being subjugated by one central Father-like power aligned with modernity, the countryside is overrun with "sons" (guerrillas and soldiers) violently—not discursively—competing to advance an ideological Father. The result is a sense of terror that is unlikely to stabilize in the short term.

Conclusion

The situation for indigenous cultures in *Men With Guns* is perhaps more bleak than for the Texans in *Lone Star*. As long as the indigenous cultures—the salt people, the cane people, the coffee people; the Kuna speakers, Tzotzil speakers, Nahuatl speakers— remain isolated, and do not venture into the capital and back, their cultures remain, supposedly, pure. However, they have no way of knowing if the guerrillas are coming to their villages. They can only hope they do not. *Men With Guns* opens with a framing narrative featuring a clairvoyant Kuna woman who tells her daughter that the doctor is coming, that he is looking for people he will not find. But she waits for the doctor partly because she is waiting for medical help: she was not "clairvoyant enough" to avoid stepping on a land mine. A lack of knowledge beyond the local offers a certain freedom, but it is a mitigated freedom. Although "ancient knowledge" is valuable and necessary for the Indians' sense of identity, that sort of knowledge is not necessarily the "right" knowledge—or at least, it may not protect them.

Similarly, when asked if Cerca del Cielo was a metaphor for the United States, Sayles noted that for some Indians, it would be for it is just as distant, just as unreal (Smith 246). As a hidden spot on an unnamed Latin American mountain, Cerca del Cielo will remain a refugee's paradise as long as no one chops down trees for firewood or starts growing food. Should the refugees begin to settle, Cerca del Cielo would no longer be myth but fact. The army—or the guerrillas—would find it, and the last resort would vanish. As Conejo says, "They're free to starve." However, more than likely it will be discovered by American eco-tourists who want to meet the last of the indigenous peoples, conveniently located on a beautiful mountaintop.

What does still offer hope, however, despite the cynicism almost unavoidable in knowing too much, are community and desire. For the moment, Cerca del Cielo remains intact, too remote to be bothered. It also, for the moment, has a doctor—Domingo. The paternal legacy that Fuentes thought he had to pass down to his students—his "direct" heirs—has instead become the property of a deserter and a ragged camp of survivors. The influence this legacy will have on the operations of the state cannot yet be foreseen, but in altering Domingo's relationship to the dominant fiction, it will surely alter this village's notions of masculinity.

Sam and Pilar pay for their desire and knowledge of their origins, personally and emotionally, but they already know that social morality is something constructed, not natural. Only the generation that knows Buddy's secret needs to be spared the recognition of incest. When the generation that created Buddy's legend has past, and his story no longer needs telling, it can be consciously—and guiltlessly—left fallow; that particular paternal legacy can die.

According to these two films, unconventional paternal legacies are inevitable in a hybrid society. Also according to these two films, there is little chance of finding a society on the Western Hemisphere that is *not* already hybrid. Peaceful existence in societies that know themselves as hybrid may be difficult, however, at least for a time. Men with guns usually only want to follow one story, and tend to make knowledge of others come at a price. But the knowledge is inevitable; and if it is men with guns who make such knowledge violent to come by, then the more stories they are forced to know, the better for society as a whole.

WORKS CITED

Adams, Thelma. "'Guns' Takes Aim at Latin Killing Fields." *New York Post*. http://www.nypostonline.com/reviews/movies/830.html. 5 May 1998.
"*Arriba* Sayles!" *Esquire* 129.3 (1998): 42.
Bakhtin, Mikhail M. *The Dialogic Imagination*. Austin: U of Texas P, 1986.
Bhabha, Homi, ed. *Nation and Narration*. London: Routledge, 1990.
Brennan, Tim. "The National Longing for Form." *Nation and Narration*. Ed. Homi Bhabha. London: Routledge, 1990. 44–70.
Bruner, E. M. "Transformation of Self in Tourism." *Annals of Tourism Research* 18.2 (1991): 238–50.
Freud, Sigmund. *Three Case Histories*. New York: Touchstone/Simon and Schuster, 1996.
———. "Totem and Taboo." 1913. *The Standard Edition of the Complete Psychological Works of Sigmund Freud*. Trans. and ed. James Strachey. Vol. 13. London: Hogarth, 1955. 1–162.
Hollinshead, Keith. "Tourism, Hybridity, and Ambiguity: The Relevance of Bhabha's 'Third Space' Cultures." *Journal of Leisure Research* 30.1 (1998): 121–57.
Lone Star. Directed by John Sayles. Rio Dulce/Castle Rock Entertainment, 1996.
Marks, Laura. "A Deleuzian Politics of Hybrid Cinema." *Screen* 35.3 (1994): 244–64.
Men With Guns/Hombres Armados. Directed by John Sayles. Anarchists' Convention Productions/Lexington Road Pictures/Clear Blue Sky Productions, 1997.
Nagel, Joane. "Masculinity and Nationalism: Gender and Sexuality in the Making of Nations." *Ethnic and Racial Studies* 21.2 (1998): 242–69.
Pratt, Mary Louise. Imperial Eyes: *Travel Writing and Transculturation*. London: Routledge, 1992.
Rodriguez, Luis. "*Hombres Armados* (*Men With Guns*)." *New York Times*,

30 March 1997, Section 2, 4.
Selwyn, Tom, ed. *The Tourist Image: Myths and Myth-Making in Tourism.* Chichester: John Wiley, 1996.
Silverman, Kaja. *Male Subjectivity at the Margins.* London: Routledge, 1992.
Smith, Gavin. *Sayles on Sayles.* London: Faber and Faber, 1998.
Sommer, Doris. "Irresistible Romance: The Foundational Fictions of Latin America." *Nation and Narration.* Ed. Homi Bhabha. London: Routledge, 1990. 71–98.
Staiger, Janet. "Hybrid or Inbred: The Purity Hypothesis and Hollywood Genre History." *Film Criticism* 22.1 (1997): 5–20.
West, Dennis, and Joan M. West. "Borders and Boundaries: An Interview with John Sayles." *Cineaste* 22.3 (1996): 14–17.
Young, Robert J. C. *Colonial Desire: Hybridity in Theory, Culture, and Race.* London: Routledge, 1995.

11

The Space of Ambiguity:
Representations of Nature in *Limbo*

Laura Barrett

The title and opening credits of John Sayles's *Limbo* appear against a travelogue, in which a stream of salmon is supplanted by a row of kitschy souvenirs—adorable stuffed bears whose harmlessness is only heightened by the attached price tags. While the fish offer the first representation of nature in a film preoccupied with definitions of nature and thus stand in opposition to the artificial toy bears, we learn from Sayles's commentary on the DVD that the salmon swim not in the Pacific Ocean but in a man-made hatchery. This small but significant moment prefigures one of the crucial themes of *Limbo*: the ambiguous nature of nature. How do our representations of nature help to constitute nature itself?[1] That question is partly answered in the film's pseudo-documentary, in which an anonymous male voice-over talks about "America's last frontier," a "land [which] abounds with creatures great and small, strange and majestic" as the camera settles on a grandmotherly woman who is being hugged by a man dressed as a polar bear. The image of a totem pole that separates these defanged and declawed stuffed bears further generalizes the commodification of the natural world to include the Esquimo, whose contributions to Alaska are extolled as their miniature representations are pieced together in a doll factory. Vacationing septuagenarians awkwardly board canoes while the voice-over describes Alaska as a "land appealing to the bold and adventurous, to men and women willing to risk their lives for the promise of untold fortune." This promotional verbiage is grounded in twentieth-century discourse about Alaska, as evinced in *National Geographic*'s June 1975 issue featuring Alaska, titled "Our Last Great Wilderness" and a contemporaneous National Park Service film portraying Alaska as the "last great wilderness" (Nash 294). Ironically, in determining that Alaska's most valuable resource is space, environmentalists and policy makers mandated that a "third of Alaska will, in the foreseeable future, be wild by default of development" (Nash 315). The unlikely partnership of development and wilderness is at the heart of *Limbo*, Sayles's 1999 film concerned with the spaces between life and death, nature and culture. Indeed, what makes *Limbo* so fascinating is its slipperiness, its unwillingness to fall easily into the dogma that critics often find hard to take in Sayles's films. *Limbo*'s ruminations on the relationship between humans and nature are especially hard to pin down, as it initially seems to endorse an engagement with and understanding of nature reminiscent of literary modernism only to move toward a more postmodern view of nature, one that recognizes, as William Cronon notes, that "[i]deas of nature never exist outside a cultural context, and the meanings we assign to nature cannot help reflecting that context" ("Introduction: In Search of Nature," 35).

With the conclusion of the opening credits, the film moves from pseudo-documentary format to the scene of a fish cannery, where an employee, mimicking the voice from the promotional film, pitches the idea of turning the factory—after it has been disinfected—into a tourist attraction, one possible exhibit offering a worker holding "fake" fish guts. Such an appreciation of the fake and a corresponding depreciation of the real are recalled through the ironic juxtaposition of tourists and residents for whom the same seedy bar is respectively a charming anachronism and a welcome respite from manual labor. The theme of reality's replacement with fabrication is continued in the following scene, as an entrepreneur, using his daughter's wedding reception as an opportunity to pitch an idea, discusses business with a representative from the logging industry. The natural world is valuable in Alaska, as evinced by the logger who wants to make millions cutting the trees. The entrepreneur argues against clear-cutting but not for environmental reasons. "It's ugly," claims the developer, who is in the business of making things picturesque: "We'll show them a little Indian fish camp, some totem poles maybe. We show them a black bear foraging for breakfast in the early morning mist. Cut the trees in the interior; turn it into a parking lot. Just quit with the chainsaws when you get to where people can see." His proposal to transform Alaska into a giant theme park boasting various attractions, including "The Whales Causeway," "Island of the Raven People," "Kingdom of the Salmon," and "Lumberland," replete with a "turn-of-the-century sawmill with a little water-power generator and a gift shop," is just another example of the "Disneyfication" of America, a process that mythologizes and sanitizes the past, cleansing it of violence and brutality. The developer, in fact, argues that his business plan goes "one step beyond Disney" since it proposes "not bigger and better facsimiles of nature but nature itself," as he advises potential investors to "[t]hink of Alaska as one big theme park."[2]

What is at stake in the battle over Alaska's resources is the concept of nature in American culture, a subject Sayles has tackled before—as a scriptwriter for *Piranha*, in which nature exacts its revenge after the military machine and real estate speculators have inadvertently colluded to wreak havoc in an isolated mountain retreat. To draw visitors, developers transform the area into a parody of itself, redesigning the river as a quaint mode of transportation. In a separate episode of reconstructing nature, military experiments result in a particularly brutal and efficient brand of piranha. The protagonist, an unemployed smelter whose job has been obliterated by real estate development, kills the piranha through pollution, a plot device that makes the point that the line between the natural and the artificial is fading fast. In *Sunshine State* (2002), four golfers, acting as a perverse Greek chorus, discuss the nature of nature. The most dogmatic one argues that "nature is overrated," only to be deflated as his fellow player responds, "Yes, but we'll miss it when it's gone," a statement made doubly ironic as the speakers are revealed to be playing golf in the median of a busy thoroughfare. Ostensibly, what these men miss is a piece of land laid bare by bulldozers, only to be rebuilt with artificial hills and lakes, new groves of bushes and trees, covered by sod, and punctured by perfectly round holes—not nature at all, hardly even the simulation of nature, simply a board on which humans play a game.

As *Limbo* so clearly demonstrates, the commercialization of nature results in the displacement of the original through a succession of representations:[3] "The Island of the Raven People" will displace an educational program from *The Learning Channel* which has displaced a *National Geographic* essay which has displaced a moment in history. Living in a world defined by the images that it has created, the entrepreneur in *Limbo* chooses to ignore that the replica of the past that he is producing has little to do with the Alaska of a century ago, and most of the tourists who pay the admission price will not notice the difference either. "That's history . . . not industry," the entrepreneur says without a trace of irony. "History is our future here."[4] But what Disneyland and Lumberland ultimately reveal is that Jean Baudrillard's thesis is correct: "Disneyland exists in order to hide that it is the 'real' country, all of 'real' America that is Disneyland. . . . Disneyland is presented as imaginary in order to make us believe that the rest is real, whereas all of Los Angeles and the America that surrounds it are no longer real, but belong to the hyperreal order and to the order of simulation" (12), an assertion illustrated by Sayles's most recent films, especially in the transformation of Alaskans' stories into tales for tourists in *Limbo*, and the use of coastal Florida as a canvas for greedy businessmen in *Sunshine State*, which, as Kent Jones notes, is "incisive . . . on the way history is used as a tool to increase commerce" (22). In an interview, Sayles has noted that Alaska serves as an excellent metaphor for the shift in the United States economy from manufacturing to service. The working pier that was Fisherman's Wharf in San Francisco has been replaced by restaurants, "and now, fish don't come in there anymore, unless it's on a University Press truck. So it's become a boutique about what used to happen" (Woodford 240), in much the same way that the speculators in *Limbo* plan to create Lumberland, a theme park that will commemorate the loss of the wilderness that it guarantees.

Although characters like *Limbo*'s Joe Gastineau, a former athlete and fisherman, live in Alaska precisely because it is real, the order of simulation seems to be creeping northward. When asked why he loves fishing, Joe responds in Hemingway-like fashion, "It's the thing itself. You go out; you find the fish; you pull him out of the water. Everything else is second-hand," a statement that seems to reify the traditional binary of modernism/postmodernism, in which the latter term is affiliated with the replacement of nature and reality by simulation, and the former evokes the truth and authenticity that evolves through a relationship with the natural world, as evinced in Joe's statement that "Every man's true desire is to work in the great outdoors." Joe's sentiments suggest the notion that modernism equals respect for nature and postmodernism amounts to its eradication. What seems to be destroying Alaska is the lack of authentic en-

In *Limbo*, Joe Gastineau (David Strathairn) is a former athlete and fisherman who lives in Alaska because it is real. *"LIMBO" © 1999 Global Entertainment Productions GmbH & Co. Medien KG and SPE German Finance Co. Inc. All Rights Reserved. Courtesy of Columbia Pictures.*

gagement with the natural world. Tourists can pretend that they have seen Alaska, but behind the picturesque and harmless facade is the clear-cut forest. In her article "Is Nature Necessary?" Dana Phillips suggests, along with Fredric Jameson and others, that the postmodern condition constitutes a break with history and nature, "a simulated plenum . . . [in which r]epresentation has supplanted presence" (206). The spectacular aspect of postmodernism, "the gaze . . . of a new kind of commodity fetishist" (206), encourages humans to move in a simulated nature, looking rather than acting. The epitome of postmodernism for Phillips is "a new form of fishing practice called CPR, . . . which stands . . . for 'Catch, Photograph, and Release'" ("Is Nature Necessary?" 209). Phillips argues that the replacement of killing with photographing fish is a debasement of the sport, an "erasure of the distinction between life and death, nature and culture" ("Is Nature Necessary?" 209). The illusion of death implicit in CPR echoes Sayles's description of the "illusion of risk" that marks humans' relationships with one another and with nature (Kirkland).[5] "[P]eople," Sayles observes, "are romantic about nature, but nature is not romantic about people. Only if you find yourself in nature by accident, unprepared, do you realize just how hard it is to survive. Most people don't want to rough it that much. They might want to go down the river, but they want the river guides there when it's time to eat" (Sherman).

If the semblance of nature is the subject of *Limbo*, then the semblance of history is at stake in *Sunshine State*, which depicts Florida's ubiquitous golf courses, theme parks, opulent communities, kitschy tourist attractions (one of which simulates mermaids in synchronized water ballet), and predatory developers as the epitome of what Jameson has described as the depthlessness of postmodern experience. That depthlessness is embodied by *Sunshine State*'s Francine Pickney, the chair of Buccaneer Days, an elaborate but pathetic series of events replete with history lessons and intended to evoke civic pride and generate tourism in the town of Delrona Beach, Florida. After an arsonist torches a replica of a pirate ship and her event fails due to lack of attendance, Francine laments: "People don't understand how hard it is to invent a tradition." The tradition, like the pirate ship, "a marketing tool that represents a romantically enhanced past" (Jones 22), disintegrates precisely because it has no substance. Inventing a tradition necessitates writing or rewriting the past, re-presenting a simulacrum, a copy of an original that never existed, like the many Florida developments that mimic Small Town USA, communities that allude to a past that existed only in our collective imaginations.

In contrast to the spectacle of postmodernism is ostensibly the engagement of modernism. Replacing the voyeuristic gaze of postmodernism is the contemplative gaze of modernism, which enables the viewer to experience nature rather than merely look upon it. Phillips defines the modernist project as "an affirmation of the self in a transcendent moment of realization in which the dross of culture (language, sexuality, history) is clarified, melting away to reveal the roots of culture in nature, and human nature" ("Is Nature Necessary?" 205) and notes that "Hemingway's stripped-down, spare modernism has as its goal a basic transformation . . . effected through a redemptive artistic project or therapeutic experience," a "therapeutic experience" that is often found in what Phillips calls "'blood sport' (bullfighting, big game hunting, fishing, war)," which allows participants to "uncover a more fundamental reality" (205–6).

Joe Gastineau's nearly devotional relationship with fishing connects him to Hemingway's Nick Adams, who wrestles with his recent war experience by fishing the "Big, Two-Hearted River," and thus seems to place him snugly in the category of modernist heroes for whom nature offers salvation from the perils of civilization. However, the "more fundamental reality" that Joe seems to understand from his tragic engagement with nature leads him away from fishing and humans. The tempest that breaks Joe's will, destroys his career, kills his shipmates, and nearly kills him occurs on one of his beloved fishing expeditions. So, just as we have comfortably settled into the binary notion that modernism equals respect for nature and postmodernism amounts to its eradication, *Limbo* shifts gears. Moreover, the film's depiction of the newly arrived lesbian couple—Frankie and Lou—complicates facile categorization. Smart, educated, ambitious, both have moved to Alaska to make money, their latest scheme being to bring alpacas to the region to carry gear on hiking trips. They find themselves in a war of wills with Harmon King, a longtime local recently put out of a job by the closing of the cannery. Harmon would rather fish for a living but Frankie and Lou have custody of his fishing license and his boat, *The Raven*, because he has defaulted on his work for the women. The law is on their side, a fact they know well because they have law degrees, but sentiment is on Harmon's side. He needs to make a living in a town where unemployment is rampant and economic misery a fact of life. Frankie, on the other hand, is so out of her element that she misuses fishing and nautical terminology, an argot that sits no better on Lou just because she wields it correctly. Nevertheless, these women, outsiders who demonstrate no special affinity for the land or the people, provide the catalyst for Joe's reengagement with nature by hiring him to fish on *The Raven*. Meanwhile, Harmon, whose bravado, cynicism, and ostensible connection with "the real" suggest a modernist hero, is rendered suspect when he shoots a halibut that he cannot reel in, an act that Lou compares to a "gangland killing."[6] At this moment at least, the seemingly authentic local resident is no more attuned to the natural world than are the developers. And, ironically, Frankie and Lou's scheme to use alpacas as beasts of burden for tourists' gear may not be as environmentally destructive as more "authentic" industries. As Sayles noted in an interview, the closing of the pulp mill in Fort Henry has had ambiguous repercussions:

> While in human terms there's something sad about that, in raw, ecological, "don't-cut-it-down" terms, tourism might end up being a cleaner, less destructive industry. In Juneau, during the Gold Rush days, for example, they weren't finding veins of gold that you could chip out with a pickax. They were taking huge rocks and stamping them in machines that ran twenty-four hours a day, year after year after year, and the noise was deafening. That mountain is honeycombed with holes and is lucky it's still standing.... [A]lthough these changes have been tough on some people, it may be better ecologically for the state. If you're a tree, you might be in better shape now. (West and West 28–29)

The local people suffer financially and psychologically as their industries evaporate; however, "the town smells better," as Joe observes.

The characters' varying and inconsistent responses to the natural world reflect one of the paradoxes at the heart of American culture: the simultaneous erosion of and desire for wilderness. More than forty years after Frederick Jackson Turner argued that the American frontier had disappeared, Robert Marshall, in his comments to a congressional committee studying Alaska's resources, affirmed Turner's claim that the frontier was crucial in the making of Americans and American culture by lauding the "pioneer conditions" and the "emotional values of the frontier" afforded by Alaska.[7] As Roderick Nash notes, "[h]ere was the first, inevitably controversial, call not just for wilderness preservation but for a permanent American frontier" (288). But a desire for wilderness demands a definition of wilderness, which is hard to establish. "Wilderness," as Nash notes, seems to stem from early Teutonic and Norse languages from the word "will" as in "willful" or "willed," which engendered the word "wild." Eventually, the term "wilderness" took on a moral connotation as a "region where a person was likely to get into a disordered, confused, or 'wild' condition" (2). Yet, while the term implies a space hostile to humans, it may also be understood as "beautiful, friendly, and capable of elevating and delighting the beholder [. . . as well as providing] a sanctuary . . . from the pressures of civilization" (4). Recently, it has come to mean a place "where man himself is a visitor who does not remain" (5). "Because of this subjectivity," Nash observes, "a universally acceptable definition of wilderness is elusive. One man's wilderness may be another's roadside picnic ground" (1).

The characters in Sayles's short stories are defined by those elusive—and often dangerously misguided—definitions of wilderness. In "Breed," a hitchhiker traveling west from New Jersey must adjust to the actual West rather than the one he has experienced through literature and Hollywood. While Brian measures "The West" (as he calls it in his mind) against films starring Audie Murphy and Randolph Scott, he discovers young men—driving cars named after horses, "Pintos, and Mavericks, Mustangs and Broncos"—who castrate their own horses so they "turn into cows" (Sayles 222, 216). His first chronicled encounter in South Dakota is with Cody Sprague, a man whose claim to fame is a "Wild West Buckin' Bison Ride," which has been rendered obsolete by the construction of the interstate. As it turns out, even Sprague is from the East. In "Golden State," another story from the same collection, Brian comes across a group of alcoholics with nicknames like Daniel Boone and Cervantes who regale him with stories of why they came to California. One is tempted by the prospect of being the "next Tarzan" (Sayles 244) and another by brochures for business opportunities: "'I remember the one [brochure] that hooked us, can still see the picture in my head. Pretty girl standing under this tree just dripping with big fat oranges. 'Money does grow on trees,' it said, 'in the Golden State'" (Sayles 245). Brian confesses to a less lofty goal: "'Where else is there to go?'" (Sayles 246), a question that simultaneously reveals the hype of California as the promised land and confirms that importance of the frontier in the American imagination. His new friend's response, moreover, further supports Turner's thesis: "'Sometimes,' said Daniel Boone staring out over the water, 'I get the feeling that if I concentrated, I could just drift on west, out across the ocean, past all the limits, into another dimension'" (Sayles 246). The West, then, is both more and less than landscape; it is an idea, an imaginary space that encapsulates a history of competing visions of nature.

That desire to pass the limits of civilization and enter the frontier is most dramatically illustrated in Sayles's award-winning story "I-80 Nebraska, M.490–M.205," in which truck drivers communicating via CB radio are taunted by the voice of Ryder P. Moses, a spectral trucker whose destination is unclear ("'I copied him going eastbound.' 'I copied him westbound.' 'I copied him standing still on an overpass'" [Sayles 296]) and whose philosophy is arcane ("'The Interstate goes on forever and you never have to get off. . . . You're beyond the laws of nature, time, gravity, friction, forget them. The only way to win is never to stop'" [Sayles 311–12]). His goal to defy time and space is accomplished when he smashes his truck into an overpass, an act he describes as "'Going west'" (Sayles 313), an echo of Horace Greeley's famous dictum and Huckleberry Finn's ingenuous resolution. The need to "go west" is metaphorically tantamount to a need for open spaces, fewer people, more wilderness, and while this is certainly a very real desire, it is nevertheless a desire promulgated by literature, art, advertising, economics. In varying eras, the land in North America has been considered a sacred space, a howling wilderness, the literalization of the pastoral, the sublime connection to God, an obstacle in the path of railroad tracks as well as, ironically, an incentive to travel the rails. The varied responses are cultural—the Puritans and Native Americans saw different landscapes—as well as temporal, which allowed the colonists' relationship with the land to change over time. Even our view of ecology has changed, moving from Theodore Roosevelt's vision of preserving natural areas so that humans could enjoy them (that is, fish the rivers, hunt the game) to the view held by many current environmentalists who believe that nature has value in and of itself, not in terms of human use. It is a commonplace among landscape photographers that visitors to Yosemite National Park do not really see the park; they see Ansel Adams's images—from calendars, postcards, coffee table books, posters. What we see is largely a product of what we have been taught to see.[8]

Perhaps the most formative story we tell ourselves about nature is the pastoral, the literary genre that, like Phillips's view of modernism and Joe's description of fishing, extols the virtues of human interaction with nature. Not surprisingly, Phillips identifies the "postmodern pastoral" as a genre in which "the familiar oppositions on which the pastoral depends appear to have broken down," resulting in "the expression of a perpetually frustrated pastoral impulse or desire" ("Don DeLillo's Postmodern Pastoral," 236), a desire blocked in part because of the absence of nature. However, the transcendence of civilization achieved through a pastoral idyll or a modernist bullfight relegates the natural world to little more than a mantra or icon. Even the most innocuous of transcendental moments in Hemingway's fiction requires a sacrifice from the natural world, illustrated by one character's version of Grace, offered after a particularly fruitful morning of fishing: "Let us rejoice in our blessings. Let us utilize the fowls of the air. Let us utilize the product of the wine" (Hemingway 122). In *The Ecology of Eden*, Evan Eisenberg notes that the pastoral continues to haunt our thoughts—in novels, films, televisions, music, ballet, and especially in the proliferation of suburban developments. "Arcadia represents a balance between nature and culture" (164), but he acknowledges that such a balance cannot be maintained because it presupposes a lack of change, a perfect timelessness, a point illustrated by the absence of children in a genre notable for its courtships and romances (147, 150). The pastoral is even more problematic in Carolyn Merchant's analysis. A genre that relegates nature to "a refuge from the ills and anxieties of urban life through a return to an unblemished Golden Age, . . . the pastoral tradition . . . contain[s] the implication that nature when plowed and cultivated could be used as a commodity and manipulated as a resource" (*The Death of Nature*, 7–8). Glen A. Love agrees: "[T]he pastoral mode, in an important sense, reflects the same sort of anthropocentric assumptions which are in such dire need of reassessment. Literary pastoral traditionally posits a natural world, a green world, to which sophisticated urbanites withdraw in search of the lessons of simplicity which only nature can teach" (231).[9] Such anthropocentric assumptions remind us that nature is, as Cronon perceives, a "profoundly human construction. . . . [T]he way we describe and understand that world is so entangled with our own values and assumptions that the two can never be fully separated" ("Introduction: In Search of Nature," 25).[10] In *The End of Nature*, Bill McKibben argues that nature is over in the sense that the rain that falls from the skies today differs from that of the nineteenth century because of chlorofluorocarbons released by air conditioners and automobiles, but, as Peter Goin notes, humans have lived in a transformed environment since the development of agriculture in the Neolithic age. "In the final analysis," Goin argues, "nature is an illusion, more cultural idea than physical reality" (51).

Sayles's reliance on the concept of limbo, both for his title and for the film's enigmatic conclusion, is fitting in a work that explores inherently slippery terms. The word "limbo" comes from the Latin term "limbus," meaning "border," or "edge," and thus continues a theme central to so many of Sayles's films. Amy Kaminsky observes Sayles's "obsession with the border and its sites of crossing" (105), illustrated by place-names—Frontera and Rio—in *Lone Star:* "Literally and metaphorically, borders are liminal spaces, dangerous places of passage from one territory—or one identity—to another" (91). According to Victor Turner, what gives the liminal its "peculiar unity" is its paradoxical indefinability: It is "that which is neither this nor that, and yet is both" (qtd. in Kaminsky).[11] Theologically, the word refers to the state of souls who died before Christ's ascension; it also designates the permanent place of the unbaptized who are excluded from the sight of God's face on account of original sin alone. Belonging neither in heaven nor hell, these souls are placed in limbo, a "condition of unknowable outcome," as Sayles defines the term (Kemp). Aside from its religious meaning, it connotes an "unfavorable place or condition," especially "a condition of neglect or oblivion to which persons or things are consigned when regarded as outworn, useless, or absurd," and suggests a place or duration of confinement or exclusion (*Compact Edition of the Oxford English Dictionary*). For Sayles, "limbo is a state that people get trapped in," whose only exit is "risk [which] involves not knowing what's going to happen next, or how it's going to work" (West and West 29). While the term "limbo," of course, allows Sayles to refute binaries and to embrace open-endedness and ambiguity in a very dramatic way, it also compels viewers to consider the film's pervasive Judeo-Christian imagery, which is integral in our understanding of nature.

In Genesis we have the paradigmatic story of man's dominion over nature, a dominion that seems to result in harmony with nature and ease with human nature. That harmony, however, is endangered from the beginning: embedded in the nurturing garden is a snake and forbidden fruit. Upon disobeying God's command to refrain from eating the fruit of the tree of knowledge of good and evil, Adam and Eve must live by the sweat of their brow, using the land to survive. The concomitant punishment of pain during childbirth only serves to heighten the negative connotation of physical labor and, by association, of the land itself. Moreover, in response to that original sin, which prevents the virtuous and faithful from seeing God, is the creation of limbo, a place that dramatizes our eviction from the garden, and our antagonistic relationship with land. The Garden of Eden, then, is a story we tell ourselves to explain our conflicted attitude toward nature, to reconcile our appreciation of its bounty and sublimity with our dread of its indifference and destructiveness. According to Merchant, the "declensionist and tragic" plot of Genesis, in which "the valence of woman. . . . and nature is bad," gives rise to a recovery plot ("Reinventing Eden," 133). That recovery plot, in which men have the power to recreate the garden on earth through labor, specifically the taming and cultivation of the land, is organized around three subplots: Christian religion, modern science, and capitalism.

> The End Drama envisions a reunification of the earth with God, . . . in which the redeemed earthly garden merges into a higher heavenly paradise. . . . Mechanistic science supplies the instrumental knowledge for reinventing the garden on earth . . . by subdu[ing] and dominat[ing] nature. . . . The origin of capitalism is a movement from a desert back to a garden through the transformation of undeveloped nature into a state of civility and order. (Merchant, "Reinventing Eden," 134–36)[12]

The fall from grace is implied in *Limbo*, illustrated by Alaska's failing economy, threatened environment, and increasing surrealism as predatory businessmen ensure a commercial fall into hyperdevelopment and simulacra. But it is also apparent in the characters' sense of entrapment, engendering lethargy in Joe's case, bitterness in Donna's, and a desperation so frantic in Noelle that she seems like an animal eager to chew off its own paw to escape. The sacred and secular recovery plots are also present in Sayles's film. The work on mainland Alaska—the development of real estate, tourism, and other commercial endeavors—in many ways constitutes the recovery plot that Merchant describes, a plot located in the intersection of Christianity, capitalism, and science. But that plot seems to be failing, on a global level—in its devastation of the environment—as well as on a local level—in

Limbo: The Space of Ambiguity

The isolation and primitivism of the island where Donna (Mary Elizabeth Mastrantonio) and Joe (David Strathairn) are stranded evokes garden imagery, but this is no Garden of Eden. *"LIMBO" © 1999 Global Entertainment Productin GmbH & Co. Medien KG and SPE German Finance Co. Inc. All Rights Reserved Courtesy of Columbia Pictures.*

its impoverishment of the lower classes. On a character level, the recovery is only a bit more optimistic. The movement from the mainland to the island (made by Donna and her daughter Noelle, as well as Joe and his half-brother Bobby) begins with the revelation that Donna "hates nature," an assessment offered by her daughter, a vegan who invents stories about babies born with gills rather than lungs. Noelle's fancy about her own affinity with the natural world is itself shaken by her seasickness during a storm. Bobby's murder at the hands of drug dealers is the final blow in the journey. After the fall, then, Joe, Donna, and Noelle find themselves in a wilderness where weather is intemperate, food scarce, and self-consciousness profound. Unlike the unabashed nudity in Paradise, these characters awkwardly remove their wet clothing merely to prevent exposure. While the isolation and primitivism of the island strongly evokes garden imagery, this is no Garden of Eden.[13]

In Christian theology, the recovery calls for the incarnation of Jesus Christ, whose sacrifice redeems humans from that original sin committed in the Garden of Eden. As the names blatantly suggest, Joe, Donna, and Noelle[14] serve as contemporary counterparts to Joseph, Mary, and Jesus. When Joe sees Noelle, dressed in a white uniform, serving hors d'oeuvres at the wedding, he teasingly says, "You look like an angel," and we soon learn that Noelle's surname is, in fact, "de Angelo."[15] But this is a troubled holy family. A less than ideal mother, Donna de Angelo moves casually from one failed romantic relationship to the next, fueling her righteous indignation and dragging her despairing daughter behind her. And as Noelle rehearses their history of moves, the viewer realizes Donna's selfish and irresponsible behavior constitutes her as an anti-Madonna. Joe Gastineau, a handyman (sometime fisherman, pulp mill worker, and no doubt carpenter) who has retreated emotionally to the point of invisibility, grows into his role as Joseph in the second half of the film when he promises to take care of Noelle. The daughter, a storyteller so alienated from her peers and distanced from her mother that she cuts herself (suggesting stigmata) to manifest her emotional pain, makes a disturbing Christ figure. Offering such a dubious recovery plot renders a global redemption out of the question and makes even these characters' personal redemption less than certain.

The secular recovery is no more comforting. In that plot, Noelle, Donna, and Joe rehearse the roles of their predecessors on the island, Annemarie and her parents. Joe surmises that the family came because "they had a scheme," which, he assumes, is the only reason white men ever left the mainland. "Land was cheap; they hunted, fished, raised foxes for their pelts." As it turns out, Joe is precisely correct. Noelle discovers the diary of a young girl, Annemarie, whose father, a former logger injured in a fall, moved his family to this remote island off the coast of Alaska to make their fortune. They could, he posited, "live in the great outdoors and operate their own business," a line which simultaneously echoes Joe's own feelings about "work[ing] in the great outdoors" and invokes an entire history of pastoralism. While the actual diary entries conclude early in the family's story, Noelle invents entries as a means to communicate her anger with her mother. Those entries catalog the deterioration of a family as they encounter the hardships of living in an isolated and inhospitable environment, hardships that include their economic ruination after their foxes are killed. The environment, Joe explains, is so maddening that "by the middle of winter up here people kill each other just because they're bored," a statement that recalls the barflies in the Golden Nugget discussing the inevitable winter suicides on the mainland.

Noelle's imagined entries appear to begin with the birthing of the vixens, followed hard upon by the realization that the fox mother ate one of her litter. Subsequently, her fictionalized entries describe the escalating madness of the mother, who burns her husband with bacon grease and eventually hangs herself, leaving behind a note confessing to the massacre of a litter of infant foxes, whom the insane woman believed were Satan's handmaidens. Described in gruesome terms, the corpses of the foxes illustrate Noelle's disgust for the perpetrator of the crime and accompanying pity for the daughter and the father. Indeed, the mother, who is described as "hiss[ing]" into her daughter's ear, is herself demonized. However, the slaughter should remind us that the foxes were being bred for their skins, so our disgust with the mother is hypocritical: the father, too, would have killed the foxes, the only difference being that his motivation would have been profit.[16] The father with whom Noelle so clearly sympathizes has endangered his family—physically and psychologically—by removing them to an island apparently uninhabited by other people. His former occupation, moreover, connects him with the representative of the logging industry, a guest at the wedding, who wants to clear-cut the Alaskan forests.

Beyond the confines of the diary, the difficulty of classifying characters as "good" or "bad" is perhaps most dramatically embodied in the persona of "Smiling Jack," who may or may not surrender his economic allegiance to the drug dealers. As a result, the audience imagines whether the helicopter's return signals rescue or assassination while Sayles carefully uses a fade to white as a conclusion,[17] and wonders whether the three stranded protagonists will be "saved." But the binary of "saved" and "damned" is no more useful in this film than the schism between nature and culture. In Sayles's film, whose very title problematizes traditional binaries, "limbo" becomes the site of contestation of opposites, a place in which the journey, the process and not the destination, is the point.[18]

The indeterminate ending of *Limbo* irritates, outrages, and confuses audiences because it offers no easy answers, but this is a trademark of Sayles's films, including *Lone Star*'s concluding command, "Forget the Alamo," a line that seems to dismiss rather blithely a complicated past very late in a film whose point is how much the past affects the present. *Men With Guns* never determines whether the promised land in the sky exists; we only know the young girl will continue to search for it. The end of *Limbo* provides the lack of closure that many readers have come to expect from postmodern narrative. The postmodern turn toward language as "constitutive of the *meaningful* world that humans inhabit, and less and less seen as representative of an independent reality" fittingly gives rise to a postmodern environmental ethics that is "always situated in language. . . . [and that] acknowledge[s] that there are no privileged positions outside language, no foundational places upon which individuals can stand to build apodictic truth," according to Oelschlaeger (*Postmodern Environmental Ethics*, 5, 9).[19] Indeed, it could well be argued that the transformation for the three protagonists comes not through an encounter with nature but with language, Noelle's stories—about a human infant who is born with gills rather than lungs, and a young woman who desires to forego her humanity so that her soul, that of a she-wolf or of a soaring bird, might be rescued from its loneliness and alienation by Fox-man. The diary entries that she invents are parables, in which she plots her relationship with her mother through a fictional mother. Sayles is interested in "how people use stories . . . to define themselves," as illustrated in the anecdotes Alaskans share with each other, the songs that Donna sings, and the stories that Noelle creates (West and West 30). As a first-person account from a child's perspective, the diary—both Annemarie's printed words and Noelle's imagined ones—silences the fictional parents; Noelle, moreover, effectively silences her own mother by refusing to read (or invent) more entries on quiet, dull evenings in the dilapidated cabin. But while Noelle's last entry, describing both the mother's suicide and the confession, would seem to foreclose discussion, Donna, having realized that the diary entries stem from Noelle's imagination, uses it to comfort her daughter, to assure her that, unlike Annemarie's mother, she will never leave her daughter. Noelle's testament works in bringing her news to her mother.

    Postmodernism's acknowledgment of the formative impact of language on our understanding of the world negates, for many, the possibility of sublimity, which suggests the overwhelming of reason, a combination of elation and fear, in which one's "mind is so entirely filled with its objects, that it cannot contain any other" (Burke 53). The apparently transcendental encounter with a sublime object robs the viewer of words and renders analysis impossible—at least for a moment.[20] Indeed, Christopher Hitt argues that acknowledging a nature apart from language is precisely what is necessary for an ecologically responsible relationship with nature, and he sees in the discourse of the sublime the possibility "that we might step outside the confines of language" (614). In Hitt's formulation of an "ecological sublime," the sublime rupture that accounts for a "disequilibrium between mind and object" does not give way to the restoration of equilibrium, a restoration that "validat[es] the individual's dominion over the nonhuman world" (608). "Ideally, then, an ecological sublime would offer a new kind of transcendence which would resist the traditional reinscription of humankind's supremacy over nature" (Hitt 609), a supremacy made possible by language.

The ostensible incongruity of language and sublimity seems to leave little room for the exalted in *Limbo*, a film that has made clear the construction of nature. However, as Donna, Joe, and Noelle may be rescued or killed, their approach to the helicopter is simultaneously one of elation and fear, a combination evoked by an encounter with the sublime, dramatically rendered by the conclusion's fade to white. In *Limbo* we see the characters' encounter with sublimity after we have been made aware of the importance of language on their understanding of the world, each other, and themselves. They stand in silence in the final scene, but not because language is irrelevant to them. Refusing to offer the solace of solution, Sayles's indeterminate ending suggests the unpresentability of reality that is the hallmark of the postmodern sublime for Jean-François Lyotard, but not at the expense of language's impact on our reception of the world. These characters can face the mystery, the uncertainty of the sublime precisely because of language, albeit language disguised, and their enlightenment is not the quiet epiphany of a solitary Hemingway hero fishing a deserted river; nor does it arrive with the drama of a Thomas Cole painting. It is instead an enlightenment born of listening and speaking—a language that can muddle as much as it clarifies, a language that constructs our understanding of the world just as it reveals that construction. Yet again, Sayles explodes the binaries of modernism and postmodernism, a paradigm that seemed to offer a choice of sublimity or language, by offering both.

NOTES

1. In an interview with Bill Moyers, Sayles makes a similar point about representations of history: "[I]n America . . . we . . . rewrite [history], to sanitize it, to make it into a story. . . . The Navajo people . . . have a tourist rain dance and their own rain dance; at what point when you're putting on the paint for the hundredth time or the thousandth time, does it start to affect the real rain dance" (Moyers).

2. The proliferation of simulacra is evident in the roster of Bobby's clients: a *National Geographic* crew and Hollywood real estate honchos. Indeed, when Bobby enters the Golden Nugget for the first time in many years he compares it to a wax museum, noting how "life-like" the patrons look in postures that have not changed in years.

3. As Candace Slater notes, the romanticization of such places as the Amazonian rain forest are "destructive in their tendency to supplant something that actually exists" (129).

4. In addition to chronicling characters' uneasy relationships with the past, Sayles's films often address the tension between past and present, a tension whose roots lie in the disparate pasts experienced by various people. As Todd F. Davis and Kenneth Womack observe, Hollis Pogue's recounting of Buddy's rise to sheriff in *Lone Star* is revealed through Sayles's use of summary to be merely one "'version' of history. Sayles's use of summary prods the viewer toward an understanding that history is personal, political, and, perhaps most important, contextual; his decision to use the generic conventions of the murder mystery, moreover, supports the idea that the truth of the past is always shifting in relation to the vantage point of the observer." The murder mystery reveals that "the objective act of the crime is lost to the past and may only be discovered through the myriad tales of those who live on" (Davis and Womack).

5. Sayles has stated that *Limbo* is about the "differences between the illusion of risk and real risk" (Kirkland).

6. It is worth noting that Harmon surrendered the title to his boat because he feared the bank would repossess it.

7. Robert Marshall was an explorer and leader in wilderness preservation in the 1920s and 1930s. Quoted in Nash.

8. See Barrett and White for an extended discussion of this subject.

9. Love calls for a new pastoralism that would require "that contact with the green world be acknowledged as something more than a temporary excursion into simplicity which exists primarily for the sake of its eventual renunciation and a return to the 'real' world at the end" (234–35).

10. In his essay "The Trouble with Wilderness; or, Getting Back to the Wrong Nature," Cronon notes that in nature people find "the false hope of an escape from responsibility, the illusion that we can somehow wipe clean the slate of our past and return to the tabula rasa that supposedly existed before we began to leave our marks on the world. The dream of an unworked natural landscape is very much the fantasy of people who have never themselves had to work the land to make a living" (80).

11. Joan M. West and Dennis West identify *Limbo* as "an unusual film in terms of genre expectations—it's part romance, part crime story, part troubled teen biography, and part Jack Londonesque survival tale" (30). Such hybridity of form itself represents a sort of border crossing.

12. According to Max Oelschlaeger, modernism, which "reinforc[ed] the Judeo-Christian perspective on nature and time, ... effected an ideological conversion of the wilderness into material nature, both as an object of scientific inquiry and as the means to fuel economic progress" (68–69).

13. In his commentary on the DVD, Sayles notes that "nature had to be manipulated during filming": later in the day's shooting, after the tide had moved, rocks were shifted to new locations to mimic their placement in earlier scenes. And, ironically, though it rained constantly during filming, they had to create rain because they needed heavier downpours and backlight. Finally, when the three protagonists first arrive on the island, cold and shivering and in danger of hypothermia, they strip in front of a tree, a tree onto which moss had to be stapled because campfires had burned the actual moss. Although the crew attempted to cover up the evidence of their interference, Sayles wondered if later visitors would be troubled by the preponderance of props in the natural environment.

14. The word "noel" comes from the Latin and French words for "birthday." In its capitalized form, "Noel" means Christmas. Furthering the parallel to the holy family is the fact that Noelle is not Joe's child.

15. Indeed, the film is filled with religious echoes: one of the men who drowns on Joe's ship, *Arctic Dawn*, is named Lester Pope, and song lyrics like "My life with you has become a living hell" and "Loving you is hell enough for me" remind us of the theological significance of the film's title, as does Bobby's description of the importance of the scout who was supposed to recruit Joe before the latter's knee troubles ended his career: "In basketball, it's like God sending the Angel Gabriel to check out your moves." When Joe asks Donna why she continues to sing for a living when the obstacles seem greater than the reward, she answers that singing provides "moments of grace," opportunities to communicate with others, to make a connection.

16. In his commentary on the DVD, Sayles points out the brutality of the history of fox hunting, including the Russians' technique of letting loose birds, which would disappear as the fox population multiplied.

17. "For me, a fade to white is like going to the infinite. It says nothing ends or begins here, we are bringing you to a certain moment, and you don't know what happens next" (Sherman).

18. Linda Hutcheon cites "border tensions" in postmodernism as the transgression of boundaries between genres, disciplines, discourses, high and mass culture, practice and theory (118). Donald Crimp notes that "hybridization," the mixing of heterogeneous media, genres, projects, and materials, violates the purity of modernist art (77).

19. Viewing ecology as the "essential Post-Modern science," a science that asserts that "all living and non-living things on the globe are interconnected, or capable of being linked," Charles Jencks argues that environmental issues demonstrated the limits of modernism, a philosophy that separates knowledge (58–59). However, for Phillips, the new ecology resembles the instability and indeterminateness of postmodernism ("Ecocriticism, Literary Theory, and the Truth of Ecology," 580).

20. While conceptualization fails in our encounter with the sublime, Immanuel Kant's subsequent description of the sublime subordinates emotion to reason, allowing the mind to master the situation. Through the return of reason we emerge whole from the sublime experience, effectively alienating subject and object.

WORKS CITED

Barrett, Laura, and Daniel White. "The Reconstruction of Nature: Postmodern Ecology and the Kissimmee River Restoration Project." *From Virgin Land to Disney World: Nature and Its Discontents in the USA of Yesterday and Today*. Ed. Bernd Herzogenrath. Amsterdam: Rodopi, 2002. 229–50.

Baudrillard, Jean. *Simulacra and Simulation*. Trans. Sheila F. Glaser. Ann Arbor: U of Michigan P, 1994.

Burke, Edmund. *A Philosophical Enquiry into the Origin of Our Ideas of the Sublime and Beautiful*. 1757. Ed. Adam Phillips. New York: Oxford UP, 1998.

Compact Edition of the Oxford English Dictionary. 1971. Oxford: Oxford UP, 1981.

Crimp, Douglas. "Pictures." *Art after Modernism: Rethinking Representation*. Ed. Brian Wallis. New York: New Museum of Contemporary Art, 1984. 175–80.

Cronon, William. "Introduction: In Search of Nature." *Uncommon Ground: Toward Reinventing Nature*. Ed. William Cronon. New York: Norton, 1995. 23–68.

———. "The Trouble with Wilderness: or, Getting Back to the Wrong Nature." *Uncommon Ground: Toward Reinventing Nature*. Ed. William Cronon. New York: Norton, 1995. 69–90.

Davis, Todd F., and Kenneth Womack. "Forget the Alamo: Reading the Ethics of Style in John Sayles's *Lone Star*." *Style* 32.3 (1998): 471–85. *Wilson Select Plus*. OCLC. 4 October 2001.

Eisenberg, Evan. *The Ecology of Eden*. New York: Knopf, 1998.

Goin, Peter. "Humanature's River." *Geographical Review* 87 (1997): 47–57.
Hemingway, Ernest. *The Sun Also Rises.* 1926. New York: Collier, 1986.
Hitt, Christopher. "Toward an Ecological Sublime." *New Literary History* 30.3 (1999): 603–24.
Hutcheon, Linda. *The Politics of Postmodernism.* New York: Routledge, 1989.
Jencks, Charles. *What Is Post-Modernism?* 3rd ed. New York: St. Martin's, 1986.
Jones, Kent. "The Lay of the Land." *Film Comment* 38.3 (2002): 22–24.
Kaminsky, Amy. "Identity at the Border: Narrative Strategies in Maria Novaro's *El Jardin del Edén* and John Sayles's *Lone Star.*" *Studies in Twentieth-Century Literature* 25.1 (2001): 91–117. Wilson Select Plus. OCLC. 17 May 2002.
Kemp, Philip. "*Limbo.*" *Sight and Sound* 10.2 (2000): 47–8. Wilson Select Plus. OCLC. 15 May 2002.
Kirkland, Bruce. "Sayles Brings Us into His Limbo." *Toronto Sun,* 24 June 2002. http://www.canoe.ca/JamMoviesArtistsS/sayles_john.html. 20 February 2005.
Limbo. Directed by John Sayles. Sony Pictures' Screen Gems, 1999. DVD.
Lone Star. Directed by John Sayles. Columbia Pictures, 1996. Videocassette.
Love, Glen A. "Revaluing Nature: Toward an Ecological Criticism." *The Ecocriticism Reader: Landmarks in Literary Ecology.* Ed. Cheryll Glotfelty and Harold Fromm. Athens: U of Georgia P, 1996. 225–40.
McKibben, Bill. *The End of Nature.* New York: Anchor, 1989.
Men With Guns (Hombres Armados). Directed by John Sayles. Sony Pictures Classics, 1998. Videocassette.
Merchant, Carolyn. *The Death of Nature: Women, Ecology, and the Scientific Revolution.* San Francisco: HarperCollins, 1990.
———. "Reinventing Eden: Western Culture as a Recovery Narrative." *Uncommon Ground: Toward Reinventing Nature.* Ed. William Cronon. New York: Norton, 1995. 132–70.
Moyers, Bill. "Bill Moyers Interviews John Sayles." *Now with Bill Moyers.* PBS. http://www.pbs.org/now/arts/sunshine.html. 12 September 2002.
Nash, Roderick. *Wilderness and the American Mind.* 3rd ed. New Haven: Yale UP, 1982.
National Geographic (special section). "Alaska: Our Last Great Wilderness." 147.6 (1975): 730–91.
Oelschlaeger, Max. *The Idea of Wilderness: From Prehistory to the Age of Ecology.* New Haven: Yale UP, 1991.
———, ed. *Postmodern Environmental Ethics.* New York: State U of New York P, 1995.
Phillips, Dana. "Don DeLillo's Postmodern Pastoral." *Reading the Earth.* Ed. Michael P. Branch et al. Moscow: U of Idaho P, 1998. 235–46.

———. "Ecocriticism, Literary Theory, and the Truth of Ecology." *New Literary History* 30.3 (1999): 577–602.

———. "Is Nature Necessary?" *The Ecocriticism Reader: Landmarks in Literary Ecology*. Ed. Cheryll Glotfelty and Harold Fromm. Athens: U of Georgia P, 1996. 204–22.

Piranha. Directed by Joe Dante. New World Pictures, 1978. Videocassette.

Sayles, John. *The Anarchists' Convention*. Boston: Little, Brown, 1979.

Sherman, Betsy. "For Filmmaker Sayles, Risk Is Starting Point." *Boston Globe*, 4 June 1999. http://www.boston.com/globe...ker_sayles_risk_is_starting_point.shtm. 24 June 2002.

Slater, Candace. "Amazonia as Edenic Narrative." *Uncommon Ground: Toward Reinventing Nature*. Ed. William Cronon. New York: Norton, 1995. 114–31.

Sunshine State. Directed by John Sayles. Sony Pictures Classics, 2002.

West, Joan M., and Dennis West. "Not Playing By the Usual Rules: An Interview with John Sayles." *Cineaste* 24.4 (1999): 28–31. *Wilson Select Plus*. OCLC. 4 October 2001.

Woodford, Riley. "Q & A: John Sayles." *John Sayles: Interviews*. Ed. Diane Carson. Jackson: UP of Mississippi, 1999. 239–47.

ANNOTATED RESOURCES

While all of John Sayles's movies are fairly well covered by the popular and industry press, only *Lone Star* and *Men With Guns* have received a significant measure of attention from film and cultural historians. The following does not offer an exhaustive survey of everything written by or about John Sayles, but rather a select listing and brief description of books, individual essays, and interview collections that offer insightful perspectives on the director's work. We also include some Web sites that should be helpful to other scholars in pursuing research on Sayles.

We should also note that as of this writing, all but two (*Baby It's You* and *City of Hope*) of Sayles's films are available on DVD, those marked with an asterisk accompanied by director's commentary: *Return of the Secaucus Seven,* Lianna,* Brother from Another Planet,* Eight Men Out, Passion Fish, The Secret of Roan Inish,* Matewan, Lone Star, Men With Guns,* Limbo,* Sunshine State,* Casa de los Babys,* and *Silver City*. The perspicaciousness about goals and techniques evident in published interviews with Sayles emerges with equal force in these commentaries.

PRINT RESOURCES

Ardolino, Frank. "Ceremonies of Innocence and Experience in *Bull Durham, Field of Dreams,* and *Eight Men Out*." *Journal of Popular Film and Television* 18 (Summer 1990): 43–51.

Ardolino examines three baseball-themed movies released in 1988–89 that, he argues, use the sport to gauge an individual's worth as well as express fantasies of "national spirit." While *Field of Dreams* and *Bull Durham* explore the mystical powers of baseball as examples of a "New Age Populism," *Eight Men Out* enacts players' fall from grace. At the same time, all of the films address how "sons [are] manipulated and corrupted by the dark fathers who control the game."

Aufderheide, Patricia. "Filmmaking as Storytelling." *Cineaste* 15.4 (1987): 12–15.

In this short but revealing interview, Sayles discusses stories told in linear and nonlinear fashion, as well as his own methods of visualizing the scripts he has written.

Bakewell, Geoffrey W. "Oedipus Tex: *Lone Star*, Tragedy, and Postmodernism." *Classical and Modern Literature* 22.1 (2002): 35–48.

Bakewell reads *Lone Star* as neotragedy, both indebted to and a reworking of the oedipal myth. He demonstrates how the film mobilizes tropes of the postmodern, including irony, parody, a self-conscious historicity and use of symbol, and particularly its revelation that incest, "one of our most enduring societal taboos is in fact more a cultural construct than a stable moral value."

Bould, Mark. *Lone Star: The Cinema of John Sayles*. London: Wallflower, 2007.

A critical assessment of Sayles's work from a Marxist/materialist perspective. One of Wallflower's "Director's Cut" series, this monograph will be suitable for introducing advanced undergraduates and graduates to Sayles's oeuvre.

Boyd, Melba. "But Not the Blackness of Space: *The Brother from Another Planet* as Icon from the Underground." *Journal of the Fantastic in the Arts* 2.2 (1989): 95–107.

In this provocative essay, Boyd proposes a link between "the Brother" and the antislavery underground movement, as she illuminates metaphoric connections between the film and nineteenth-century U.S. history.

Campbell, Neil. "'Forget the Alamo': History, Legend, and Memory in John Sayles' *Lone Star*." *Memory and Popular Film*. Ed. Paul Grainge. Manchester: Manchester UP, 2003. 162–79.

For Campbell, *Lone Star* is a central popular document of the 1990s that renegotiates major conflicts manifest in the "shifting cultural landscapes" of the United States during the decade. He argues that the film offers viewers complex redefinitions of power relations while also challenging their sense of a coherent personal and national identity, two chief components of what for Campbell is a new vision for depicting history and public memory onscreen.

Carnes, Mark. *Past Imperfect: History According to the Movies.* New York: Henry Holt, 1995.

This book compiles essays by historians on the cinematic representation of their area of specialty and the problems associated with reconciling a commitment to historical accuracy and fidelity with the demands of popular narrative. Labor historian Eric Foner discusses *Matewan*.

Carson, Diane, ed. *John Sayles: Interviews.* Conversations with Filmmakers Series. Jackson: UP of Mississippi, 1999.

A compilation of popular press interviews with the director about his fiction, film, and television work. The introduction offers a very good overview of Sayles's career and chief thematic concerns, which makes it particularly useful for advanced undergraduate courses.

Davis, Todd F., and Kenneth Womack. "Forget the Alamo: Reading the Ethics of Style in John Sayles's *Lone Star*." *Style* 32.3 (1998): 471–85.

The authors employ Genette's principles of narrative (e.g., summary, ellipsis) to examine the "moral impact" of Sayles's style. Use of incest as metaphor in *Lone Star*, they argue, is Sayles's strategy for eliciting in spectators an understanding of how their shared history results in ethical dilemmas that eventually confront them in the present.

Dubofsky, Melvyn. "*Matewan*." *Labor History* 31.4 (1990): 488–91.

Dubofsky offers a generally negative assessment of Sayles's portrayal of coal miners' organizational history in *Matewan*, suggesting that he "abuses history as much as he uses it."

Embry, Marcus. "A Postcolonial Tale of Complicity: The 'Angel of History' and *Men With Guns*." *Discourse: Journal for Theoretical Studies in Media and Culture* 21.2 (1999): 163–80.

Embry addresses *Men With Guns* from a postcolonial perspective that problematizes simplistic oppositions between colonizer/colonized. He argues that reviewers' frequent omission of the film's bracketing narrative (the woman who speaks in Kuna to her daughter about the story to come) suggests they missed the complexity of the film's challenge to character identification and thus viewers' complicity in the events shown. Thus, *Men With Guns* reflexively "implicates cinematic representation itself in the violence in Latin America."

Fishbein, Leslie. "John Sayles' *Matewan:* Violence and Nostalgia." *Film and History* 18 (1998): 63–67.

This article praises the care with which Sayles represents historical violence in *Matewan*, in particular his subtle employment of a "socialist-realist" aesthetic in which the hero's nonviolent stand is neither romanticized nor his death in a gunfight directly shown.

Handley, George B. "Oedipus in the Americas: *Lone Star* and the Reinvention of American Studies." *Forum for Modern Language Studies* 40.2 (2004): 160–81.

Handley suggests that the importance of *Lone Star* has been misunderstood by Americanists, arguing that "the danger of postnational longing among U.S. cultural critics . . . is that it can become an Oedipal delusion if we believe that by running ourselves out of town or across borders, we will be free of our origins and identity."

Holmlund, Christine. "When Is a Lesbian Not a Lesbian? The Lesbian Continuum and the Mainstream Femme Film." *Camera Obscura* 25/26 (January–May 1991): 145–78.

Holmlund surveys critical responses to the "femme" lesbian in four films made in the 1980s, including Sayles's *Lianna*. She uses the intense debate over whether the film employed a nonvoyeuristic female gaze to support her overall argument that it is impossible to generalize about an "imaginary lesbian reader." For Holmlund, such a tactic ignores the "diversity, variability, and tenuousness of the necessary identities and identifications that structure [film] viewing."

Kaminsky, Amy. "Identity at the Border: Narrative Strategies in Maria Novaro's *El Jardín del Edén* and John Sayles's *Lone Star*." *Studies in 20th Century Literature* 25.1 (2001): 91–117.

Kaminsky explores these two films as examples of "border cinema," in which cultural ritual is engaged as a means to negotiate characters' "safe passage" across dangerous liminal sites. In *Lone Star*, a ritualized version of the paternity plot ("who is my father?") serves this function, although Sayles undermines its service of patriarchy by making it a question important for *both* son and daughter to ask.

Kellman, Steven G. "Sayles Goes Spanish: *Hombres Armados*." *American Studies in Scandinavia* 32.1 (2000): 54–64.

For Kellman, Sayles's *Men With Guns* is a "daring case of cinematic translingualism." He argues that the director's strategy to shoot almost exclusively in Spanish and indigenous dialects for a predominantly North American audience encouraged his spectators to interrogate their own "willful ignorance" about the relationship between violence and geopolitics in the Western Hemisphere (and elsewhere).

Kraver, Jeraldine R. "Mining Zola's Naturalism: Creating Coherence in the Coal Pits in *Germinal*, *King Coal*, and *Matewan*." *Excavatio: Emile Zola and Naturalism* 13 (2000): 214–24.

Kraver offers a sensitive, close examination of key works of naturalist fiction by Emile Zola and Upton Sinclair with Sayles's film about coal miners. She argues that like the fictional protagonists, Danny Radnor "embraces the central optimism of tragedy" in rejecting a religious faith incommensurate with miners' lives in favor of collective social action.

Levy, Emanuel. *Cinema of Outsiders: The Rise of American Independent Film*. New York: New York UP, 1999.

This is a well-researched study and a commonly used survey text for university courses on the subject. However, while Levy describes Sayles as the "uncrowned father of the new independent cinema" whose work is preeminently and uniformly about "outsiders," still he recirculates a critical commonplace that the director is uncinematic, his movies basically "photographed scripts."

Limón, José E. "Tex-Sex-Mex: American Identities, Lone Stars and the Politics of Racialized Sexuality." *American Literary History* 9.3 (1997): 598–616.

In his analysis of gender, racial representation, and colonialism in *High Noon* and *Lone Star*, Limón compares how a particular cultural iconography is used to represent Anglo-American/Mexican relations in ways that move beyond stereotypes toward a "politically critical ambivalence." He argues that the Sayles film uses the relationship between Sam and Pilar as an allegory for the resolution of this historical ambivalence, even destabilizing those systems of social relations that uphold it.

Magowan, Kim. "'Blood Only Means What You Let It': Incest and Miscegenation in John Sayles's *Lone Star.*" *Film Quarterly* 57.1 (2003): 20–31.

Magowan argues that in this film, Sayles provocatively endorses incest by mobilizing a racial politics that no longer condemns miscegenation. The historical taboos against both, common in Southern cultural narratives, are subjectivized and thus rendered subject to negotiation.

Molyneaux, Gerard. *John Sayles: An Unauthorized Biography of the Pioneering Indie Filmmaker.* Los Angeles: Renaissance, 2000.

An account of Sayles's life and films for a general readership that (despite the subtitle) interpolates many friendly interviews with members of the director's family and professional circle in the course of its chapters.

Packer, George. "Representing Chicanas?: The Poetics of History, Desire, and Identity in the Lone Star States." *Journal of the American Studies Association of Texas* 29 (October 1998): 18–38.

Packer offers an insightful analysis of *Lone Star*'s representation of Mexican American characters and culture in Texas, and what these representations suggest in terms of identity politics in the region.

Pribram, E. Deidre. *Cinema and Culture: Independent Filmmaking in the United States, 1980–2001*. New York: Peter Lang, 2002.

Analyzing her subject as a discursive formation, Pribram investigates four sets of discourses—those pertaining to representation; material and institutional concerns; interpretive, audience, or reception settings; or cultural or historical issues—that comprise independent filmmaking in the United States during the last twenty years. While like many other critics Pribram describes Sayles's work as "stylistically straightforward," she does note his innovative exploration of "multiple and shifting perspectives."

Quart, Leonard, and William Kornblum. "Film and the Inner City." *Dissent* 47.2 (1999): 97–104.

Largely a discussion in a political periodical of the portrayal of inner-city life as a backdrop for films, this essay examines *City of Hope* as well as Spike Lee's work. The authors focus on how the use of these urban landscapes shapes the action that ensues within the genre film.

Roberts, Nora Ruth. "John Sayles and the Un'Disappearance' of the Working Class: The Vitality of Our History." *Against the Current* 12.4 (1997): 39–42.

In this brief article, Roberts positively assesses Sayles's treatment of the American working class in *Matewan*, *Eight Men Out*, and *Lone Star*, particularly what she views as the director's depiction of their history in "dramatic, involving and nonpreacherly" terms.

Rodriguez, Ralph. "*Men With Guns:* The Stories John Sayles Can't Tell." *The End of Cinema as We Know It: American Film in the Nineties*. Ed. Jon Lewis. New York: New York UP, 2001. 168–74.

This brief essay explores the contradictions of Sayles's address of political and historical issues in *Men With Guns* as a racial and ethnic "outsider." Unlike other similar movies of the 1990s, the film tackles complicated topics in a sensitive way, but Rodriguez suggests that its real strength lies in its implicit acknowledgment of the provisional status of historical narrative, that "no storyteller or historian can tell the whole story."

Ryan, Jack. *John Sayles, Filmmaker: A Critical Study of the Independent Writer-Director.* Jefferson, NC: McFarland, 1998.

This work devotes separate chapters to Sayles's feature films from *Return of the Secaucus Seven* through *Men With Guns*, discussing funding, plot, characters, setting, dialogue, and political sensibility. Ryan also traces various parameters of Sayles's technical development, such as his camera work, editing, mise-en-scène, and use of sound and music.

Sarris, Andrew. "*Baby It's You:* An Honest Man Becomes a True Filmmaker." *Film Comment* 29 (May/June 1993): 28–30.

After seeing *Passion Fish*—which Sarris describes as one of the "best films of 1992"—the chief proponent of auteurism in the United States offers a reassessment of Sayles's work, having previously described it as "cinematic spinach." This film, argues Sarris, marks the writer's evolution into a filmmaker who now understands the "magical ecstasies of mise-en-scène."

Sayles, John. *Thinking in Pictures: How Movies Really Get Made.* 2nd ed. New York: Da Capo, 2003.

This is a slightly revised new edition of Sayles's original primer on indie filmmaking (published in 1987 by Houghton Mifflin) that uses his experiences on *Matewan* to explain how to write, finance, and shoot low-budget productions. The subtitle was changed from "The Making of the Movie *Matewan*," and it also has a new introduction by the director. Otherwise, this edition is little altered from the first, with separate chapters on screenwriting, directing, editing, and so on. It also has location photographs, sketches, and the complete shooting script.

Scobey, David. "*Eight Men Out.*" *American Historical Review* 95.4 (1990): 1143–46.

Scobey assesses the representation of historical components in Sayles's "Black Sox" film from the perspective of a professional historian.

Smith, Gavin, ed. *Sayles on Sayles*. London: Faber and Faber, 1998.

This collection offers original interviews with Sayles, conducted by Smith—a contributing editor to *Film Comment*—on the director's work up to *Men With Guns*.

ELECTRONIC RESOURCES

The following Web sites also provide invaluable (and the most recent) information on the director's work:

http://www.johnsayles.com

Formerly known as the John Sayles Borderstop, this is the Web site for all things Sayles. Best for finding the latest interviews and materials about Sayles's current films, fiction, and upcoming projects.

http://www.johnsaylesretro.com/nav-interview.html

The Independent Film Channel's (IFC) Web site for the Sayles Retrospective in 2002. The concise timeline of key events in Sayles's life and career is especially useful.

http://www.sensesofcinema.com/contents/directors/04/sayles.html

Good overview of Sayles's career, with a number of helpful links to interviews and articles.

http://www.williams.edu/resources/chapin/collect/sayles.html

This is a link to the holdings of the John Sayles Archive at Williams College. The collection includes drafts and complete scripts, production materials, character notes, correspondence, reviews, drafts, and galley pages of the fiction (as well as some of Sayles's student writing), and "extensive files of miscellaneous articles about Sayles and references to his work."

CONTRIBUTORS

Cynthia Baron teaches in the film and American culture studies programs at Bowling Green State University. She has a background in experimental and low-budget filmmaking and her academic research has focused on film performance, women's labor in the film industry, and Hollywood in the cold war era.

Laura Barrett is associate professor of English in the Harriet L. Wilkes Honors College of Florida Atlantic University. Her work on modern and postmodern American literature has appeared in *Modern Fiction Studies, Studies in the Novel*, and *Western American Literature*. She coauthored an article with Daniel R. White titled "The Re-Construction of Nature: Postmodern Ecology and the Kissimmee River Restoration Project," for the collection *Nature and Its Discontents in the USA of Yesterday and Today*.

Mark Bould is senior lecturer in the School of Cultural Studies at the University of the West of England, Bristol. He has published on Marxism, science fiction, and film noir. He is currently completing a book on John Sayles's work titled *The Cinema of John Sayles: A Lone Star* (Wallflower, 2007).

Hamilton Carroll received his PhD from Indiana University in 2003 and is currently a Marion L. Brittain Fellow in the School of Literature, Communication, and Culture at Georgia Institute of Technology. His dissertation addressed cultural representations of the nation-state in the age of the postnational, with specific emphasis on contemporary film and fiction.

Diane Carson is professor of film studies at St. Louis Community College at Meramec. She is the editor of *John Sayles: Interviews* (UP of Mississippi, 1999) and coeditor of *Multiple Voices in Feminist Criticism* (U of Minnesota P, 1994), *Shared Differences: Multicultural Media and Practical Pedagogy* (U of Illinois P, 1995), and *More Than a Method: Trends and Traditions* *in Contemporary Film Performance* (Wayne State UP, 2004), in which her article on Chris Cooper's performance style appears. She contributed an essay on Sayles to *Contemporary American Independent Film* (Routledge, 2005).

Susan Felleman is assistant professor of cinema studies at Southern Illinois University, Carbondale. She is the author of *Botticelli in Hollywood: The Films of Albert Lewin* (Twayne, 1997), *Baring the Device: Art and Psyche on Screen* (forthcoming from U of Texas P), and numerous other publications on film and art.

Rebecca M. Gordon is affiliated with the Film and TV Studies Department and the Latin American, Latino, and Caribbean Studies Program at Dartmouth College. She completed a dual-doctorate at Indiana University in English and American Studies. She specializes in spectatorship, historical reception studies, emotion and cognition, and film aesthetics, with additional research interests ranging from cognitive philosophy to Latino studies. Her publications include essays and reviews in *Film Quarterly*, *Film-Philosophy*, and *Scope*.

Heidi Kenaga received her PhD from the University of Wisconsin–Madison. She teaches film, television, and literature courses at the University of Memphis. Dr. Kenaga's essays on aspects of 1920s' American cinema and culture have appeared in anthologies in the United States and the United Kingdom. Her research interests include U.S. studio history during the 1920s and 1930s (particularly industrial and corporate practices, women's labor, and audienceship and reception), the relationship between "middlebrow" culture and Hollywood, and contemporary independent cinema.

Martin F. Norden teaches film as professor of communication at the University of Massachusetts–Amherst. He is the author of *The Cinema of Isolation: A History of Disability in the Movies* (Rutgers UP, 1994) and has also done extensive work on women in early Hollywood. He is the editor of the forthcoming book *The Changing Face of Evil in Film and Television* (Editions Rodopi).

Klaus Rieser is assistant professor in the Department of American Studies at the University of Graz, Austria. His major areas of teaching and research comprise U.S. film, gender, multiethnicity, and cultural studies. He is the author of a book on the representation and the metaphorical functions of U.S. immigration in film, *Passagen zum Ende des Regenbogens* (Trier: WVT, 1996), has recently finished a book on masculinity and film titled *Borderlines and Passages: Liminal Masculinities in Film* (Essen: Die Blaue Eule, forthcoming 2005), and is currently coediting an anthology titled *US Icons and Iconicity*.

Greg M. Smith is associate professor of communication and graduate director of the Moving Image Studies program at Georgia State University. His most recent book is *Film Structure and the Emotion System* (Cambridge UP, 2003). He is editor of *On a Silver Platter: CD-ROMs and the Promises of a New Technology* (New York UP, 1999) and coedited *Passionate Views: Film, Cognition, and Emotion* (Johns Hopkins UP, 1999).

Maureen Turim is professor of English and film studies at the University of Florida. She is the author of *Flashbacks in Film: Memory and History* (Routledge, 1989) and *The Films of Oshima Nagisa: Images of a Japanese Iconoclast* (U of California P, 1998). Professor Turim has also published over sixty essays in anthologies and journals on a wide range of theoretical, historical, and aesthetic issues in cinema and video, cultural studies, and psychoanalytic and feminist theory.

Mika Turim-Nygren is Maureen Turim's daughter. She began working on this project in collaboration with her mother at the beginning of her high school career. She is now preparing to enter the Honors program at the University of Florida on a National Merit Scholarship, where she hopes to major in English with a focus in creative writing and literary criticism.

Alex Woloch is an associate professor of English at Stanford University. He is the author of *The One vs. the Many: Minor Characters and the Space of the Protagonist in the Novel* (Princeton UP, 2003) and the coeditor, with Peter Brooks, of *Whose Freud? The Place of Psychoanalysis in Contemporary Culture* (Yale UP, 2000).

INDEX

Aaron, Caroline, 97
Adams, Ansel, 247
Adorno, Theodor, 152
African Americans, 6, 64, 77n9, 87–90, 96–98, 99n5, 99nn7–8, 105–6, 114n1, 115n6, 123–24
Alexander, Jace, 108, 121
Alexander, John, 83
Ali, 99n5
"aliens." *See* science fiction
Alligator, 79
Altman, Robert, 117, 124
American Gigolo, 24
American Graffiti, 151–52
Anderson, Benedict, 205, 206
Anderson, Carolyn, 112
Andrew, Geoff, 27, 33
Andromeda Strain, The, 98
Ansen, David, 28
Appadurai, Arjun. *See* Nestor Garcia Canclini
Arnott, Mark, 65
Arquette, Rosanna, 28, 30, 71, 88
art cinema, 2, 10
Apollo 13, 13
Auerbach, Erich, 58, 76n4
Aufderheide, Patricia, 113
auteur, 1–2, 75n2, 76n2, 117
Auty, Chris, 28

Babies and Banners, 34
Baby It's You, 4, 5, 22, 30, 41n1, 62, 88, 131; and *American Graffiti*, 69; analysis of scenes in, 71–74; and *The Big Chill*, 69; critical reception of, 28; and Paramount, 5, 14n2, 28–29, 68–75
Bad Boys, 99n5

Badge of Evil (novel). See *Touch of Evil*
Bad Lieutenant, 35
Bakewell, Geoffrey, 172n1
Ballhaus, Michael, 131
Bambara, Toni Cade, 42n3
Baran, Edward, 91
Baron, Cynthia, 45n11
Baron, David, 125
Barrett, Laura, 256n8
Bassett, Angela, 122
Baudelaire, 120, 132n2
Baudrillard, Jean, 241
Bazin, André, 4, 41, 55, 56, 58–59, 76n5
Beetle, The (novel), 84
Behlmer, Rudy, 44n10
Being There, 98
Benjamin, Walter, 132n2
Benson, Sheila, 28
Bernardi, Daniel, 98n3
Bertolucci, Bernardo, 152
Berry, John, 38
Bhabha, Homi, 197, 207, 229, 234
Big Chill, The, 69, 129
Biskind, Peter, 39
Black, Gregory, 25–26, 44n10
Blacklist, The, 25
Blade Runner, 80, 98n1
Blood Simple, 34
Bloom, Harold, 8–9, 159, 170
Blue Collar, 18, 30
Bodnar, John, 18, 42n4
Body Heat, 5
Bonavoglia, Angela, 28
Booker, M. Keith, 20, 23, 42n4
Bould, Mark, 98n1
Brennan, Tim, 233–34
Bridgewater, Dee Dee, 80

Brier, Stephen, 103
Brogan, Hugh, 100n11
Brother from Another Planet, The, 5, 6, 12, 22, 34, 36, 41n1, 57, 62, 69, 75, 77nn8–9, 79–102, 179; analysis of scenes in, 81–82, 90–91; as critique of commodity consumption, 80, 89–93; final shot of, 81, 96–98; images in, 80–81, 90–91, 93–96; immigrants/immigration in, 82, 87, 94–96, 99n4, 99–100n10–11; as "postfuturist" science fiction, 79–80; and *Men in Black*, 80, 86–87; racial politics of, 87–90, 96–98; representation of the "alien" in, 80, 86–88; silence of main character, 63–64; Statue of Liberty, 80–82, 88, 93–96, 100n12; use of special effects in, 87
Bruzzi, Stella, 18
Bulworth, 18
Buñuel, Luis, 7, 125–27, 128, 132n5
Burke, Edmund, 255
Burmester, Leo, 57
Bush, George W., 12, 14n3
By Man's Law, 25

Canclini, Nestor Garcia, 198–99
Cannes Film Festival, 103
Carrey, Jim, 129
Carson, Diane, 2, 13, 33, 35–36, 56, 69, 70, 75, 202, 203, 204, 210
Casa de los Babys, 3, 5, 12, 41–42n1
Cassavetes Award, John, 1
censorship. *See* popular Hollywood filmmaking
Chandler, Raymond, 159, 165, 172n2
Child of the Western Isles (novel). See *The Secret of the Ron Mor Skerry*
Children of Paradise, 37

China Syndrome, The, 46n15
Chinatown, 5, 9,
Choose Me, 34
Christensen, Terry, 20
Christian imagery, 6, 105–14, 249–52, 257nn14–15
Ciccolella, Jude, 119
Cineaste, 229
Citizen Kane, 159, 164, 172n5, 218
City of Hope, 2, 6–7, 14n7, 21, 31, 32, 41n1, 57, 117–33; community or "tribes" in, 117–18, 121, 122–23, 129, 130–32; ensemble cast of, 117–18, 124–25, 128–32, 180; and *Grand Canyon*, 129–30, 131; and *Nashville*, 124–25; and *Phantom of Liberty*, 126–28, 132n5; and *La Ronde*, 125–26, 127, 132n4; use of "trades" [long takes] in, 6–7, 118–31, 132n1, 133n8
Civil Action, A, 20
Clapp, Gordon, 65, 100n13, 108
Classification and Rating Administration (CARA), 26, 44n10
Cohn, Lawrence, 42n1
Cole, Thomas, 255
Colon, Miriam, 122
Combs, James E., 20
Combs, Sara T., 20
Comito, Terry, 166
commodities/commodification, 5–6, 80, 90–93, 95–96, 97–98
community, 7, 117–33, 135–36, 150, 154, 183–84
Conformist, The [*Il Conformista*], 152
Connell, Robert, 174, 175–76, 178, 187–89
consumerism, 121
contemporary independent filmmaking (U.S.), 2, 3–4, 11, 16–50
Cook, David A., 41, 44n11

Cooper, Chris, 12, 23, 30, 53, 105, 121
Coppola, Francis Ford, 1
Corliss, Richard, 36–37
Corrigan, Tim, 1
Courtney, Jeni, 137
Cousineau, Maggie, 65
Cox, Dan, 29
Crime de Monsieur Lange, Le, 165
Crimp, Donald, 258n18
Cronon, William, 239, 248, 257n10
Crowdus, Gary, 121
Cruz, Tania, 232
Csicsery-Ronay, Istvan, Jr., 83–85, 87, 95
CSU (Conference of Studio Unions), 45n11
Curtis, Liane, 90

D'Alessandro, Anthony, 42n1
Daring, Mason, 111
Dash, Julie, 42n3
Dassin, Jules, 38
Daughters of the Dust, 42n3
Davis, Thulani, 114n1
Davis, Todd F., 172n3, 256n4
Day the Earth Stood Still, The, 85, 115n5
Deer Hunter, The, 30
DeKoven, Marianne, 19
Delgado, Damian, 202, 203
Demeter, John, 34
Denby, David, 28
Denison, Anthony John, 120
Derrida, Jacques, 150
Dickens, Hazel, 110–11
Dietrich, Marlene, 167
Dillinger in Hollywood: New and Selected Short Stories, 14n1
Dirlik, Arif, 200–1
Dirty Dancing, 34
Dirty Dozen, The, 129
"Disneyfication," 233, 239–40, 241
Dissanayake, Wimal, 194
Dissent, 59–60

Dmytryk, Edward, 38
Douglas, R. M., 145
Dracula (novel), 84
Dragnet (television series), 98
Dubofsky, Melvyn, 104

Earth vs. the Flying Saucers, 85
Ebert, Roger, 7, 181, 192n5
Edge of the World, The, 135–36
Edwards, Daryl, 124
Eight Men Out, 3, 5, 7, 21, 32, 36, 41n1, 57, 117, 130, 131, 133n8
Eisenberg, Evan, 248
Embry, Marcus, 14n6
Empire Strikes Back, The, 69
Endfield, Cy, 38
Enemy of the State, 99n5
Engels, Frederick, 93
ER (television series), 128
Erickson, Ingrid M., 163
Erin Brockovich, 20
Esquire, 230
E.T. the Extra-Terrestrial, 86

Fahrenheit 9/11, 34
Faison, Frank, 119
Fanny and Alexander, 34
Faulkner, James, 163, 167
Featherstone, Mike, 208
Ferncase, Richard, 34
Fiedler, Leslie, 177
F.I.S.T., 18, 30
Flaherty, Robert, 135, 136
flaneur. *See* Baudelaire
Fonda-Bonardi, Claudia, 36
Foner, Eric, 104, 115n3
Foner, Philip S., 19
Force of Evil, 20, 42n3
Ford, Harrison, 189
Ford, John, 136, 159, 165, 167–70, 172n6
Foster, Gloria, 119
Foucault, Michel, 184, 192n6
Framing Blackness, 97
Frazier, Randy, 92

Fresh Prince of Bel-Air, The (television series), 99n5
Freud, Sigmund, 8, 142, 158–59, 160, 161, 162, 163, 171, 172n7, 187, 218, 220, 221, 223, 225, 226–27, 232–33; "Civilization and Its Discontents," 163; oedipal narratives, 158–73, 174–93, 215–37; Oedipus complex, 159, 160, 215, 220, 221, 226–27; Oedipus myth, 9, 158, 159, 167, 176; preoedipal mother, 142–43; psychoanalytic theories, 7, 8, 139, 142–43, 158–64, 171, 186; "Rat Man," 218, 225, 227; "return of the repressed," 159, 161–62; *Three Case Histories*, 218, 225; "Totem and Taboo," 159–60, 227, 232–33; the Unconscious, 8, 159, 163–64
From Dawn to Dusk, 19
Fry, Rosalie K., 135, 136, 149

Gallun, Raymond Z., 85
Garafola, Lynn, 30
Garnett, Rhys, 84–85
Genesis myth, 249–50
genre, 5, 54, 62, 70, 165–71
Gershon, Gina, 122
Gianos, Phillip L., 25, 42n4
Giant, 172n6
Girgus, Sam, 172n6
Glauberman, Naomi, 36
Glover, Danny, 130
Godfather, The, 30
Goin, Peter, 11, 249
Gomery, Douglas, 167–68, 170
González, Dan Rivera, 224
Gordon, Carl, 92
Graff, Todd, 121
Grand Canyon, 129–30, 131
Grand Illusion, 9, 159, 165
Greeley, Horace, 247
Grody, Kathryn, 76–77n7, 199

Grossberg, Lawrence, 189–90
Guerrero, Ed, 97
Gunton, Bob, 105

Hamilton, Richard, 83
Hammett, Dashiell, 159, 165, 172n2
Handley, George B., 14n5
Hanks, Tom, 129, 189
Harlan County, 34
Hartley, Hal, 192n4
Hartzler, Jonas, 115n7
Hauerwas, Stanley, 14n3
Haynes, Todd, 33
Hemingway, Ernest, 244, 248, 255
historical events, representation of, 6, 53–55, 61, 64, 65, 75n1, 103–5, 112–13
Hitchcock, Alfred, 57
Hitt, Christopher, 255
Hoberman, J., 33
Hollinshead, Keith, 230–31, 234
Horne, Gerald, 28
Horrocks, Roger. *See* Joane Nagel
Hoynes, William, 18, 32
HUAC (House Un-American Activities Committee), 23, 45n11
Huston, John, 38
Hutcheon, Linda, 258n18
"hybridity" in Sayles's films, 9–10, 62–63, 216–17, 228, 229, 257n11

IA (International Alliance of Theatrical Stage Employees), 44–45n11
IFC Films, 12
immigration/immigrants, 42n2, 80, 81, 82, 83, 86–88, 94–96, 99n4, 99n7, 99–100nn10–11, 103, 190, 215
Independence Day, 86, 99n5
Independent Spirit Award, 103
In the Company of Men, 43n6

Invaders from Mars, 85
Invasion of the Body Snatchers (1956), 85
Invasion of the Body Snatchers (1978), 98
It Came From Outer Space, 85
It Happened One Night, 18

Jameson, Fredric, 80, 151–52, 242, 243
Jansen, Sue Curry, 24
Jarmusch, Jim, 56, 192n4
Jencks, Charles, 258n19
JFK, 20
Johnston, Trevor, 114
Jones, Dorothy, 44n10
Jones, James Earl, 105
Jones, Kent, 241, 243
Jones, Tommy Lee, 83
Jordan, Daniel P., 113
Jungle, The, 25
Jurassic Park IV, 13

Kaminsky, Amy, 249
Kant, Immanuel, 258n20
Kasdan, Lawrence, 69, 129–30
Kazan, Elia, 38
Kellner, Douglas, 21–22, 40, 46n15
Kemp, Philip, 33, 168, 172n5, 181, 249
Kephart, Edwin, 36
Kidd, Kenneth B., 156n2
Kipen, David, 43n6
Kirkland, Bruce, 243, 256n5
Klady, Leonard, 42n1
Kline, Kevin, 129
Kolker, Robert, 75–76n2
Kristofferson, Kris, 165
Kyles, Dwania, 92

labor history films, 34
L.A. Law (television series), 32
Lane, Fredric, 82
Learning Channel, The (cable television), 240
Lears, T. J. Jackson, 2

Lee, Spike, 1, 33, 56
Le Fevre, Adam, 65
Leff, Leonard L., 44n10
"left-leaning films," 20–21, 22, 23–24, 30, 42nn3–4
Leslie, Esther, 99n5
Leone, Marianne, 119
Levy, Emanuel, 4, 33, 52, 56, 211, 212
Lewis, Jon, 25, 26, 27, 39, 44n10, 45n11
Lewis, Ronald, 104
Lianna, 3, 5, 12, 22, 41n1, 57, 75, 174
Limbo, 2, 11–12, 41n1, 61–63, 64, 71, 77n7, 131, 179, 238–60; Alaska as "last wilderness" in, 238–39; analysis of opening scenes in, 238–40; Christian theology in, 249–52, 257nn14–15; "Disneyfication" of Alaska, 239–40, 241; ending of, 62, 253–54; gay characters in, 244–45; as generic hybrid, 62–63, 257n11; liminality in, 249, 253; nature/wilderness in, 241–43, 244–49; as postmodern narrative, 254–56; storytelling in, 254–55; sublimity in, 254–55; and tourism industry, 61–62, 238–40, 241–43
Lipsitz, George, 24, 27, 29, 39, 44n10
Lone Star, 1, 2, 7–9, 11, 14nn4–5, 21, 31, 32, 34, 41n1, 53, 54, 61, 75n1, 117, 130, 131, 158–73, 179, 215–37; as border story, 162–63, 229–30; critical reception of, 7–8; as "hybrid" film, 216–17, 228; incest in, 164, 165, 168, 172n4, 219–20, 235; influence of *Chinatown* on, 165; influence of *Citizen Kane* on, 159, 164, 172n5, 218; influence of *The Man Who Shot Liberty Valance* on, 165,

Lone Star (continued)
  167–71; influence of Renoir on, 164–65; influence of *Touch of Evil* on, 165–67; publication of script, 14n4; as revisionist western, 62, 167–71; tourism in, 233; transition shots into the past in, 8, 162–63, 218–19
Long Goodbye, The, 5
long takes, 6–7, 8, 17, 21, 33, 63, 164–65
Los Gusanos (novel), 14n1
Losey, Joseph, 38
Lost in Space (television series), 86
Love, Glen A., 248, 256n9
Lucas, George, 69
Lukács, Georg, 4, 51–52, 58, 60, 75
Luppi, Federico, 10, 53, 195, 212, 221, 224
Lynch, John, 141
Lynch, Susan, 145
Lyons, Charles, 27, 31, 43n7–8, 44n10
Lyotard, Jean-François, 255

MacArthur Award, John D. and Catherine T., 1
MacMillan, Bruce, 113
Magnificent Ambersons, The, 37
Magowan, Kim, 165, 172n4
Mair, Jan, 99n5
Maltby, Richard, 44n10
Maltin, Leonard, 181
Man of Aran, 135
Man Who Shot Liberty Valance, The, 9, 159, 165, 167–71
Man Who Wasn't There, The, 5
Marks, Laura, 228, 229
Marsh, Richard, 84
Marshall, Robert, 245, 256n7
Martin, Steve, 130
Martinez, Vanessa, 62
Martyr to His Cause, A, 19
Marx, Karl, 93, 150
masculinity, 9, 174–93, 215–37
Masterson, Whit, 165
Mastrantonio, Mary Elizabeth, 62, 251
Matewan, 6, 7, 9, 13, 14n3, 14n7, 22, 30, 31, 36, 41–42n1, 53, 56, 57, 61, 103–16, 117, 130, 131, 174–93; Christian imagery in, 104, 105–11; as critique of male hegemony, 185–91; "exit politics" in, 185, 187–88; female characters in, 175, 177, 180–81, 184; historical veracity of, 6, 19, 75n1, 103–04, 112–13; music in, 180; plot summary of, 191n1; publication of script, 14n4; representation of hero in, 105, 115n5, 175–78, 182–83, 186–88, 190–91; secondary characters in, 180–81; as western, 105, 176–77
McCarthy, Colman, 14n3
McClintock, Anne, 95–96
McDonnell, Mary, 23, 53
McGhee, Dorothy, 115n4
McKibben, Bill, 248
Mean Streets, 30
Mellen, Joan, 127
Memento, 4
Men in Black, 5, 80, 82, 86–87, 99n6
"Men in Black," 5–6, 80, 97
Men With Guns [*Hombres Armados*], 2, 9–10, 12, 14nn6–7, 18, 22, 41n1, 53, 61, 62–63, 64, 130, 174–93, 194–214, 215–37; "Alliance for Progress," 201–02, 212, 213n3; Cerca del Cielo, 191n1, 202, 210, 231, 235, 254; consumption in, 198–99; as critique of male hegemony, 185–88, 190–91; as "foreign film," 209–210, 213n6; as "hybrid film," 216–17, 228–29; Latin American literary traditions and, 222–23; multiple language use, 181–82, 209–10; plot summary of, 191–92n1; publication of

script, 14n4; representation of hero in, 175–76, 177–78, 179; storytelling in, 210–12; tourists/tourism in, 195, 199–200, 203–07, 209–10, 212, 230–33; urban vs. rural spaces in, 197–98
Merchant, Carolyn, 248, 250
Merritt, Greg, 33, 46n15
Mette, Nancy, 108
Meyer, David S., 18, 32
Michaud, Jean. *See* Keith Hollinshead
Mignolo, Walter D., 201, 213n5
Mike, Spike, Slackers, & Dykes, 1
Miller, Frank, 27, 44n10
Mimic, 13
Mission Impossible, 129
Missing, 46n15
modernism/postmodernism, 11–12, 35, 80, 151, 177, 204, 239, 241–44, 247, 254, 256, 257n12, 258nn18–19
Mogambo, 98
Molyneaux, Gerard, 14n2, 46n15
Morton, Joe, 31, 63, 64, 81, 91, 119, 129
Mostel, Josh, 105, 124
Motion Picture Alliance for the Preservation of American Ideals, 45n11
Moyers, Bill, 256n1
Moylan, Tom, 89, 90–91
MPAA (Motion Picture Association of America), 26, 29, 44–45nn10–11
MPPA (Motion Picture Producers' Association), 44n11
MPPDA (Motion Picture Producers and Distributors of America), 26, 43–44nn10–11, 45n11
Mr. Deeds Goes to Town, 18
Mulvey, Laura, 170–71, 174, 176–77, 190
Munt, Ian, 205–06
Murphy, Audie, 246
Murphy, Michael, 12

My Life as a Dog, 34

NAFTA (North American Free Trade Agreement), 215, 217
Nagel, Joane, 227–28
"narrative avant-garde," 3, 37–38
nation/nationality, representation of, 9–11, 194–214, 215–37
Nash, Roderick, 239, 245–46
Nashville, 124–25
National Film Preservation Board's Film Registry, 1
National Geographic, 238, 240, 256n2
National Park Service, 238–39
nature, 11–12, 61–62, 238–60
Neale, Steve, 174, 176, 192n3
neoconservatism, 12, 16, 18, 22, 27, 29, 30, 39, 42n3, 46n15, 111
Neve, Brian, 20, 42n3
Nevins, Joseph, 98n4, 100n10
New Left, 59–60, 64–66, 68
Newsome, Herbert, 91
Nichols, John, 45n12
nonviolence, 6, 14n3, 106–7, 182–83, 186–87
Norma Rae, 18, 46n15
Northern Lights, 34
nostalgia, 4, 7, 52–55, 60, 64, 68–69, 70–72, 74–75, 151–54, 168, 170, 205–06

Oelschlaeger, Max, 254, 257n12
Oldham, Will, 105, 110
Ophuls, Max, 7, 125–26, 128
Ozaki, Yei Theodora, 148

Packer, George, 38, 39, 59–60, 76n6
Pale Rider, 115n5
Paris, Texas, 34
Passanante, Jean, 64, 100n13
Passion Fish, 1, 3, 5, 7, 14n4, 41n1, 53, 174, 179
pastoralism, 247–48, 252, 256n9
Patinkin, Mandy, 76–77n7, 199
Paycheck, 20
Pease, Donald, 196

Peña, Elizabeth, 53
Phantom of Liberty, The, 7, 125, 126–28, 132n5
Phillips, Dana, 242–43, 243–44, 247–48, 258n19
Phipps, Keith, 24
π [*Pi*], 4
Pierson, John, 1, 34
Piranha, 79, 240
Polanski, Roman, 159
political films, 18, 20–24, 42n4, 46n15
Political Film Society, 14n7, 103
Polonsky, Abraham, 27, 38
popular Hollywood filmmaking, 3, 11, 118, 181; centrality of stars to, 128–29; depiction of community in, 129; political censorship and, 3, 16–50, 43n5, 43–45nn8–11;
populist films, 18, 38
postmodernism and language, 254–56
"postnational cinema," 10, 194–214
Powell, Michael, 135
Pratt, Mary Louise, 222
Prendergast, Christopher, 76n3
Prevert, Jacques, 37

Pribram, E. Deidre, 3, 29, 33–34, 35, 36, 37, 40, 44n10, 46n15
Primary Colors, 18
PCA (Production Code Administration), 43–44n10
Progressive, The, 14n3
Public Enemy, 99n8
public spaces, 121
Puette, William J., 30, 45–46n14
Pulitzer, Joseph, 94
Pullman, Bill, 86
Purdy, Jim, 44n10

Quart, Leonard, 121
Quartermass trilogy, 85
Quick and the Dead, The, 13
Quiet Man, The, 136

Rabinow, Paul, 192n6
race/racism, 5–6, 26, 27, 77n9, 80, 83, 84, 85–86, 87–90, 96–98, 99n7, 100n10, 129, 167, 186, 188, 189
Ray, Nicholas, 27, 38
Raymond, Bill, 120
Reagan era, 6, 17–18, 29, 59, 60–61, 111–12, 115n8
realism/social realism in Sayles's films, 4, 17, 19, 36, 51–78, 135, 150, 164, 166
reflexivity in Sayles's films, 4, 54, 64–65, 68, 77n7, 114, 195
religious fundamentalism in U.S., 6, 112–13
Renoir, Jean, 37, 41, 159, 164–65
Renzi, Maggie, 41n1, 64, 97, 119
Reservoir Dogs, 4
Return of the Secaucus Seven, 1, 4, 12, 17, 18, 21, 22, 41–42n1, 57, 60, 61, 64–69, 74, 76n2, 77nn10–11, 78n13, 100n13, 117, 130; and *The Big Chill*, 69, 129; as key contemporary independent film, 34; multiple perspectives in, 36–37; nostalgia in, 53–55, 64, 68, 74; publication of script, 14n4
Return to the Edge of the World. See *The Edge of the World*
Richardson, Robert, 118, 121, 131, 133n8
Ricoeur, Paul. See Tim Brennan
"right-leaning films," 21–22, 24
Rikowski, Glenn, 99n9
Ritt, Martin, 38
Rocky, 30
Rodriguez, Luis, 228–29
Rodriguez, Ralph, 14n6
Roffman, Peter, 44n10
Roger & Me, 34
Rogin, Michael, 29
Roman, Monica, 45n13
Ronde, La, 7, 125–26, 127, 132n4
Roosevelt, Theodore, 247

INDEX

Rosen, David, 42n1
Rosenbaum, Jonathan, 17, 24, 32, 35, 43n6
Ross, Steven J., 18–19, 20, 25, 42n2, 42n4, 43n5, 43n9, 44n11
Rossen, Robert, 58
Rubin, Gayle, 226
Rules of the Game, The, 37
Ryan, Jack, 96, 112, 124, 172n2, 172n5
Ryan, Michael, 21–22, 40, 46n15
Ryan, Susan, 181

Salt of the Earth, 64
Salvador, 46n15
Sardar, Ziauddin, 84
Sarris, Andrew, 37
Saturday Night Fever, 30
Sayles, John, as actor in his films, 6, 57–58, 97, 112–13, 121; aesthetic concerns of, 4, 12, 33–35, 36–37, 55; archives at Williams College, 12; as auteur, 40, 52, 56–57, 59; awards won by, 1, 13–14n1, 14n7, 103; as "father" of contemporary independent cinema, 3, 52, 46n15; as fiction writer, 4, 13–14n1; on Freud, 8, 158–59; interest in storytelling technique, 7–9, 11–12, 52, 55, 117, 135; list of important political films, 42n4; production practices of, 13; progressivism of, 6, 16–24, 27–28, 30–32, 35–41, 69, 174, 178; use of ensemble casts by, 6–7, 9, 117–33, 179–82; use of Steadicam by, 6, 117–18, 125, 128, 131; and *Thinking in Pictures: The Making of the Movie* Matewan, 13, 181; work as script doctor, 13
Schamus, James, 39–40
Schatz, Thomas, 169
science fiction, 5–6, 62, 64, 77n9, 79–102, 105, 115n5; representation of "aliens," 80–87, 98–99n4
Scorsese, Martin, 56, 76n2
Scott, Randolph, 246
Screen Actors Guild, 45n11
Searchers, The, 172n6
Secret of Roan Inish, The, 7, 41n1, 131, 134–57, 174; analysis of scenes in, 138–39; differences from source novel, 155–56; folklore/myth and, 135, 144–50; location shooting in Ireland, 135–36; psychoanalytic approach to, 139, 142–44; representation of work, 150–51; selkies in, 134, 136, 140, 141–49, 155–56; storytelling in, 140–42, 146–47, 153–54
Secret of the Ron Mor Skerry, The (novel), 135, 136
sex, lies, and videotape, 34
Shane, 115n5
Shannon's Deal (television series), 32, 41n1
Sheriff, Sidney, Jr., 89
Sherman, Betsy, 243, 257n17
Shohat, Ella, 208–09, 212, 213n4
Shull, Michael Slade, 18, 25, 42n4
Siegel, Carol, 187–88
Silkwood, 46n15
Silver City, 3, 12, 14n4, 14n7, 17, 22–23, 41–42n1
Silverman, Kaja, 192n3, 215, 220, 226–27
Simmons, Jerold L., 44n10
Simon, Ronald, 28
Sirk, Douglas, 27
Six Millon Dollar Man (television series), 98
Skinner, B. F., 158
Slater, Candace, 256n3
Smiling Sam, 19
Smith, Gavin, 36, 75, 105, 112, 113, 114, 132n1, 132n3, 133n6, 133n8, 158–59, 235

Smith, Greg M., 180
Smith, Will, 87, 99n5
Sobchack, Vivian, 79–80
Society for Cinema Studies, 2
Soja, Edward, 211
Sommer, Doris, 222–23
Sorrell, Herb, 45n11
Sosa, Roberto, 195
soundtrack/dialogue, 63–64, 71–73, 77n8, 90, 110–11, 122, 180, 181–82, 209–10
South by Southwest Film Festival (2002), 12
Spano, Vincent, 28, 30, 71, 88, 120, 129
Specters of Marx, The, 150
Spectral Mother: Freud, Feminism, and Psychoanalysis, The, 142–43
Spielberg, Steven, 1
spin-off television series, 133n7
Splash, 98
Sprengnether, Madelon, 142–43
Staiger, Janet, 216, 229
Stam, Robert, 208–09, 212, 213n4
Starman, 86
Star Trek (television series), 86
Star Wars franchise, 87, 99n5
Star Wars Episode I: The Phantom Menace, 86
Statue of Liberty, 80–82, 88, 93–96
Steinbeck Award, John, 1
Stevens, Fisher, 88
Stevens, George, 172n6
Stoker, Bram, 84
Stone, Oliver, 1, 38, 59
Stop Making Sense, 34
Storming Heaven (novel), 115n2
Stranger Than Paradise, 34
Strathairn, David, 11, 62, 65, 97, 105, 119, 242, 251
Streetwise, 34
Strike at Coaldale, The, 25
sublimity, 258n20
Suleiman, Susan, 127
Sunshine State, 3, 12, 21, 22, 31, 41n1, 54, 72, 77–78n12, 117, 130, 131, 154; representation of nature in, 240–41, 243
Superman, 115n5
Sweet Hereafter, The, 43n6

Tarantino, Quentin, 33, 56
Taussig, Michael, 224
Taxi Driver, 30, 76n2
Teenage Mutant Ninja Turtles, 34
Tenney, Jack B., 45n11
Tessera. See Harold Bloom
Thing, The (1951), 85
Tighe, Kevin, 108
Tirelli, Jaime, 119
Touch of Evil, 9, 125, 159, 165–67, 170, 171
tourism/tourists, 10–11, 61, 77n7, 179, 181, 190, 194–214, 230–33, 235, 239, 241, 242, 245, 250
Trott, Karen, 64
Turner, Frederick Jackson, 245
Turner, Victor. See Amy Kaminsky

UMWA (United Mine Workers of America), 104, 105
Under Fire, 46n15
Union Dues (novel), 13n1, 60, 104
unionization, 6, 19, 26, 27, 30, 45–46n14, 103–116, 176, 177, 181, 184, 187, 188, 189, 190, 191n1; in Hollywood, 26, 44–45n11; as represented in media, 45–46n14
Union Maids, 34
urban life, representation of, 6–7, 117–33
Urry, John, 204
U.S. "good neighbor" policy, 212

Vasey, Ruth, 25, 31, 43–44n10
Vecsey, George, 104, 115n8

Wag the Dog, 18
Walbrook, Anton, 125

Walsh, Francis R., 25
Wang, Wayne, 33
War of the Worlds, The (1953 film), 85
War of the Worlds, The (novel), 84
Warshow, Robert, 168–69
Weinbaum, Stanley G., 85
Welles, Orson, 37, 38, 159, 164, 165–67
Wells, H. G., 84, 85
West, Dennis, and Joan M. West, 158, 162–63, 164, 170, 229, 245, 249, 254, 257n11
West Wing, The (television series), 128
western, the (genre) 167–71; male narcissism in, 176–77; Proppian approaches to, 170–71, 176–77
Wexler, Haskell, 103, 131, 136
What Is to Be Done? 19
White, Daniel, 256n8
White Queen (novel), 85
wilderness, in Sayles's fiction, 246–47. *See also* nature
Willemen, Paul, 174
Williams, Barbara, 120
Williams, Linda, 126–27
Wilson, David, 181

Wilson, Rob, 194
Wings of Desire, 122
Wobblies, The, 34
Woodford, Riley, 241
Womack, Kenneth, 172n3, 256n4
Wonderful Visit, The (novel), 85
work and labor, representations of, 138–39, 150–51, 153, 239, 241–42
working-class films of silent/Progressive era, 18–19, 23, 42n2, 42n4, 43n9; of studio and corporate eras, 18, 30, 34, 42n4
Woman Under the Influence, A, 34
Wright, Tom, 97
Wyatt, Justin, 24, 43n5, 44n10
Wyler, William, 55

Yanagita, Kunio, 147–48
Yosemite National Park, 247
You Can't Take It With You, 18
Young, Robert J. C., 217

Zaniello, Tom, 42n4
Zerilli, Linda, 94–95, 100n12
Zieger, Gay P., 18
Zieger, Robert P., 18
Žižek, Slavoj, 98

www.ingramcontent.com/pod-product-compliance
Lightning Source LLC
Chambersburg PA
CBHW070755230426
43665CB00017B/2368